MISSISSIPPI'S CIVIL WAR

MERCER
UNIVERSITY PRESS

Endowed by
Tom Watson Brown
and
The Watson-Brown Foundation, Inc.

MISSISSIPPI'S CIVIL WAR

A NARRATIVE HISTORY

Ben Wynne

MERCER UNIVERSITY PRESS
Macon, Georgia

ISBN 978-0-88146-512-9
MUP/P497

First Paperback Edition 2014.

Books published by Mercer University Press are printed on acid free
paper that meets the requirements of American National Standard for
Information Sciences—Permanence of Paper for Printed Library
Materials.

Library of Congress Cataloging-in-Publication Data

CIP data are available from the Library of Congress

CONTENTS

Acknowledgments   vii

List of Maps

1. A Tragic Evolution   1

2. The Call of My Country, 1861   34

3. In Defense of the State, 1862   58

4. The Turning Point, 1863   95

5. The End, 1864–1865   148

6. Reconstruction and Revision   178

Appendix   205

Bibliography   223

Index   237

To Carly

ACKNOWLEDGMENTS

This book could not have been completed without the assistance and support of many people to whom I owe a great debt. The staff at Mercer University Press has always been very kind to me, and I would like to express my appreciation in particular to Marc Jolley, Kevin C. Manus, Marsha Luttrell, and Barbara Keene. They are, collectively and individually, consummate professionals and a joy to work with. I would be remiss if I did not recognize my friend Scott Poole at the College of Charleston, a great historian who suggested that I write this book in the first place. A number of former professors and colleagues from several institutions have, through the years, allowed me to benefit from their counsel and example. They include Charles Sallis at Millsaps College, Ron Howard and Kirk Ford at Mississippi College, Robert Haws, David Sansing, Ted Ownby, Nancy Bercaw, Charles Reagan Wilson, Sheila Skemp, Michael Namorato and Charles Eagles at the University of Mississippi, and James C. Cobb of the University of Georgia. As I revised the manuscript, my friend Brant Helvenston of Live Oak, Florida, once again was kind enough to take time out of his busy schedule to review the manuscript and provide valuable input. My friend Bill Fisher of Phoenix, Arizona, a master wordsmith, also provided me with great assistance by taking the time to read and comment on the work.

In doing research for the book I benefited from the assistance of the staffs of a number of libraries, archives, and other organizations. Those located in the state of Mississippi included the Mississippi Department of Archives and History, the J. D. Williams Library at the University of Mississippi, Mitchell Memorial Library at Mississippi State University, the Cook Library at the University of

Southern Mississippi, the Millsaps-Wilson Library at Millsaps College, the Delta State University Library, the Eudora Welty Library in Jackson, the Gulfport Public Library, the Attala County Public Library in Kosciusko, the Elizabeth Jones Library in Grenada, the Oxford-Lafayette County Public Library, the Laurel-Jones County Public Library, the Evans Memorial Library in Aberdeen, the William Alexander Percy Memorial Library in Greenville, the B. S. Ricks Memorial Library in Yazoo City, the Biloxi Public Library, the Pascagoula Public Library, the Marshall County Public Library in Holly Springs, the Meridian-Lauderdale County Public Library, the Bryan Public Library in West Point, the Carnegie Library in Okolona, the Warren County-Vicksburg Public Library, the Jennie Stephens Smith Library in New Albany, the Lowndes County Public Library in Columbus, the Lee County Public Library in Tupelo, the Florence Public Library, the McComb Public Library, the Lincoln County Public Library in Brookhaven, the Iuka Public Library, the Copiah-Jefferson Regional Library in Hazelhurst, the Madison Public Library, the Vicksburg Old Courthouse Museum, the Vicksburg National Military Park, Shiloh National Military Park, the Corinth Civil War Interpretive Center, the Northeast Mississippi Museum at Corinth, the Marshall County Museum at Holly Springs, the Columbus Mississippi Convention and Visitors Bureau, the Natchez Mississippi Convention and Visitors Bureau, and the Old Capital Museum in Jackson.

Institutions or organizations outside the state of Mississippi that were very helpful included the Tennessee State Library and Archives, the Alabama Department of Archives and History, the Georgia Department of Archives and History, the Southern Historical Collection at the University of North Carolina, the Robert W. Woodruff Library at Emory University, the Odum Library at Valdosta State University, the Illinois Historical Society, the Moultrie Georgia Public Library, the Chicago Historical Society, the Memphis Tennessee Public Library, the Carnegie Library in Pittsburgh, Pennsylvania, and the Library of Congress and National Archives in Washington, DC.

I would like to thank my family and friends for their years of love and cheerleading and last, but certainly not least, I could not have produced this book without the unwavering support of my wife Carly. Not only does she encourage all of my efforts, she also exercises great patience as stacks of books, papers and other research material sometimes seem to take over our home.

LIST OF MAPS

Map 1. Mississippi in 1860 //39

Map 2. Corinth-Pittsburg Landing Vicinity, April 1862 //62

Map 3. North Mississippi, 1862 //75

Map 4. Battle of Corinth, 1862 // 78

Map 5. Grierson's Raid, 1863 // 100

Map 6. Federal Advance on Vicksburg, 1863 //104

Map 7. Sherman's Meridian Campaign, 1864 // 150

Map 8. Vicinity of Brice's Cross Roads, 1864 // 159

1. John Jones Pettus, Mississippi's governor in 1861 (Mississippi Department of Archives and History).

2. Jefferson Davis, United States senator from Mississippi and the only president of the Confederacy (National Archives).

3. Mississippians in camp early in the war (Library of Congress).

4. Mississippians in camp early in the war (Library of Congress).

5. Corinth, Mississippi, under federal occupation (Mississippi Department of Archives and History).

6. Former slaves gather at the office of the provost marshal in Corinth during federal occupation (Mississippi Department of Archives and History).

7. Confederate dead in front of Battery Robinette after the assault on the federal works at Corinth (Illinois State Historical Library).

8. The Lafayette County Courthouse in Oxford during federal occupation (*Review of Reviews*).

9. The flamboyant Earl Van Dorn, whose successful raid on the federal supply depot at Holly Springs was a major victory for the Confederacy in Mississippi (Library of Congress).

10. Pennsylvanian John C. Pemberton, defender of Vicksburg (National Archives).

11. Ulysses S. Grant, whose victory at Vicksburg set him on a course that eventually led to the White House (Library of Congress).

12. Federal ships under fire on the Mississippi as they pass the Confederate batteries at Vicksburg on April 16, 1863 (Mississippi Department of Archives and History).

13. Federal troops camp in the shadow of Wexford Lodge, also known as the Shirley House, at Vicksburg (Chicago Historical Society).

14. Grant's troops marching triumphantly into Vicksburg past the Warren County Courthouse (Mississippi Department of Archives and History).

15. An American flag flies over the Warren County Courthouse after the fall of Vicksburg (*Review of Reviews*).

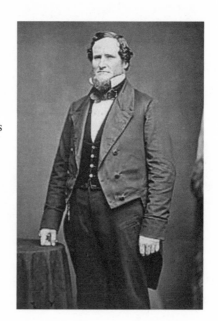

16. General William Barksdale fell with many of his fellow Mississippians at Gettysburg (Mississippi Department of Archives and History).

17. Former slaves who once belonged to Joseph Davis, the Confederate president's older brother, gather at the Davis plantation after it was seized by the federals (Vicksburg Old Courthouse Museum)

18. Jackson, Mississippi, the state capital, suffered a great deal of damage during the war (Mississippi Department of Archives and History).

19. William Tecumseh Sherman ordered his men to destroy the city of Meridian following their devastating march through central Mississippi (National Archives).

20. Edward Cary Walthall, one of Mississippi's most prominent Confederate generals (Mississippi Department of Archives and History).

21. General Stephen D. Lee commanded troops in Mississippi during the latter stages of the war (Library of Congress).

22. General Nathan Bedford Forrest, victor at Brice's Cross Roads (National Archives).

23. Charles Clark,
Mississippi's second, and
last, Confederate governor
(Mississippi Department of
Archives and History).

24. Confederate veterans from the 22nd Mississippi Infantry posed for this
photograph at their 1899 reunion (*Confederate Veteran*).

25. Reunion of Amite County's Confederate veterans around the turn of the century. Ironically, the men displayed an American flag for the photograph, the flag of the enemy in 1861 (author's collection).

26. Former soldiers along with their families and friends gathered for a photograph following a 1905 ceremony dedicating a monument to Carroll County's Confederate veterans (Mississippi Department of Archives and History).

27. The Jefferson Davis Presidential Library on the Mississippi
Gulf Coast (Carlise Womack).

1

A TRAGIC EVOLUTION

The Deed is Done, Disunion the Remedy.
Jackson Mississippian
November 9, 1860

As delegates to the Mississippi Secession Convention gathered at the state capital building in Jackson on January 9, 1861, James Lusk Alcorn knew that his cause was lost. A fifty-six-year-old planter from Coahoma County, Alcorn was one of the most respected men at the convention, and the unquestioned leader of a dwindling group of delegates who opposed disunion. He had worked tirelessly to stave off rash action, but the issue had been decided for all practical purposes several weeks earlier when Mississippians elected a decidedly pro-secession majority to the convention. During a caucus shortly before the final vote on the secession ordinance, Alcorn warned a handful of like-minded colleagues that severing ties with the Union would lead to civil war and massive loss of life, with federal soldiers trampling Mississippi's cotton fields, freeing the slaves at the point of a bayonet and forever altering the state's social system. After expending all of his energies trying to keep his state in the Union, Alcorn succumbed to the inevitable. His was the first name called as the final vote took place, and he responded by rising to address his fellow delegates. "The die is cast," he stated resolutely, but with obvious sorrow, "the Rubicon is crossed; I follow the army that goes to Rome; I vote for the ordinance."[1] In the end, secession triumphed, and Mississippi followed a course that would prove Alcorn a prophet.

In 1861, Mississippi was indeed firmly established at what one historian later described as the "storm center of secession."[2] For more than a decade radical politicians in the state had plied their trade by shouting at the top of their lungs that Mississippi was under siege. They had wheedled and humbugged the average white Mississippian into believing that the demise of his community was imminent, that everything he held sacred was about to be washed away by the rising tide of abolitionism. Playing on the white population's insecurities and race-based fears, these politicians created a climate of uncertainty that bred panic in many communities. As a result, much of Mississippi embraced the ultimate act of political defiance in 1861, and many of its citizens turned their backs on the nation of their birth. This political insurgence quickly gave way to a harsh military reality. Abraham Lincoln and the people of the non-slaveholding states would not allow the Southerners to break apart the Union, and great armies would ultimately invade the South, and Mississippi, to insure that the nation stayed whole.

Mississippi was the second state to leave the Union, following South Carolina's lead. More than 75,000 Mississippians fought for the Confederacy, some almost literally in their own backyards and others in distant locales like Virginia, Pennsylvania, or Kentucky. From a political standpoint, Mississippi contributed a number of its leaders to the Confederate Congress and provided the Confederacy with its only president. The city of Corinth, in the northern part of the state, was a vital transportation center coveted by federal military

---

[1] Lillian A. Pereyra, *James Lusk Alcorn: Persistent Whig* (Baton Rouge: Louisiana State University Press, 1966) 42–43.

[2] Reference to Percy Lee Rainwater, *Mississippi: Storm Center of Secession, 1856–1861* (Baton Rouge: Otto Claitor, 1938).

authorities as was the port city of Vicksburg on the Mississippi River. Throughout Mississippi, small towns and farms with their surrounding hills and hollows became parts of great battlefields on which United States and Confederate soldiers clashed in large numbers. Blood spilled out across the Mississippi countryside as the state's young men fell, and a social system in which half of the state's population languished in bondage began to unravel. By 1865, many white Mississippians were left in permanent mourning for lost loved ones, and for the loss of a perceived "way of life" that generations of their descendants would struggle to reconstruct, exaggerate, and glorify. At the same time, the state's former slaves had their first experience with freedom.

Mississippi may have followed a radical course in 1861, but the state was not always at the forefront of the struggle between state and federal authority. Despite a great deal of posturing by ambitious politicians, from statehood in 1817 to the mid-1850s most Mississippians were content within the Union. They lived in a frontier state where rich and poor alike wanted nothing catastrophic to alter their chances for prosperity. Cotton made some Mississippi planters wealthy within the confines of the Union, and civil agitation would only serve to cut into their profits. Likewise, the mass of poorer whites who focussed their energies on sustenance farming wanted no disruptive forces impeding their efforts to make a living. Because the first quarter century of Mississippi's existence was a formative period, local and state concerns usually took precedence over national political intrigues. Immediately following statehood, Mississippians labored to improve their state's standing in the Union. They linked their personal security and hopes for prosperity to their state's success. While slavery became an issue to be debated, and to many an institution to be defended with greater ferocity as time wore on, withdrawal from the Union was seen as a reckless alternative by most Mississippi communities for most of the antebellum period.

Mississippi entered the Union in 1817 with most of its population and wealth concentrated in the southwest, around the old Natchez District along the Mississippi River. A small number of wealthy planters who owned most of the region's slaves dominated political affairs there and had a cozy relationship with many federal officials. The planters looked to the United States government to advance their interests through expanded markets and internal improvements. They also had commercial contact with the North as part of an expanding market economy. To the east of the Natchez district, and across the Pearl River, lay the area known as the Piney Woods. This sparsely populated region was home to small farmers who worked poor soil and owned few slaves. Though some were active in civic matters, the citizens of the Piney Woods did not have the resources to compete politically with their more affluent neighbors. They struggled for a voice in state affairs and had little time or inclination to consider events on the national level.

For more than a decade after statehood, most of Mississippi remained the domain of the Choctaw and Chickasaw Indians. The tribes had inhabited the land for centuries but, like their brethren throughout North America, they were doomed by the white man's concept of property acquisition and ownership. Through treaties in the 1820s and 1830s the federal government forced the Indians off the land, opening millions of acres in Mississippi for settlement. The removal of the Indians signaled the beginning of a great land boom and a sharp change in the state's political environment. New counties came into being as thousands of settlers flooded into Mississippi to start new lives. Most of the settlers came from the Southern states on the Atlantic seaboard, bringing with them the Jeffersonian ideal of the independent yeoman farmer. In 1832, a constitutional convention met and adopted a new, more democratic state constitution that reflected Mississippi's population shift and wrested political power from the old Natchez elite.

The settlement of Mississippi beginning in the 1820s followed traditional patterns of American westward expansion. The call of new land and the quest for prosperity drew thousands of dissatisfied residents from the older states to a new life in a rugged, sometimes uninviting wilderness. Some of these settlers even established homes in Mississippi before the government officially organized the Indian holdings. For many the move west was part of a family tradition. The family histories of many settlers included a father and mother born in

Virginia, the Carolinas, or Georgia, older children born in Alabama or Tennessee, and younger children born as true first-generation Mississippians. Although no one knew it at the time, many of the small sons that these immigrants brought with them, or those born in Mississippi soon after their family's arrival, would serve in the Confederate army. Unlike their parents, the legacy of these children as pioneer settlers ultimately gave way to a collective legacy of defeat that branded them as casualties of a unique regional identity.

As their populations increased following statehood in 1817, new counties very quickly produced dozens of small communities with families trying to recreate some semblance of the social environment that they had known in the East. Establishing themselves as part of a community was important to the immigrants because the process also established their identities in the new land. In the East, they had been able to draw comfort from the social and cultural interaction within their communities. The familiarity of neighborhood bred a sense of security, and a community hierarchy fostered order and stability. By immigrating to the frontier, settlers had broken old community ties and cast themselves socially adrift. As a result they tried to either transplant or create a sense of community in their new home as quickly as possible. They sought to bring order to their new, usually isolated social universe. Without order there could be no community cohesion and subsequently no feeling of security so vital for community prosperity and expansion. From a practical standpoint, the burden of taming the Mississippi wilderness would be lightened with cooperative effort. To build vibrant communities settlers would have to carve roads through forests, construct public buildings and establish local networks of commerce. More hands would make the work easier.

As new communities developed, social hierarchies evolved within their bounds. Some settlers had come to Mississippi with more goods than their new neighbors, and thus were already more prosperous. Others initially had little, but having arrived early were able to acquire prime land on which they could work their way up in a relatively short time. Through means that they already possessed, hard work, or the right combination of ambition and blind luck, some citizens prospered more than others and through their wealth established themselves as community leaders. Their neighbors were willing to follow their lead in various civic matters, either by calling on them for advice or by electing them to public office. A crude class system developed that would soon be better defined through intermarriage among the more prominent families. Although the class system of the Mississippi frontier was fluid, within a generation somewhat sharper distinctions would develop between the few in the state with significant means, and the bulk of he population that usually found themselves struggling. In 1861, these community hierarchies would help provide the chain of command for local military units going off to war. In the early stages of the conflict, military qualifications in many cases took a back seat to political or economic influence as volunteers looked for men to lead them.

Mississippi's reaction to the Nullification Crisis of 1832–1833 reflected its citizens' satisfaction within the Union, and the mindset of the state's residents with regard to the concept of states' rights and secession at that particular time. The crisis began as a dispute between the state of South Carolina and the federal government over a series of national tariffs that the South Carolinians as well as many other southerners viewed as excessive. US Senator John C. Calhoun, a champion of states' rights, led South Carolina's protest against the actions of the federal government and its chief executive, the formidable Andrew Jackson. Calhoun argued that a state had the right to nullify a federal law if that state believed that the law was unconstitutional or in any way infringed upon the rights of its citizens. Furthermore, if the state and the federal government continued to disagree on the nature of a law, then the state could exercise its ultimate authority and leave the Union. Because the rest of the South traditionally opposed the "Yankee Tariff" on the grounds that it favored Northern manufacturers, Calhoun believed that the other Southern states would fall in line behind South Carolina, threaten radical action if the tariff was left in place, and by presenting a united front force the federal government to change the law. In the end, however, Calhoun overestimated the other states' commitment to Southern solidarity and underestimated their loyalty to Andrew Jackson.

In Mississippi, there was no more admired figure in the 1830s than Andrew Jackson. His record as a war hero captivated the population and tens of thousands of recent immigrants to the state credited Jackson personally with removing the Indians and making available the land on which they settled. To many he was a role model, a fellow westerner who had risen to great heights as the product of a frontier society. While many of Mississippi's citizens may have sympathized with Calhoun and his ideas about the tariff, they loved Jackson and the "rise of the common man" that he represented. In turn, much of Mississippi's political community pledged their support to Jackson and the United States government in the face of South Carolina's plea for Southern unity and threats of secession. As the crisis peaked the Mississippi legislature denounced the tariff but with equal fervor denounced South Carolina's stance against the federal government, and particularly the act of secession as dangerous and "contrary to the letter and spirit of the Constitution." The lawmakers also emphatically offered support to the president "in the full exercise of his legitimate powers to restore peace and harmony to our distracted country and to maintain, unsullied and unimpaired, the honor, the independence and integrity of the Union."[3] As Mississippi's leading politicians pledged their loyalty to the Union, a great wave of patriotism swept through the countryside. In 1833, Mississippi had been a state for less than two decades and its citizens had no intention of leaving the security of the Union because of a philosophical squabble over the nature of federal authority.

Lost in the shuffle was the dissenting opinion, which would give birth to a political movement radically grounded in the concept of states' rights. As other Mississippians celebrated the Union, a vocal

---

[3] Massachusetts, *State Papers on Nullification: Including the Acts of the Convention of the people of South Carolina, Assembled at Columbia, November 19, 1832 and March 11, 1833; The Proclamation of the President of the United States, and the Proceedings of the Several State Legislatures Which Have Acted Upon the Subject* (Boston: Dutton and Wentworth, 1834) 231.

minority of the state's political operatives warned of disaster if
Mississippi and the rest of the South did not stand behind Calhoun.
Their rhetoric was predictable, and alarmist. They attacked the tariff
as an oppressive economic plot hatched by Northern business
interests to exploit the South and thereby corrupt the values upon
which the federal government was founded. They argued that an
individual state, as a voluntary member of the national compact,
reserved the right to judge the constitutionality of federal laws.
Coupled with these arguments, usually indirectly, was the inference
that outside influences in any form represented a potential threat to
the institution of slavery. By evoking the potential threat to slavery,
Mississippi nullifiers added an emotional element to their argument,
an element that could generate attention in a way that abstract
political ideology could not. Congress eventually passed a
compromise tariff that diffused the situation, but in Mississippi and
the rest of the South the concept of states' rights and the protection
of slavery became inextricably linked. Over the next quarter century
the two concepts would become one, and the minority argument of
1833 would become the majority opinion of 1861.

Calhoun's greatest supporter and the unchallenged leader of the
nullification movement in Mississippi was John Anthony Quitman.
From the 1830s until his death in 1859, the overbearing Quitman
never wavered in his extreme views regarding states' rights, slavery,
and the limits of federal authority. Through the ups and downs of the
1840s and 1850s the rapidly emerging states' rights wing of
Mississippi's Democratic Party looked to him for counsel and
leadership. As one of the state's most prominent politicians for most
of his adult life, Quitman made sure that his extreme views were
always part of any debate on the inflammatory sectional issues of the
day. He was enamored with the concept of secession as the ultimate
show of state authority and few doubted that Quitman's ghost looked
on approvingly as Mississippi finally left the Union in 1861.

Ironically, the man who became a spokesman for Southern
radicals was born in the North. Quitman came into the world in
Rhinebeck, New York, on September 1, 1799. The son of a Lutheran
minister, he studied law and in 1821 moved to Natchez on the

Mississippi River where he was determined to make a name for himself. He established a law practice and rapidly ascended the Natchez social ladder. Within a decade his work as an attorney coupled with successful land speculation made Quitman a member of the prominent planter class in the city. He entered politics, first securing a place in the state legislature in the 1820s and later serving as governor. Quitman was a states' rights ideologue even before he embraced Calhoun's nullification theory. At the heart of his concerns was a self-serving perception of the tariff and other federal political activity as a threat to Mississippi's plantation elite. He believed that any federal legislation that favored Northern manufacturers, as the tariff did, was by definition harmful to the South and particularly to the South's political ruling class. More importantly, he feared early on that the institution of slavery was vulnerable to outside pressures originating in the North, regardless of who was in the White House, and he watched with increasing alarm the rise of the abolitionist movement in the non-slaveholding states. Northerners, he believed, had taken "Indians and negroes under their special care," and were determined to "regulate all our domestic legislation" with regard to slavery.[4] On the eve of secession Southern radicals would quote Calhoun prodigiously, but in Mississippi those who favored their state's withdrawal from the Union also quoted Quitman.

The catalyst for the increase in radical thought and political rhetoric in Mississippi, and in the rest of the South, was the Mexican War. The war was primarily a Southern undertaking promoted in the name of Manifest Destiny by expansionist president James K. Polk of Tennessee and his Southern supporters in Congress. The annexation of Texas in 1845 had given the United States another slave state and Southern political leaders had dreams of expanding slavery to the Pacific Ocean and perhaps even south into Central America. The primary impediment to their dreams of expansion was the fact that

---

[4] Robert E. May, *John A. Quitman, Old South Crusader* (Baton Rouge: Louisiana State University Press, 1985) 42–49; J. F. H. Claiborne to John A. Quitman, October 20, 1830, in John Francis Hamtramck Claiborne, *Life and Correspondence of John A. Quitman*, vol. 1 (New York: Harper and Bros., 1860) 95–96.

much of the western lands coveted by the Southerners belonged to Mexico. As a result, the United States in effect picked a fight with its neighbor to the south, turning a border dispute along the Rio Grande and Nueces Rivers in south Texas into a full-scale war.

Mississippians, like other Southerners, were enthusiastic in their support for the Mexican War. The state contributed three regiments to the conflict, the most prominent of which was the 1st Mississippi Regiment, which was assembled at Vicksburg and commanded by Colonel Jefferson Davis. Once the United States declared war, communities around the state sent their young men off to Mexico with great fanfare. Parades, parties, and speeches by long-winded politicians were the order of the day as the volunteers, their friends, and their families united behind the effort. Few doubted that Mississippi's sons would carry the day and make their communities proud.

Despite the fact that the United States was fighting with questionable motives against an overmatched enemy, and that more Americans died from disease during the struggle than from combat wounds, the Mexican War was viewed by many as a triumph for Mississippi and the other Southern states that contributed volunteers. The war produced nationally acclaimed Mississippi war heroes, including Davis, but more importantly it produced community heroes as well. Mississippi's veterans returned to small towns around the state with firmly established reputations as honorable men who did their part in upholding the strong military tradition of the South. Those who died during the struggle became community martyrs, men to be emulated and whose memory should be cherished. The participation of community sons had also localized the war and given individual communities a stake in its outcome. The men had represented their communities well, and throughout Mississippi the soldiers' service and the war's outcome were celebrated as community victories.

In addition to bolstering community pride, the Mexican War had other far reaching influences on many Mississippi locales. Just as the participation of community sons localized the military conflict, it also localized subsequent national issues that the war's outcome created. Paramount among these was the issue of the spread of slavery into the newly acquired western territories. In 1846, Pennsylvania representative David Wilmot introduced into the House of Representatives an amendment to an appropriations bill that denied the introduction of slavery into any territory acquired by the United States as a result of the war with Mexico. Though the so-called Wilmot Proviso failed to become law, it helped polarize national sentiment with regard to the expansion of slavery. It also helped the cause of states' rights extremists in the South who hoped to convince the masses that a shadowy abolitionist conspiracy aimed at destroying the "Southern way of life" was underway in the North. For many Mississippians the Wilmot Proviso and other proposals to halt slavery's expansion in the years following the war became not merely the distant maneuverings of anti-slavery politicians at the national level. They represented an effort to deny the South the spoils of war that community sons had helped win and, as such, were an insult to the individual community's support for the war effort. These were affronts that could not, and would not, be easily forgotten. As sectional tensions increased, one Mississippi politician reminded his constituents again and again that all Mississippians "have been virtually excluded from their just rights in the greater portion, if not all, of the vast and rich territories acquired from Mexico in the late war; and thus, by unjust and insulting discrimination, the advantages and benefits of the Union have been denied them."[5] Political implications aside, the war with Mexico and particularly the participation of so many Mississippians was also important because it established a standard of personal and community honor through military service for the next generation of white males in the state. As talk of war and the call for volunteer soldiers grew louder in 1861, young men in Mississippi did not have to look far for examples to emulate.

From 1840 to 1860, Mississippi continued to grow and evolve, and its total population more than doubled to almost 800,000 residents. By 1860 many local communities were well established and

---

[5] *Mississippian* (Jackson), November 1, 1850, 2.

networks of dirt roads linked towns with one another, and with the state's developing markets. Improvements in communication and transportation also allowed local communities access to information about events taking place outside their immediate vicinity, and some of the news that the citizenry heard alarmed them. In 1840, white Mississippians in many newly settled areas of the state busied themselves building new lives with little concern about national events. Twenty years later they had created their communities, and the social infrastructure of their state, but a threat to their hard-won security seemed to loom close on the horizon. Community newspapers that reported local events also kept readers apprised of state and national politics, usually with a partisan slant and under inflammatory headlines designed to grab the reader's attention. The outside world encroached on even the most isolated settlements in Mississippi, making it difficult for anyone to ignore the most singularly significant issue of the day.

By 1860 Mississippi's social, economic, and political institutions were hopelessly entangled in the web of slavery. An increasing dependence on staple agriculture created a slave-based cotton culture that affected all of the state's white residents to one degree or another. During the 1850s, Mississippi established itself as the nation's top cotton producer and by the end of the decade the state was generating over a million ginned bales of cotton annually to lead the Southern states and contribute more than one-fifth to the US total. For the well-heeled planters of the era, the 1850s were a time of great prosperity, evidenced by the fact that during that ten-year period the value of farm lands in Mississippi increased by almost 200 percent. Likewise, the number of slaves in Mississippi increased during the period and by the eve of the Civil War slaves represented 55 percent of the state's total population.

MISSISSIPPI POPULATION STATISTICS
(percentage of the total)

Year	Free	Slave	Total
1840	179,074 (47.8)	195,211 (52.2)	374,285
1850	295,718 (48.8)	309,874 (51.2)	605,592
1860	353,899 (44.8)	436,631 (55.2)	790,530

From the end of the Mexican War the slavery issue dominated Mississippi politics. It helped destroy the state's Whig Party, which was perceived by many as having Northern sympathies, and ultimately allowed the radical states' rights wing of the Democratic Party to emerge unchallenged. A fledgling states' rights movement had developed in Mississippi in response to the Nullification Crisis of the early 1830s, but once that crisis passed radical leaders were unable to influence significant numbers of voters. Following the Mexican War, however, states' rights advocates pointed to the Wilmot Proviso and speeches by various Northern politicians as evidence of an abolitionist conspiracy in the North. They used fear to draw voters to their cause through exhaustive rhetoric that centered around the demise of slavery and the subsequent breakdown of Southern communities, and white culture in general, once emancipation had taken place. This argument was increasingly potent in a state where the white population in 1860 was in the minority.

One of the best practitioners of this alarmist political strategy was Albert Gallatin Brown, who held various political offices and was arguably the most popular politician in Mississippi during the antebellum period. Brown was born in South Carolina in 1813 and at the age of ten migrated to Copiah County, Mississippi, with his family. He attended Jefferson College near Natchez and Mississippi College in Clinton, studied law and was admitted to the bar in 1833. An energetic and highly ambitious young man, Brown wasted no time beginning a law practice and a political career. He was elected to the Mississippi legislature where he served two terms and in 1838, when he was only twenty-five years old, he won election to the

United States House of Representatives. Five years later Mississippians elected Brown as their governor, making him the state's youngest chief executive ever. He later returned to Congress and during the 1850s, as sectional tensions increased, represented Mississippi alongside Jefferson Davis in the United States Senate. Like Davis, Brown resigned his seat once Mississippi left the union in January 1861.

Brown's rise to prominence was notable because it paralleled the growing sectional nature of state and national politics. Brown's career was built on the votes of small slaveholders, non-slaveholders of moderate means, and poor whites who barely scratched out a living on the state's poorest soil. Many of these Mississippians lived in the eastern half of the state and felt threatened by the rapid expansion of plantation agriculture. Some of their anxieties were economic. They could not compete with the large planters, were jealous of accumulated wealth, and were sensitive to their place in the state's economic and political mix. Others had deeper fears. From a social standpoint, the economic inferiority of poorer whites in relation to the planters made them all the more conscious of their own social superiority in relation to the slave population. This translated into a fierce defense of slavery in the poor white community despite the fact that the institution did not benefit them financially and actually served to fill the economic coffers of the wealthy planters whom they distrusted. In short, even the poorest white male realized that he would never languish at the bottom of the state's social system as long as the institution of slavery existed. Such attitudes made poor whites susceptible to pro-slavery demagogic appeals.

Brown won seats in the state and national legislatures by championing the interests of the small farmer of eastern and south Mississippi against the wealthy river counties. As slavery spread, however, Brown dedicated himself to racially based politics. He won election to high office and became one of the premier demagogues of the antebellum period through the use of a consistently sectional platform that emphasized the ills of emancipation. "Disunion is a fearful thing," he said in 1860, "but emancipation is worse. Better leave the Union in the open face of day, than be lighted from it at midnight by the arsonist's torch."

In Washington, Brown was vocal during what many referred to as the nation's "first secession crisis" in 1850. The status of slavery in the newly acquired western territories created the crisis, fueling the fires of debate in Congress and creating a great deal of ill will between the slave states and the free states. A number of important issues were in play but paramount were the status of slavery in California (which was poised to enter the Union), slavery and the slave trade in the District of Columbia, and the passage of a new fugitive slave law. The debate was tailor-made for states' rights demagogues like Brown and John A. Quitman, both of whom railed against what they claimed was a massive abolitionist conspiracy in the North. "Pray to God and keep your powder dry" was Brown's advice to a large crowd in Jackson during a passionate tirade defending slavery and the Southern way of life. For the first time, a good number of Mississippians wondered aloud if their state might leave the Union, with some rumors including the caveat that if all the slave states left the Union to form a Southern confederacy, Brown or Quitman might serve as the new nation's first president. The crisis eventually passed as a result of what would be called the Compromise of 1850, postponing radical action by the South. Still, Southern political leaders were not satisfied and Mississippi's congressional delegation protested any restrictions that the compromise placed on slavery anywhere in the United States. Their constituents were generally more moderate in tone, suspicious of growing opposition to slavery in the North but unwilling to break up the Union over the issue.

After extensive debate the Mississippi legislature voted to accept the Compromise of 1850, and in 1851 the state narrowly elected a governor who had run on a pro-Union platform. After violent civil strife over slavery tore apart Kansas in 1854, however, states' rights politicians had enough rhetorical ammunition to make the abolitionist threat seem real in the minds of many Mississippians. The same year the formation of the Republican Party, with an agenda that included stopping the expansion of slavery, reinforced the idea that anti-slavery ideologues were organizing to gain control of the federal government in hopes of destroying the social, political, and economic institutions of slave-holding states. For the rest of the decade, Mississippi Democrats consolidated their strength around a strict states' rights platform that was complex, but had at its foundation the protection of slavery at all costs. Their position left no room for compromise and, at the end of the 1850s, lit the fuse that would ignite civil war.

After 1855 Democratic candidates carried most of Mississippi in state and national elections, and ambitious politicians vying for leadership positions within the Democratic Party knew that they could not suceed without embracing states' rights. Political leaders at the local level used states' rights rhetoric in speeches that, while not necessarily inciting their constituents to radical action, made sectional tensions a part of local conversation. More and more communities around the state held meetings to discuss political issues of the day, all of which were to one degree or another tied to the slavery debate. These meetings did not usually advocate secession as a singular course of action, but they did cross an important threshold in that most recognized secession as a possible solution to the state's problems. Such discussions also brought the slavery question into individual communities and planted it firmly at the doorstep of anyone who took part in day-to-day community discourse.

Ambitious politicians reveled in the fears of their constituents and exploited community anxieties in speech after speech. If abolitionists in the Northern states get their way, the rhetoric insisted, the South's economy would be ruined and freed slaves would wreak havoc, demanding social equality and most likely causing a race war in which thousands would die. Such horrific predictions terrified those Mississippi citizens who had worked for decades to build up their communities and to establish the security that those communities provided.

Radical politicians spoke to crowds all over the state, and their strategy was apparent. While extremist elements of the Democratic Party became dominant in Mississippi by preaching states' rights, there was only one states' right that could stir the emotion of white masses regardless of their economic circumstance. To an increasing number of white Mississippians the threat to slavery was seen not simply as a threat to the property of slaveholders. Many believed the radical politicians as they argued that the demise of the institution would quickly lead to societal degeneration, chaos and violence that would expose all whites to, as one newspaper phrased it, "the butchery of African assassins." Mississippi's Democratic leaders took advantage of the fears that the Southern wing of their national organization had helped create by constantly reminding the masses that the Democratic Party was the party of the South, and the only political party that could fend off the abolitionist threat. By inciting fear among their constituents, states' rights Democrats ran roughshod over what little political competition existed at both the local and state levels as the decade wore on. They continued their rhetorical onslaught through the 1850s until most voices of reason in their party had been either converted or silenced. According to one politician of the era, many average citizens eventually accepted states' rights rhetoric as fact simply because it "had been so often sounded in their ears that they had become somewhat accustomed to it." In 1859 John Jones Pettus, the uncompromising states' rights candidate of the Democratic Party, won the race for governor in a landslide, garnering more than three-quarters of the total vote.[6]

The perceived threat to the institution of slavery was an effective tool for extremist politicians because it tended to unite most white Mississippians, rich or poor, slaveholding or not. Throughout the South, racism left most whites in a dilemma that would not reconcile itself. Although literally surrounded by blacks, they could not conceive of a society in which the races were equal. Slavery defined the self-perception of every white Southerner. For the planter elite, slavery signified power, status, and paternalistic control of not only their slaves but, as fellow dependants in the household, of their wives and children as well. The ability of white males to hold property established the social order in the South, and included claims over

---

[6] *Mississippian* (Jackson), March 7, 1851, 3; John W. Wood, *Union and Secession in Mississippi* (Memphis: Saunders, Parrish, and Whitmore Printers, 1863) 13.

their dependants based in both custom and law. For the large planter, a disruption of the slave system meant a disruption of his societal authority and the "natural" relationship between the male head of the family and his charges.

The impact was similar on poorer, non-slaveholding white males. Though not directly involved as slaveholders, they recognized the social impact that the demise of slavery would have on their world. Regardless of their economic condition, they drew strength and self-esteem simply from the fact that they were white males and heads of their own households. Their white skin bonded them to their more affluent planter neighbors, with whom they periodically interacted. They recognized the importance of property as the traditional barometer of independence and feared a future in which they might compete with free blacks for land or in the labor market. From a psychological standpoint, the South's slave-based society allowed poorer white males the comfort of viewing themselves as free men in a society where most of the population—white women and children along with slaves—were denied the rights of citizens. They defined their own independence through the bondage of others and believed that the demise of slavery would irreversibly harm their position in Southern society. The small farmers' race-based "equality" with wealthy planters was illusionary, but their fears were ripe for exploitation by secessionist politicians as sectional tensions increased.

Mississippi's 1859 gubernatorial election served notice that the state's political course had taken a radical turn. States' rights Democrats secured the nomination of John Jones Pettus, a Tennessee transplant who had been a member of Mississippi's political community since the 1840s. Pettus began his career representing Kemper County in the state legislature and later served as the president of the state senate. Described by a contemporary as "a disunion man of the most unmitigated order," he ran on a platform that included heavily arming the state to defend the institution of slavery should a Republican be elected to head the federal government in 1860.[7] Fight the abolitionist threat or perish became the Democratic rallying cry as the party's candidates saturated the state with harsh rhetoric designed to appeal to the deepest race-based fears of Mississippi whites. A patchwork coalition of former Whigs and disaffected Democrats known benignly as the Opposition Party tried to mount a challenge to Pettus but their candidate, Harvey W. Walter, stood little chance. During the first week of October 1859 the unrepentant Pettus crushed Walter by a final count of 34,559 to 10,308, carrying all but three of the state's counties. In four counties, Franklin, Jackson, Marion, and Rankin, Walter did not receive a single vote. Democrats won the other major state races by margins of over three to one and also filled the state's seats in the United States House of Representatives. After the election, William L. Sharkey, a former Whig and the Opposition Party's most prominent leader gave an address in which he predicted dark times ahead:

> It is a cause of regret that we cannot pass in silence over the question of slavery.... A few fanatics at the North and a few alarmists and disunionists at the South, keep it up for their own purposes. It is made by them the chief ingredients in elections and it is thrust into all the deliberations in Congress.... It is daily making us more and more sectional and more and more inimical; and that it must seriously endanger our national existence none will deny.[8]

As if to confirm everything that states' rights politicians had said during the campaign, the fanatical abolitionist John Brown launched his famous raid on Harper's Ferry, Virginia, in the interim between Pettus's election and his inauguration. Though unsuccessful, Brown's attempt to capture a federal arsenal and provoke a slave rebellion struck fear in the hearts of whites throughout the South. Many in the North condemned the violence, but many others lauded Brown's

---

[7] Reuben Davis, *Recollections of Mississippi and Mississippians*, rev. ed. (Hattiesburg: University and College Press of Mississippi, 1972) 378.

[8] William L. Sharkey to Henry Dickinson, September 3, 1859, McGavock Family Papers, Tennessee State Library and Archives, Nashville, Tennessee.

efforts as the notion of a vast abolitionist conspiracy became believable in the minds of many Southerners. Pettus devoted much of his spirited inaugural address to the sectional conflict and the Northern "dogma of equality of the negro to the white man." For months after the Harper's Ferry raid Democratic newspapers exploited the fears of the electorate by printing account after account of rumored slave atrocities taking place in the border states, in the South, and around Mississippi. In Natchez, the Democratic *Daily Courier* alarmed many of its readers by informing them that maps of Mississippi were found among John Brown's papers. In Aberdeen, the *Sunny South* called Brown's raid simply "The Beginning of the End."[9]

In reality, white anxiety regarding major slave revolts was unfounded. While individual slaves from time to time might attempt to flee, circumstances in Mississippi dictated that there was little chance of a large-scale slave rebellion breaking out, even in those parts of the state with the highest slave populations. As sectional tensions increased during the 1850s Mississippi slaveholders became increasingly concerned about security to the point of obsession. They tightened their control over their slaves, making it almost impossible for them to organize even had they sought to, and the slaves themselves knew that any act of agitation would be met with swift and brutal retribution. By 1859, paranoid slaveholders and many non-slaveholders alike were heavily armed and always on the lookout for anything even slightly out of the ordinary. In addition, those slaves with the ability to lead a revolt were usually those with the most to lose. Because of their competence their masters had likely placed them in positions of responsibility on the farm or plantation, and given them special privileges. They had their families to consider, not to mention their own lives. For all of these reasons a major slave rebellion during which large numbers of slaves rose up

---

[9] For detailed accounts of reaction in Mississippi to John Brown's raid, see Donald Brooks Kelley, "Harper's Ferry: Prelude to Crisis in Mississippi," *Journal of Mississippi History* 27/4 (November 1965): 351–72; and Adrienne Cole Phillips, "The Mississippi Press's Response to John Brown's Raid," *Journal of Mississippi History* 48/2 (May 1986): 119–34.

and killed their masters was the least common form of slave resistance in the antebellum South, though it was the most feared by whites.

Whether threats to their safety were real or imagined, Mississippi whites, especially those involved in state government, took them seriously. The year 1860 saw Mississippi fortify itself for whatever trials might lay in the future. The state legislature appropriated $150,000 for arming and reorganizing the state's militia and many counties began producing new volunteer "Home Guard" units. Governor Pettus was forced to devote more and more time to military concerns as his office was inundated with requests from all over the state for military supplies.

Meanwhile, in Washington DC, the nation was unraveling in part because the national Democratic Party was fracturing. During spring 1860, the slavery issue irreparably divided the Democrats, thus ensuring a Republican victory in the presidential election the following fall. The Democratic National Convention met in Charleston, South Carolina, in April and there Northern Democrats passed resolutions endorsing the concept of popular sovereignty—with the people of a given territory or state voting on the issue—as a solution to the slavery debate. Democratic delegates from the South condemned popular sovereignty and any other form of compromise on the slavery issue, insisting on federal protection of the institution in all states and territories. Mississippi's United States senator Albert Gallatin Brown issued a statement that summed up the South's ambitions: "The whole power of the government," he wrote, "in all its departments, is to be used, as soon as we get hold of it, to protect our slave property in the territories and on the high seas, in the same way and to the same extent that other kinds of property are protected."[10] Mississippi sent an eleven-man delegation to the convention, led by staunch states' rights advocate David C. Glenn and including newspaper publisher Ethelbert Barksdale, owner of the influential Jackson *Mississippian*. Both Glenn and Barksdale addressed

---

[10] Dunbar Rowland, *Encyclopedia of Mississippi History*, 4 vols. (Madison WI: Selwyn A. Brant, 1907) 1:633.

the convention, stating that there could be no compromise on the slavery issue, and that the concept of popular sovereignty was unacceptable to Mississippi Democrats.

The convention as a whole eventually voted to endorse popular sovereignty. In response, Mississippi's delegation and those from seven other states of the lower South walked out on the proceedings. "Go your way and we will go ours," Glenn said to his Northern brethren as the assembly broke up, "The South leaves you."[11] Eventually the two wings of the party met separately to nominate candidates for president. Northern Democrats nominated Stephen Douglas of Illinois while the Southern states' rights advocates chose the vice president of the United States, Kentuckian John C. Breckinridge, as their candidate. Along with Republican nominee Abraham Lincoln, a fourth candidate rounded out the field in the general election. John Bell of Tennessee represented the Constitutional Union Party, an upstart organization that hoped to become an effective agent for compromise. Bell and his followers argued that Southerners should fight for their rights within the Union, and did their best to side-step any inflammatory political discussions of slavery. This moderate strategy would garner significant support in some parts of the South, but the Constitutional Union Party was not destined to carry the day in a region still haunted by the ghost of John Brown.

In Mississippi, many in the so-called Opposition Party backed Bell and did their best to counter Breckinridge's candidacy during the 1860 contest but, as was the case in the most recent statewide elections, States' Rights Democrats were dominant. Douglas had little support in the state and Lincoln was not even placed on the ballot. The rhetorical crux of the contest between Breckinridge and Bell was familiar. Mississippi Democrats trumpeted the states' rights doctrine while the Opposition, now operating under the banner of Constitutional Unionists, warned voters of hidden agendas and the desperate need to protect the Union of their forefathers. In the press,

---

[11] Quoted in Robert W. Dubay, *John Jones Pettus, Mississippi Fire-Eater: His Life and Times, 1813–1867* (Jackson: University Press of Mississippi, 1975) 58.

both sides used language colored by military imagery. Democratic papers warned readers to "gird on your armor and prove the title of your property by your trusty swords," while Bell's supporters advised the voting public to "buckle on your armor and go forth to do battle for the success of Union candidates." Opposition stalwart William Sharkey toured the state giving speeches that in actuality were more anti-Breckinridge than pro-Bell. He knew that his party's only chance was to convince Mississippi voters that the states' rights Democrats were committed to a dangerous course that would take the South out of the Union and lead to bloody civil war. As the election grew closer the rhetoric grew harsher, with Sharkey emphasizing secession's violent consequences in an attempt to "outscare" the Democrats. "If a state goes out of the Union," he stated time and again, "she must prepare to wade through blood."[12]

Though Sharkey was respected around the state, his words of warning were not enough to stop the Democrats. In November, Lincoln, whose countenance one Mississippi Democratic editor described as being "strongly marked with the blood of his negro ancestry," was elected president of the United States, polarizing sectional sentiment. Breckinridge carried Mississippi over Bell by a vote of 39,962 to 24,693 with Douglas garnering 3,597. Bell's support came from traditional anti-Democratic strongholds along the Mississippi River and the northeast part of the state where there were relatively few slaves or slaveholders.

Following the election of Lincoln, events moved quickly in Mississippi. In the state capitol, the *Mississippian* reflected the dominant mood in an editorial titled "The Deed Is Done, Disunion the Remedy" published soon after Lincoln's victory. From the governor's mansion, Pettus called the legislature into extraordinary session scheduled for November 26. He also invited Mississippi's congressional delegation to meet with him at the mansion a few days prior to the session to discuss a course of action. Four days before the legislature met, Mississippi's United States senators Jefferson Davis and Albert Gallatin Brown, and representatives Reuben Davis, Otho

---

[12] Quoted in Rainwater, *Storm Center of Secession*, 150.

R. Singleton, William Barksdale, and Lucius Q. C. Lamar met with Pettus in Jackson. Secession was considered inevitable, but there were stark differences of opinion on how secession might be accomplished. Jefferson Davis, Brown, and Lamar counseled caution, believing that Mississippi should leave the Union only in concert with other Southern states. Davis in particular believed that peaceable secession was impossible, and that the federal government would crush Mississippi if the state acted alone. On the other hand, Reuben Davis, Singleton, and Barksdale supported immediate secession. Favoring immediate action as well, Pettus cast the deciding vote for the group despite spirited attempts to change his mind. Those in the minority finally acquiesced so the group could publicly claim unanimity. On November 26, Pettus addressed the state legislature, advising that withdrawal from the Union was the only alternative to "Black Republican politics and free Negro morals." Believing that such a withdrawal from the Union would be only temporary, and filled with a certain degree of misguided missionary zeal, he told the assembly that it was time for Mississippi to "go down into Egypt while Herod rules in Judea." Ten thousand copies of Pettus's address were printed and distributed to the public as the legislature passed resolutions calling for a secession convention to meet the following month. Resolutions defending slavery as the ultimate states' right and condemning alleged Northern abuses of the Constitution were also proposed and passed one after another in rapid succession.[13]

In December 1860, Mississippians elected delegates to the state secession convention on a county-by-county basis. Candidates for these positions were not necessarily nominated on a particular platform, although their thoughts regarding the secession question were usually well known to local voters. In general, county conventions that nominated candidates did not establish strict guidelines for delegates with regard to voting, choosing instead to allow the delegates to exercise their best judgment during deliberations. While the procedures used by each county during the process were not uniform, in most counties elections involved

---

[13] Quoted in Robert W. Dubay, *John Jones Pettus*, 70.

candidates who favored separate state secession and those leaning toward Southern cooperation. Cooperationists generally took the stand that Lincoln's election alone was not a reason to disrupt the Union. Only after all options within the Union had been exhausted, they argued, should Mississippi consider secession, and then only in concert with the other Southern states. Within this conservative group, the exact options that individual candidates were willing to explore varied, as did the lengths to which they were willing to go to keep Mississippi in the Union. In general, few candidates labeled as cooperationists were firmly against the *right* of the state to secede, but most were opponents of *immediate* secession without at least some lengthy discussions on the matter. The position of separate state secessionist candidates was more concise. They united in support of Mississippi's immediate secession, and cooperation with the other Southern states after secession had taken place.

Those Mississippians who opposed secession realized that the canvas for convention delegates was the final opportunity to advance their agenda and hopefully dilute the strength of radical states' righters. They painted secessionists as demagogues who were creating problems that did not exist, or at least did not exist to the extent that secessionists claimed. However, by 1860, the national political climate had changed. Events of the previous decade, especially John Brown's violent activities in Kansas and Virginia, seemed to prove that the secessionist threat was real, a position that states' rights Democrats had promoted for years. As a result, on the eve of the election of convention delegates it was difficult to convince most voters that the threat of abolitionism was nothing more than a political contrivance.

Still, those who favored keeping the Union intact would not give up without a fight. William Sharkey, their most prominent spokesman, toured the state promoting pro-Union meetings while James L. Alcorn conducted a strenuous campaign against secession in the Mississippi Delta. In Attala County, John W. Wood campaigned as a cooperationist but made it clear that he favored Mississippi remaining in the United States. A thirty-seven-year-old attorney from Kosciusko, Wood was more ideologue than politician, a rarity among the men pursuing seats at the convention. "We have heard much said about the right of secession," he said in one speech, "but there is no such right." Wood also was quick to point out the realities of life in an independent Mississippi, where "we shall lose our nationality" and be thrown into economic chaos, unable to support an army, internal improvements, or even the most basic governmental infrastructure. He concluded that once Mississippi left the Union "the rich man's property will be ruinously depreciated, the poor man will be robbed of the reward of his daily labor… and lawless violence and anarchy [will] take the place of law and order."[14]

Although the label included men of varied political leanings, during the actual canvas the term "cooperationist" generally came to mean anyone who was not for immediate secession. Most Cooperationists believed that the South had rights under the Constitution and that secession meant giving up those rights. They maintained that while Lincoln's election was legal from a technical standpoint, it violated the spirit of the Constitution. It represented not the mandate of the people of the United States, but the mandate of the Northern states, which were presumably united in their prejudices against the South's people and institutions. Most Cooperationists candidates, regardless of their degree of support for a more moderate course, were quick to ask their fellow citizens "Shall we abandon all…. Shall we give up all without an effort? Shall we not rather demand a full performance of the covenants of the Constitution?" Using the same line of thinking, more dedicated Union men claimed that Mississippi was on the verge of "committing suicide" and disparaged "the Scripture-quoting Pettus" for advocating a course of action "equaled in its cowardice only by its extreme silliness."[15]

Anti-secession sentiment persisted in the counties along the Mississippi River, the northeast and in parts of the Piney Woods, and those areas chose delegates to the convention with Unionist leanings. However, in the end the majority of the state elected men who either

[14] Wood, *Union and Secession in Mississippi*, 10–19.
[15] Quoted in Rainwater, *Storm Center of Secession*, 181.

leaned toward secession or were avowed secessionists. This was due to the fact that most of the state's counties were Democratic, and even though the general population was probably more moderate in their thinking than their political leaders, the Democratic Party remained the party of states' rights. To make a name for himself within the Democratic Party in Mississippi, a politician had to stand firm in his conviction to the states' rights doctrine, and to secession as a method of redress against Northern abuses.

Although returns were close in a number of counties, secessionists carried the day in the election of convention delegates for several reasons. Few counties ran a strictly pro-Union ticket while most candidates throughout the state believed in the legality and legitimacy of the concept of secession. In addition, voter turnout was significantly lower for the election of convention delegates than for the previous presidential election. Approximately 68,000 voters took part in the presidential election while only about 38,000 cast ballots for convention delegates. The lighter turnout favored the secessionists and was possibly a concession by many fence-straddling moderates that Lincoln's election had decided the issue. In general, many voters who had supported Bell were willing to support more radical action now that a Republican was poised to occupy the White House. After Lincoln's election, secessionists and much of the public in general were more agitated with regard to the slavery issue. Secessionists also were more likely to use various forms of intimidation to accomplish their object. While this could take the form of actual physical confrontations, it usually meant that those disagreeing with secession were simply ostracized in their communities. Such was the case with John H. Aughey, who later claimed that as he cast his vote for a pro-Union candidate in Choctaw County, he did so "amidst the frowns, murmurs, and threats of the judges and bystanders" at the polls.[16]

---

[16] Quoted in Glover Moore, "Separation from the Union, 1854–1861," in Richard Aubrey McLemore, ed., *A History of Mississippi*, 2 vols. (Hattiesburg MS: University & College Press, 1973) 1:443.

The triumph of fire-eating Democrats was apparent as the convention met on January 7, 1861. According to one participant, "the advocates of immediate and independent action were complete masters of the situation, and from the first day's meeting... it was manifest to the most superficial observer that the die had been cast already." A number of delegates voiced opposition to disunion, but conciliatory rhetoric quickly faded in the face of a decidedly pro-secession majority. The convention elected William S. Barry, a former United States congressman and resolute secessionist from Lowndes County, president of the body on the third ballot. Barry received fifty-eight of ninety-seven votes cast while James L. Alcorn placed a distant second with fourteen. On the convention's first day, the body established a committee of fifteen members to draw up an ordinance of secession. A native Georgian who would become one the most influential politicians in Mississippi history chaired the committee, and penned the bulk of the ordinance himself.

Lucius Quintus Cincinnatus Lamar was born into an already prominent family in Putnam County, Georgia, in 1825. His father was a noted lawyer and judge and his uncle, Mirabeau Lamar, served as the second president of the Republic of Texas. Lucius graduated from Emory College, studied law and gained admission to the bar in 1847. Two years later, he moved to Oxford, Mississippi, where he practiced law and served as professor of mathematics at the University of Mississippi. He moved back to Georgia but returned to Mississippi and won election to the United States House of Representatives, serving from 1857 to 1860 when he resigned to take a seat at the Mississippi Secession Convention as a representative from Lafayette County. A moderate compared to men like Pettus or Albert Gallatin Brown, Lamar had a keen political sense and when it became apparent that Mississippi was destined to leave the Union, he positioned himself at the forefront of the effort, writing the state's secession ordinance. Once the war began, Lamar served briefly as a Confederate officer but was plagued by poor health. In 1862, he became the Confederate envoy to Russia, France, and England, though technically in an unofficial capacity since those nations did not recognize the Confederacy. After the war Lamar once again taught at the University of Mississippi but soon became involved in Reconstruction politics. Elected to the US Senate, he helped the Democratic Party regain control of the state and ultimately became Mississippi's most powerful political voice at the national level. Lamar served in the cabinet of President Grover Cleveland and in 1888 Cleveland appointed the Mississippian to the Supreme Court, where he served until his death in 1893.

Before the final vote on Lamar's ordinance, three amendments to fend off immediate secession came before the convention and were handily defeated. The first, offered by J. Shall Yerger of Washington County, held that Mississippi should undertake the fight for its rights as part of the existing Union. This proposal was defeated by a vote of seventy-eight to twenty-one. The convention also voted down by seventy-four to twenty-five an amendment advanced by Alcorn that would have delayed any action until the other Deep South states had seceded. Walker Brooke of Warren County proposed the amendment that made the best showing. It provided that a secession ordinance should not go into effect until ratified by the state's voters in a popular referendum. This proposal lost by a vote of seventy to twenty-nine.

After the three amendments failed, it was apparent that the secession ordinance would pass overwhelmingly. As a result Alcorn, the acknowledged leader of the pro-Union opposition, urged his like-minded colleagues to support the impending mandate of the convention. While Alcorn's aim was to promote unity once Mississippi's fate was decided, he also had a political agenda. As a savvy politician he realized that further protests against the ordinance might prove detrimental to his political future. He did not want the state to leave the Union, but once it did he had little choice but to go with it or risk committing political suicide.

On January 9, Mississippi's Ordinance of Secession passed by a vote of eighty-four to fifteen. Afterwards, one observer heard a number of convention delegates naively claim that secession was "but a demonstration inviting concessions [from the North], which concessions will promptly be made and the disrupted Union fully restored within the next twelve months."[17] The fifteen delegates who voted against the ordinance represented the pro-Union faction's last stand in the state. Most came from scattered counties that had traditionally been Whig and later Opposition strongholds, or areas where non-slaveholders had acute suspicions about the motives of Democratic leaders. Once the votes were counted, however, even most of the dissenters signed the document. Only John J. Thornton of Rankin County and John W. Wood of Attala County, both confirmed Union men, failed to affix their names to the Mississippi's Ordinance of Secession.

In addition to passing the secession ordinance, the convention published a document outlining the delegates' reasons for voting in favor of radical action. Alexander M. Clayton drew up the document, which left little doubt as to what motivated Mississippi's withdrawal from the Union:

> In the momentous step which our state has taken of dissolving its connection with the government of which we so long formed a part, it is but just that we should declare the prominent reasons which have induced our course.
>
> Our position is thoroughly identified with the institution of slavery—the greatest material institution in the world. Its labor supplies the products which constitutes by far the largest and most important portions of the commerce of the earth. These products are peculiar to the climate verging on the tropical regions, and by an imperious law of nature, none but the black race can bear exposure to the tropical sun. These products have become necessities to the world, and a blow at slavery is a blow at commerce and civilization. That blow has been long aimed at the institution, and was at the point of consummation. There was no choice left to us but submission to the mandates of abolition, or a dissolution of the Union, whose principles had been subverted to work out our ruin.[18]

---

[17] Davis, *Recollections of Mississippi*, 403.

[18] Mississippi Commission on the War between the States, *Journal of the State Convention and Ordinances and Resolutions Adopted in 1861* (Jackson: Mississippi Commission on the War between the States, 1962) 86.

In Washington, Mississippi's congressional delegation resigned after the state seceded and joined other Southern congressmen in a sad trek home. The most dramatic resignation was that of Jefferson Davis, the most well-known member of the group. Davis was first elected to represent Mississippi in the House of Representatives in 1845. A graduate of the United States Military Academy, he resigned his seat in Congress to lead a Mississippi regiment during the Mexican War. Wounded at the Battle of Buena Vista, he emerged from the conflict as a bona fide war hero and national figure. His fame helped him win election to the United States Senate and he subsequently served as secretary of war in President Franklin Pierce's cabinet. Davis returned to the Senate in 1857 as one of the South's primary spokesmen, often stating his support for slavery and states' rights while holding firm to the position that the slaveholding states should fight for their rights within the federal Union. Having little other choice, he accepted secession and its consequences once the decision to secede had been made in Mississippi.

The fifty-two-year-old Davis was ill when he made his way to the senate floor to give his resignation speech on January 21, 1861. A recurring bout of neuralgia had left him bedridden for much of the previous two weeks. Still, he recognized the gravity of the situation and the importance of his appearance. The curious began arriving at the capitol steps before dawn, and onlookers soon packed the senate gallery. While four other Southerners were bidding adieu to their nation that same day, many spectators had come specifically to hear Davis, who was the most prominent figure among the departing senators. He had served with distinction in the United States Army, led the nation's war department as a cabinet secretary, and been the voice of the South in countless political debates during the volatile 1850s. Many also believed that if the seceding states formed a Southern confederacy, Davis would help lead the effort. Stated simply, Jefferson Davis was famous, and those on hand knew that they were witnessing history. The Mississippi senator's farewell address began in low tones, but his voice grew stronger and more resolute as he defended his home state, the concept of states' rights, and the inferiority of the slave. In a moment of high drama, he stated that he bore no ill will toward his Northern colleagues, wished them well, and emphasized his hopes for "peaceful relations" between his state and the United States. Davis ended his six-minute address and walked solemnly from a senate chamber echoing with thunderous applause and the sounds of open weeping. The next day he and his wife Varina boarded a train and left Washington.

Back in Mississippi the state's secession convention remained in session to take care of a variety of matters. It revised the existing state constitution and began the process of streamlining the government of what some referred to as the "Republic of Mississippi." When Jefferson Davis returned to his home state, he found that the convention had selected him to command state forces as major-general, with Christopher H. Mott, Charles Clark, James L. Alcorn, and Earl Van Dorn chosen as brigadier generals. Delegates also made provisions for a new state flag. For several weeks after secession the so-called Bonnie Blue Flag, with a single white star in the center of a blue background, was the state's unofficial standard, inspiring Henry McCarthy to write the period anthem *The Bonnie Blue Flag*. The convention eventually approved a committee report that allowed for a new state flag "of white ground, a Magnolia tree in the centre, a blue field in the upper left hand corner with a white star in the centre...to be finished with a red border and a red fringe at the extremity." After debate the convention adopted the "Magnolia Flag" as Mississippi's official banner. Finally, the gathering elected delegates to a convention in Montgomery, Alabama, for the purpose of creating a Southern confederacy. The convention adjourned on January 26 and reconvened two months later to ratify the constitution of the Confederate States of America. In the interim Jefferson Davis, the era's most reputable Mississippian on the national stage, became president of the Confederacy.

While the secession convention officially took Mississippi out of the Union, the real fight for independence had not yet begun. Bloody civil strife would soon engulf the state and the nation as years of political rhetoric evolved into deadly actions. Within a few months the grim realities of war would temper initial enthusiasm for the cause as Mississippians began to fall on battlefields near and distant.

On February 23, 1861 Abiezer Clarke Ramsey, a minister raised on the Gulf Coast, wrote a letter to his brother Andrew in Leaf, Mississippi that foreshadowed coming events. "I see no chance but a war," it read, "and when it commences it will be a war of extermination, for the South, although weak, will fight until the last man is killed."[19]

---

[19] Abiezer Clarke Ramsey to Andrew Woodside Ramsay, February 23, 1861, quoted in Cyril Edward Cain, *Four Centuries on the Pascagoula*, 2 vols. (Spartanburg SC: Reprint Company, 1983) 2:57.

2

THE CALL OF MY COUNTRY: 1861

The company has received marching orders and we shall
probably leave tomorrow. I am ready to go.[1]
Henry A. Garrett
Company A, Jeff Davis (cavalry) Legion, Natchez,
Mississippi, June 1, 1861

Like the rest of the South, Mississippi was ill prepared for the war
that loomed on the horizon in early 1861. After secession and before
joining the Confederacy the state hastily organized the Army of
Mississippi under the command of Major General Jefferson Davis.
Davis's war record and political standing made him the obvious
choice to lead the state's military and his four brigadiers, Charles
Clark, Christopher Mott, Earl Van Dorn, and James Alcorn, were
well credentialed men as well. Clark, the grandson of a Revolutionary
War veteran, was born in Cincinnati, Ohio, and came to Mississippi
as a young man during the 1830s. He served as colonel of the 2nd
Mississippi Infantry Regiment during the Mexican War and for years
was an influential member of the state legislature representing

---

[1] Quoted in John K. Bettersworth, ed., *Mississippi in the Confederacy: As They Saw
It* (Baton Rouge: Louisiana State University Press, 1961) 46–49.

Jefferson and Bolivar counties. Mott, another Mexican War veteran who had parlayed his military notoriety into a political career, represented Marshall County in the legislature. A lawyer by trade, he occupied the bench as a judge and was a law partner of US Representative Lucius Q. C. Lamar. From a purely military standpoint, Van Dorn was arguably the best qualified of the original leadership. A West Point graduate like Davis, Van Dorn was a skilled horseman who earned a number of commendations during the Mexican War. During the 1850s, he commanded the 2nd United States Cavalry to great acclaim on the southwestern frontier. Alcorn was the strictly political general in the group. He was born in Illinois and grew up in Kentucky. In the 1840s, he came to Mississippi where he built up a lucrative law practice. Alcorn represented Coahoma County in the state legislature for more than a decade and also represented the county at the secession convention.

The choice of these five men to lead the state's military represented some of the great contradictions of the era. Davis and Van Dorn, as West Point graduates, were breaking a solemn oath to protect the United States by pledging to defend an "independent" Mississippi. Both had fought for the federal government and for years Davis had been an important fixture in the federal government as a United States senator and as secretary of war. Their actions—taking up arms against the nation of their birth—squarely fit the definition of treason, but most white Mississippians viewed their efforts as noble. Van Dorn was also the only member of the original leadership who was born in the state. While much would be made of the "native soil of Mississippi" that these men went to war to defend, the others were not native to the region. Davis and Mott were Kentuckians while Clark and Alcorn were actually born on free ground in the North, a fact that did not seem to affect their ability to achieve high office in the state. In the end, independent Mississippi's first military leaders served only briefly. Jefferson Davis was selected as president of the Confederacy soon after Mississippi seceded and the other generals all resigned to join the Confederate army. Most soldiers of the Army of Mississippi followed their commanders into Confederate service as well. On one hand, it was only natural that Mississippi contribute some of its leadership and manpower to the Confederacy. However, giving up the state's men and resources to the collective effort of a Southern confederacy also represented an ironic turn of events in a state supposedly pledged to its own autonomy and suspicious of centralized political authority. After the Confederacy enacted conscription laws in spring 1862, maintaining an effective state force was no longer feasible, though home guard units and state militia continued to function in many places.

Be it state forces or the Confederate army, finding young men to serve in the ranks in 1861 was not difficult, though supplying and training them on short notice proved to be a problem. When Mississippi left the Union, Governor Pettus sent out the call for volunteers to be organized into four, twelve-month regiments, but he greatly underestimated the response to his order. Enlistment overwhelmed the initial demand for soldiers and soon more than eighty volunteer companies clamored to serve. Arms were in short supply and grumbling from restless, would-be soldiers and their frustrated commanders grew louder and louder across the state. Pettus ordered as many volunteer companies as possible to rendezvous points along the railroad at Corinth, Enterprise, Grenada, and Iuka. There the companies were organized into regiments, mustered briefly into state service and then transferred to the Confederate army. In general, ten companies from the same part of the state were banded together to form a regiment, and Confederate authorities sometimes tried to band regiments from the same state together in a common brigade.

Most Confederate soldiers served in the infantry and as a result the volunteer infantry company was the basic building block of the Confederate army. In Mississippi, as in the rest of the South, volunteer companies formed in every part of the state following secession as a great wave of patriotism swept through the countryside. More often than not community leaders, regardless of their military acumen or experience, commanded the companies as captain because to one degree or another they had helped organize and finance the undertaking. Company leaders might be lawyers, doctors, state legislators, or local planters. Some companies were named for their captain or for the town or county from which they hailed. Others were named for prominent Southerners associated with the secession movement, or for a Mississippian who had gained acclaim in the Mexican War. Upon muster into Confederate service, a single letter replaced the homespun company names that the volunteers brought with them from home. For instance the Pettus Rifles, a volunteer company named for the governor, was organized in Copiah County and eventually entered the war as Company D of the 12th Mississippi Infantry. The pine strewn hills around Morton, in Scott County, produced the Morton Pine Knots, Company H of the 20th Mississippi Infantry, while in Holmes County at Richland local men named their volunteer group after radical states' rights politician John A. Quitman. The Quitman Rifles entered the war as Company C of the 15th Mississippi Infantry. In Bolivar County, wealthy planter Miles McGehee organized a volunteer unit and sent to Memphis for cloth to make each man a summer and a winter uniform. He also contributed his own mules and wagons to haul the company's equipment and produced an extra $1000 for the company treasury. As a result of this generosity, his company was known as the Miles McGehee Rifles, and eventually entered the war as Company A of the 20th Mississippi Infantry. Such company names were not always associated with males. In Madison County, Helen Johnstone, whose family owned the massive Annandale Plantation, sponsored a company of men from Madison, Leake, and Attala Counties that organized as the "Helen Johntsone Guards." This group served the Confederacy as part of the 24th Mississippi Infantry.

One unusual name for a volunteer company came from Tippah County where a group of green recruits called themselves the "O'Connor Rifles." The name in and of itself was not odd unless placed in retrospect in the context of the times. Commanded by John H. Buchanan, the volunteer company was first organized as a militia company in 1859 in response to the Harper's Ferry Raid. The men chose the name for their unit as a tribute to Charles O'Conor (who spelled his name with only one *n*) who was not a Mississippian, or even a Southerner. O'Conor was a New York attorney and well-known member of his home state's legal community. What made him an appealing figure in the South was that through the 1850s he was an unwavering states' rights Democrat who defended slavery and insisted that the federal government had no right to tamper with the institution in any way. To many radical Southern politicians of the period, O'Conor represented an "enlightened Yankee" and his name sometimes appeared in their speeches. As a result, many in Tippah County held the New Yorker in high esteem, so much so that they named a volunteer militia company in his honor. As if to confirm that the company had done the right thing, O'Conor was one of the men who defended Jefferson Davis against treason charges after the war.

Like all young men destined for the battlefield, Mississippi's Confederate soldiers were victims of their times, growing up during an era when tensions over slavery were mounting. Most were the sons of first-generation Mississippians who had come to the Mississippi frontier in search of the traditional American dream. They sought title to their own property and the opportunity to advance themselves as far as their abilities might take them. The families of the men had acquired land and established communities. Through these communities they had established a degree of comfort and security that they hoped would aid them in their quest to advance their station in life.

Through the 1850s, however, it seemed that Mississippi's communities were in increasing danger. Had they remained isolated, the national slavery debate may not have had a great effect on them, as most of their residents owned few or no slaves. But the communities did not remain isolated. Instead they had become part of a much broader community that included all Mississippi whites and ultimately all Southern whites who were concerned about the slavery issue. By the eve of the Civil War, the slavery debate had become localized. It had trickled down from the national level through a heated rhetoric that struck at the personal identity of each Mississippian. Secessionist politicians had successfully cloaked the slavery question as a states' rights issue, underscored by easily exploitable national events.

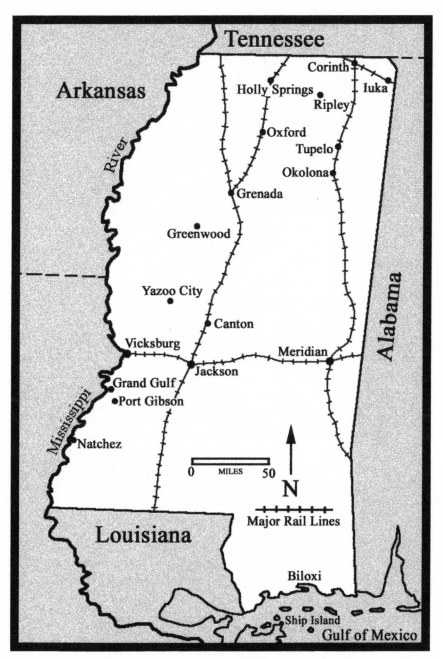

Map 1 Mississippi in 1860

All over the state young men were frantic to serve, particularly after Fort Sumter surrendered in South Carolina and President Lincoln called for 75,000 volunteers from the non-slaveholding states. At Oxford, the chancellor of the University of Mississippi pleaded with the parents of his students to keep their sons in school, but the young men were beyond his control. According to one observer, "the stirring and ear-piercing fife startle the man of peace who walks the usually quiet streets of Oxford, now filled with men in whose [face] we read war, war , war!!!" The student body dwindled as its members formed a volunteer company, the University Greys, or left for home to join local units. In fall 1861, the university closed its doors when only four students appeared for classes. Although young men across the state were caught up in the moment, many also felt a profound sense of duty. As war loomed on the horizon, Adams County native Henry A. Garrett, a recent volunteer, expressed in his diary the conflicting sentiments that were probably on the minds of many new soldiers: "it is hard to leave home when so many strong ties bind me to it, but the call of my country must be obeyed as the voice of God.... I have done my whole duty as a citizen, if not as a man."[2]

While patriotic enthusiasm throughout the state was high during early 1861, other factors also influenced volunteers to join the war effort. Mississippians who joined the Confederate army held a limited view of the dangers that they would encounter once they stopped drilling and actually began fighting. Their immediate frame of reference for combat was the Mexican War, in which the United States army, packed with Southerners, had crushed a much weaker enemy with relative ease. Few doubted that a new Southern army could repeat this feat, and it was no coincidence that some volunteer companies around the state were named for Mississippi Mexican War heroes. Conventional wisdom in the South also held that any fight with the North would be a limited struggle and that most Northerners would not fight if pressed. The ill-conceived mantra "one southern man can whip a dozen Yankees" echoed through

---

[2] Quoted in Bettersworth, ed., *Mississippi in the Confederacy*, 46–49.

communities all over the state as their young men volunteered for military service. While there were inherent dangers in joining the army, the soldiers' own mortality was only an abstract consequence to most of the men. A general feeling existed that they would fight the Yankees, defeat them handily, and be back home within a few months with tales of heroism and adventure.

Many young men also saw service in the Confederate army as a way to display their personal honor just as older members of their communities had done during the Mexican War. Their communities viewed military service as a traditional right of passage dating back to the genesis of the United States. For years, states' rights orators had made a concerted effort to compare their cause with the struggle for independence carried out by those who fought in the American Revolution. In 1861, anyone who did not agree with secession as a remedy to sectional difference risked being branded a "tory" traitor to the legacy of the revolutionary generation, and as such a traitor to their community and their heritage. Volunteer companies were indeed community enterprises in every sense of the phrase. Because they were recruited locally, they contained many relatives and friends. Most of the men who volunteered for service in a typical company had grown up together. Their grand adventure in the Confederate army represented an appealing extension of their neighborhoods, a community undertaking fortified by kinship and friendship ties. While officially they may have gone to war to defend the Confederacy, the men's initial willingness to fight sprang from the notion that they were protecting their communities along side other men who they were related to or at least knew well. They also were motivated to give a good account of themselves because they knew that those same friends and relatives would be observing their every move.

The average enlisted man in Mississippi was in his early to mid-twenties. Most of the soldiers were single and therefore better able to leave home for extended periods of time. Usually the single men owned little personal property and because the vast majority came from large families that worked small holdings, they could expect only a minimal inheritance at best. Most worked on farms either as members of their parents' household or as hired labor while others busied themselves in occupations such as blacksmith, carpenter, clerk, teacher, mechanic, shopkeeper, teamster, overseer, and in a variety of apprentice positions. These unmarried volunteers were yet to establish themselves as independent property holders with the status it afforded and, as a result, were in social limbo with regard to their standing in their communities. They had not yet found their place in society, had few responsibilities other than the daily drudgeries of mundane lives, and were likely anxious to win some type of positive reputation.

Married volunteers were little better off than their unmarried counterparts. Most were recently wed, with perhaps one or two small children. The vast majority were farmers who owned their own farms, but in most cases worked only meager holdings as they struggled to feed their families. Both husbands and wives in these households were not far removed from their parent's charge and could count on communal support for their families as the husband left home to participate in what most believed would be a relatively short conflict. In the enlisted ranks there were relatively few men who had firmly established themselves as the family patriarch of a large household.

The men elected company officers who were usually somewhat older, prominent community leaders, members of substantial families, or in most cases men who had helped organize and finance the company. The officer corps of most volunteer companies reflected peacetime, class-based community hierarchies that were not based on military background. Legislators, lawyers, doctors and men with significant property holdings would lead their companies into battle. Some would be up the task while others would quickly prove that the ability to make a good political speech or accumulate significant wealth did not translate into a cool head on the battlefield.

Conspicuous in the ranks of the volunteers were a small number of slaves. Officers often brought body servants with them into the army while others donated slaves for use by their individual companies or regiments. Occasionally small groups of non-slaveholders pitched in to hire a slave to tend their common needs.

Such arrangements were not unusual in the Confederate army, particularly during the first year of the war. Of course, the Confederate government did not recognize slaves as members of any Southern regiment and the bondsmen's duties were generally confined to cooking, cleaning, and tending horses. Despite the stereotype of the "loyal darky" that Confederate apologists would propagate in years to come, most slaves who followed their masters off to war were no more content with slavery in the Confederate army than they had been with the institution on the plantation or farm. While some slaves who traveled with the army stayed with their masters, many took advantage of battlefield confusion and ran away at the first opportunity.

Usually there was an interim of three to four weeks between the time that the companies destined for the war were organized and the time that they actually left home for Confederate service. During this period each group held rudimentary drill sessions on their local village greens. Daily drills quickly became public spectacles, enhancing community pride as local residents gathered to view the awkward transformation of their sons, grandsons, brothers and cousins from citizens to soldiers. In 1861, an Aberdeen woman wrote that after one local company organized she "was so interested in them that when I heard they were to drill I would order out my carriage and drive to where I could watch their maneuvers." The drills in Aberdeen and similar occasions around the state bolstered the feeling that the service of each local company was more of a community undertaking than a military exercise. The potential for death or life-altering wounds seemed to be the farthest thing from most of the minds of the men as they were caught up in the celebratory atmosphere of the moment. "The novelty was delightful," according to one soldier, "From sunrise to sunset it was incessant drill. At evening came parade; and when all assembled on the green, and scores of fair creatures visited the grounds, and strolled around with brothers, sons and sweethearts, we all thought it was a fine thing to be a soldier, to strut about, or dance quadrilles to the music of a town band."[3]

Before Mississippi's volunteer companies left home, they all took part in a celebration universal throughout the South in spring 1861—the presentation of the local battle flag. Though they would fight under a variety of regimental, brigade, corps, and army banners, it was the standard of the local company that gave most soldiers immediate symbolic evidence of what they were fighting for. Women in communities all over the state sewed together company battle flags with great care and presented them to volunteer companies in ceremonies conducted with the greatest degree of pomp and flowery language.

A Lauderdale County ceremony was typical. There planter Peter H. Bozeman had recruited enthusiastic local men into a volunteer company of which he served as captain. Bozeman's plantation near Alamucha served as a mustering point for the group, dubbed the Alamucha Infantry, and also hosted a large community celebration for the departing company in May 1861. From the front porch of the Bozeman home, local dignitaries praised the men in speeches that were interrupted again and again by cheers from a large crowd of well-wishers. As the assembled company looked on, Martha T. Swain, representing the local women, rose to the podium and made a moving address emphasizing chivalry and honor, bringing many in the audience to the verge of tears. Sophronia McElroy, who had relatives in the unit, then presented a large handmade flag to company officers who accepted it with appropriate remarks. After the ceremony, the Alamucha Infantrty marched 12 miles to the depot at Lockhart's Station, where another enthusiastic crowd greeted them with cheers. "Once there, great hospitality was lavished," one soldier wrote, "Salutes were fired in complement to the company and soon

---

[3] Josie Frazee Cappleman, "Local Incidents of the War between the States," in Franklin L. Riley, ed., *Publications of the Mississippi Historical Society*, vol. 4 (University: Mississippi Historical Society, 1901) 85; An English Combatant, *Battlefields of the South, From Bull Run to Fredericksburg; with Sketches of Confederate Commanders, and Gossip of the Camps* (New York: John Bradburn, 1864) 6.

the cars arrived and the company put aboard."[4] The train was bound for Corinth, where the men were mustered into Confederate service as part of the 13th Mississippi Infantry.

Similarly ceremonies took place throughout the state as excitement over the impending war peaked. In Ripley, the seat of government for Tippah County, town fathers and local women organized a parade for two volunteer companies that were destined for Corinth and service in the 2nd Mississippi Infantry. The festivities culminated on the town square with a dress review and presentation of a hand-sewn battle flag. In Holly Springs, Marshall County, young women from the Holly Springs Female Institute organized a barbecue for the men of the Jefferson Davis Rifles, which would become Company D of the 9th Mississippi. Once the men and their families, friends and admirers had eaten their fill, one of the students "who was tastefully dressed in a gray jacket and cap to correspond to the uniform of the company," gave a speech and presented a flag to the company's captain. The flag presentation ceremony involving the Water Valley Rifles took place on a large wooden stage in the center of the town of Water Valley in Yalobusha County. There, as a large crowd looked on, eleven women from the community, each representing one of the Southern states that had seceded up to that time, delivered "a beautiful bunting flag, with the name of the company and the inscription 'Our Country, Our Home' on it" to company officers. The new soldiers then left Water Valley for service in the 15th Mississippi Infantry.

During the ceremonies and parties surrounding their departure, most of the new soldiers were on their best behavior, but things changed once they boarded trains and were out of sight of their "mothers, sisters, and sweethearts." One volunteer from Yazoo County remembered his first experience with large numbers of his army brethren as a raucous occasion. As his troop train moved along

---

[4] United States War Department, comp., *The War of Rebellion: Official Records of the Union and Confederate Armies*, 130 vols. (Washington, DC: Government Printing Office, 1880–1901) ser. 2, vol. 3, n. 25, p. 290 (Afterwards this work is cited as *OR* followed by the series, volume, part, number, and page number).

a circuitous route through the state, it made a number of stops over a period of several days, accumulating more and more men until the cars were overcrowded. "Some of us were in passenger cars, but the greater number had to be put up with baggage cars having temporary seats," he wrote, "and for want of sufficient ventilation, muskets were freely used in knocking out panels to admit air." As the men moved on from place to place frivolity on board increased. According to another soldier, "Some passed days and nights, riotously, on the roof, and beguiled the time playing cards or, having violins and banjos, with singing and dancing, scarce heeding the many bridges that jeopardized their heads, or the uneasy and dangerous rolling of overloaded and ill-constructed cars."[5]

Things were no less raucous when the young men arrived at the state's major rendezvous points. Corinth in particular was a hub of activity, being situated as it was at a major rail crossroads. Most of the new soldiers there were away from home for the first time and there was a considerable amount of horseplay in and around the camps, especially during idle evening hours. Card or checker games, foot races, and wrestling were popular pastimes as was singing around the campfire and, among those with the ability, reading books and writing letters. Armed with money brought from home, however, many soldiers chose drinking as a way to occupy their time. In an effort to curb excessive frivolity, authorities usually forbid the soldiers to congregate at night in Corinth without an appropriate pass signed by their commanding officer. Although they risked stern punishment, some men insisted on smuggling liquor into camp on a regular basis. As a result, many young Mississippians who were away from home for the first time had their initial experience with distilled spirits in Confederate bivouacs. According to one annoyed observer, the men camped at Corinth "made night hideous by their song and cries, stimulated by enormous draughts of whiskey and a proportionate consumption of tobacco, by teeth and by fire."[6]

---

[5] English Combatant, *Battlefields of the South*, 9–10.
[6] Quoted in Bettersworth, ed., *Mississippi in the Confederacy*, 53.

Life leading to war

While there was great enthusiasm for the war on Mississippi soil, there was little action there in 1861. On January 11, just two days after the state left the Union, a hastily placed battery on the Mississippi River at Vicksburg fired a warning shot at the steamship *A. O. Tyler*. While the shell sailed harmlessly over the side-wheeler, many considered the incident the first hostile shot of the Civil War fired in the state. Less than two weeks later, a disorganized band of state troops commandeered the federal fort then under construction on Ship Island, several miles off the Mississippi coast. The militia held the island briefly and regular Confederate forces occupied the fort later in the year. On July 9, the United States ship *Massachusetts* came within range of Confederate batteries on the island and a twenty-minute artillery exchange ensued. Neither side suffered significant damage or casualties and the federal ship withdrew. Two months later the Confederates abandoned Ship Island, leaving it for Union forces who occupied and it on December 3 and held it for the duration of the war. On New Year's Eve 1861, Union ships from the island raided Biloxi, where they destroyed a Confederate battery. Ship Island also served as the staging point for other raids along the coast and for the federals' successful assault of New Orleans in 1862.

As the state continued preparing itself for war by enlisting soldiers, selecting commanders, and reassessing its infrastructure, it also took steps to allay some white Mississippians' greatest fear. Anxiety over the prospect of slave insurrections had not disappeared as word of John Brown's demise reached Mississippi. Indeed, it increased as the Union split apart. Rumors were rampant that abolitionists who had been sympathetic to John Brown planned to penetrate the South, arm the slaves, and provoke bloody uprisings. One rumor in particular involved an organization called the "Mississippi Society" that allegedly was operating in Illinois. According to anonymous correspondence received in the governor's office, members of the group planned to come into the state, obtain work as overseers, and from those positions organize the slaves in revolt. Rumors regarding the so-called Mississippi Society and similar organizations were unfounded, but they contributed to the general paranoia that had become almost a tradition among whites in all of the slaveholding states.

Other practical considerations contributed to the fears of Mississippi whites with regard to the control of the state's slave population. Once the war began in earnest some planters had a difficult time finding overseers to supervise their slaves. Many overseers left their plantations for the Confederate army, and the nature of the volatile Mississippi economy after secession made it difficult for many planters to find men willing to take on such work. Rampant wartime inflation produced high prices, which in turn produced demands for higher wages that some debt-ridden planters were unable to pay. In the eyes of many whites, this left far too many slaves unsupervised. Even the mildest rumor concerning slave resistance could set off a panic among whites in counties such as Adams, Hinds, Madison, or Yazoo, where slaves made up more than 70 percent of the total population. The Mississippi legislature responded to what was perceived as a growing crisis by strengthening existing state statutes dealing with abolitionists who might come south. In July 1861, lawmakers made it a felony punishable by a minimum of ten years in prison for any white to "advise or conspire with any slave or slaves to rebel against the white inhabitants of the state" or instruct any slave in "seditious, revolutionary or rebellious sentiments."[7] At the local level communities increased the size and number slave patrols using local militia and other volunteers.

During the early months of the war, a number of Mississippi units saw their first combat and suffered their first casualties on distant battlefields rather than on their native soil. Once organized, many of Mississippi's first Confederates were sent out of the state to various locations. Some eventually became part of the storied Army of Northern Virginia in the Eastern theater, or the rugged Army of Tennessee in the West. In June, the 2nd Mississippi Infantry under Colonel William C. Falkner, the 11th under Colonel William H. Moore, the 13th under Colonel William Barksdale, the 17th under Colonel Winfield Scott Featherston, and the 18th under Colonel E.

---

[7] Quoted in Bettersworth, ed., *Mississippi in the Confederacy*, 233–34.

R. Burt were in Virginia as part of the victorious Confederate force at First Bull Run. Though on the winning side, the Mississippi regiments suffered numerous casualties during the battle, as they did in subsequent struggles in the Old Dominion.

Three of the men commanding these first Mississippi units in Virginia eventually gained significant notoriety. Winfield Scott Featherston was a fixture on Mississippi's political scene for more than forty years. Born in Rutherford County, Tennessee in 1821, he was educated at various academies but eventually left school to fight in the Creek Wars. After his military service ended Featherston studied law, was admitted to the bar, and opened a successful law practice in Houston, Mississippi. He was heavily involved in Democratic politics and won election to the United States House of Representatives, where he served from 1847 to 1851. With the outbreak of the war Featherston was elected colonel of the 17th Mississippi Infantry. He led his regiment in several major engagements and was wounded during the Battle of Seven Days. Promoted to brigadier general, Featherston took command of a brigade in William W. Loring's division in Joseph Johnston's Army of Tennessee. After the war, Featherston stayed active in Democratic politics and was a pivotal figure in helping the Democrats end Reconstruction in Mississippi and regain control of the state government. He served in the state legislature and as a circuit court judge before his election to the 1891 state constitutional convention. When he died in 1891 at Holly Springs in Marshall County, Featherston was lauded as one of the most influential politicians in Mississippi's history.

William Barksdale's political standing also led him into the Confederate officer corps. Born in Tennessee like Featherston, Barksdale came to Columbus, Mississippi, as a young man. There he practiced law and edited a newspaper, the *Columbus Democrat*. He served as a captain and quartermaster of state forces during the Mexican War, and after the conflict his political career in the state flourished. Barksdale was elected to the United States House of Representatives, where he served from 1853 until his 1861 resignation three days after Mississippi severed its ties with the

Union. An aggressive and charismatic leader, he served as colonel of the 13th Mississippi Infantry and in 1862 was appointed brigadier general, eventually commanding his regiment and the 17th, 18th, and 21st Mississippi infantry regiments in "Barksdale's Mississippi Brigade" in James Longstreet's corps. Barksdale became a legend in his home state on July 2, 1863, when he was killed leading his troops at the Battle of Gettysburg. He was arguably the most famous Mississippian to die in battle during the Civil War. Year after year, decade after decade, generation after generation, white Mississippian's would speak with reverence of Barksdale's service at Gettysburg, and his last charge would be revered by many as "the grandest charge ever made by mortal man."

William Cuthbert Falkner also became a legendary Mississippian, but not for leading grand Confederate charges. Falkner was born in Knox County, Tennessee, in 1826 and, like Featherston and Barksdale, came to Mississippi as a young man. He lived for a time in Pontotoc before finally settling with relatives in Ripley. After service in the Mexican War, he returned to Ripley, opened a law practice, and lived what could only be called a colorful, though sometimes violent life. In 1849 he was involved in a feud during which he killed two men. He was acquitted of all charges on the grounds of self-defense, but gained a reputation as a man not to be trifled with. In contrast, Falkner also wrote poetry and novels that were published to some acclaim. With the outbreak of the Civil War he helped organize a volunteer company, the Magnolia Rifles, that became part of the 2nd Mississippi Infantry. The men elected Falkner colonel of the regiment but he was later defeated for reelection and left the unit. After the war Falkner played an active role in North Mississippi reconstruction. He was involved in a variety of business ventures and helped establish the Ship Island, Ripley, and Kentucky Railroad. In 1889, he was elected to the state legislature but before he could take his seat a disgruntled former business partner shot and fatally wounded him in downtown Ripley. While the one-time Confederate colonel's death was widely reported when it occurred, it was not his untimely demise or his brief Civil War service that gave him a lasting legacy. William C. Falkner ultimately gained immortality through the work of his great-grandson and namesake, the Nobel Prize-winning author William Faulkner (who spelled his name with a *u* included). The younger Faulkner, who had grown up hearing stories about the colorful colonel, used his ancestor as the model for the character Colonel Sartoris in *Flags in the Dust, The Unvanquished,* and several short stories.

For those new Mississippi recruits that were not involved, the Battle of First Bull Run caused anxiety that often bordered on panic. Many men in units yet to see action were frightened, but not for the right reasons. They had been told that the war would not last more than a few months, and that the South would easily triumph with those involved returning home bathed in glory. The Confederate victory at Bull Run seemed to indicate that this was true, and many men were desperate to participate in a battle before the war ended. They believed that returning home without seeing combat would be looked upon by their communities as disgraceful. Men from the 14th and 15th Mississippi infantry units at Union City, Tennessee, the 3rd and 7th Mississippi on the Gulf Coast, and the 5th and 10th Mississippi in Florida begged for transfers to Virginia.

Meanwhile, back in Mississippi the military and political realities of secession and war continued to set in. As Governor John Jones Pettus struggled to help his state gain a war footing in spring and summer 1861, he also had to struggle with a reelection campaign. Pettus was anxious to maintain his administration in a second two-year term but because of the climate of the times he was not optimistic. Pettus was an abrasive man. Coarse, fiery, and quick to anger, he made enemies as rapidly as he cultivated allies, and secession created for him innumerable political problems. In 1859 it had been relatively easy for him agitate the public in his favor. He had simply railed against Northern abolitionists, pounded his chest and threatened to lead his state out of the Union if its people did not receive satisfaction. By 1861, however, secession had occurred, and though patriotism ran high in the state, there was also an underlying current of uncertainty and, in some quarters, outright fear. Pettus had to deal with problems that no other chief executive had ever had to address, and with events that were unique not just to Mississippi history but to the history of the United States as well.

Pettus was vulnerable on a number of issues, but the key point on which many took the governor to task was the supplying and maintenance of Mississippi's growing number of troops. Once volunteer companies began to organize after secession, the supply of military units quickly exceeded the initial demand. "The expense of forwarding our troops arms, ammunition, tents, camp equipage, [and] clothing," Pettus wrote to Jefferson Davis as the state mobilized, "has so depleted our treasury that I am unable to pay the expenses of calling the remaining troops into camp."[8] As a result, the state government had trouble distributing supplies to the men during the period before the Mississippi units were transferred to the Confederate army. This left many companies sitting idly by, growing more and more frustrated with the state's bureaucracy as each day passed. Fired by the excitement of the times, some communities viewed the fact that their young men lacked adequate supplies as a sign of incompetence on the part of government officials, or perhaps even as an intentional slight to certain sections of the state. A few of Pettus' ideas with regard to defending Mississippi were also controversial, some to the point of being ridiculous. At one time he proposed arming as many state troops as possible with shotguns rather than rifles, and even ordered a large number for use by some of the men. When the arms arrived, however, the boxes containing them held partially assembled or antiquated weapons of little use to anyone. According to one frustrated observer, "There were guns without a vent, to be fired by live coal, guns without ramrods, barrels without stocks, stocks without barrels, guns without cocks [and] cocks without guns." About the same time Pettus, in a moment of sheer bravado, also advanced the notion that Mississippians should allow federal soldiers to invade the state because in doing so the Yankees would render themselves more vulnerable to ambush.

---

[8] "John J. Pettus to Jefferson Davis," quoted in Bettersworth, ed., *Mississippi in the Confederacy*, 50.

While he had a great deal of support among the state's political elite, Pettus also had enemies among the states' rights Democrats in Mississippi. Most were old political rivals, men who had always believed that they were superior to Pettus. Others thought that the governor was in over his head with regard to the state's military situation. In the early days following secession, it seemed that every Mississippi politician suddenly became a military strategist, and few were shy in voicing their opinions on how the state's forces should be organized and assigned. Pettus had also made bitter political enemies among those in the state who had been against secession. While Mississippi unionists were in the minority, and were far less vocal after secession occurred, they still voted and many would likely vote for the devil himself before they would cast a ballot to send Pettus back to the governor's mansion.

As other candidates made plans to unseat Pettus, the governor became despondent to the point that he considered withdrawing from the race. Political associates urged him to press on, but it seemed that his heart was not in it. Then, suddenly and dramatically, the governor's fortunes changed for the better. In September, the Confederate States of America authorized a large-scale mobilization of troops from Mississippi. As a result, thousands of idle, frustrated volunteers were suddenly off to war, and as they left their homes, another great wave of patriotism surged through the state. Communities that had been complaining for weeks about Pettus' inaction quickly rallied around their wartime governor, praising him for keeping a cool head during times of crisis. A few weeks later, the state held its election and John Jones Pettus crushed several other candidates, receiving 31,169 out of 35,621 votes cast: a landslide of more than 87 percent. In calmer times, the results would have left the incumbent governor elated, and Pettus was indeed happy with the outcome, however, he had little time to savor it. Though Pettus won re-election in a rout, the state's problems did not disappear. In fact, they became more pronounced.

Events in Virginia also weighed heavily on the Governor's mind in the aftermath of the election. On October 21, 1861, approximately 1,600 Confederates under Brigadier General Nathan Evans defeated

2,000 federal troops commanded by Brigadier General Charles P. Stone at Ball's Bluff near Leesburg, Virginia. It was a stirring victory during which the federals suffered over 900 casualties to only 149 for the Southerners. Among the Confederates who died on the battlefield was John A. Pettus, a private from the 18th Mississippi Infantry and John Jones Pettus's son. Less than a month later, the governor's other son, William Winston Pettus, left college and enlisted in the Confederate army against the wishes of his father. Hence, as he prepared for another term, Governor Pettus did so with the knowledge that Mississippi's withdrawal from the United States, an act that he had fervently promoted, had resulted in the death on one of his sons and placed his other son in extreme danger.

While many other families in Mississippi were losing their sons to the Confederate army, enthusiasm for the state's war effort was certainly not confined to the male population. "I wish a regiment of ladies could go to war," one woman wrote early on, "as I am nearly crazy to see the Yankees killed." Motivated by the excitement and uncertainty of the times, women around the state pitched in to fill important support roles for the Confederacy. Even before any major battles were fought in the state, nurses were a treasured commodity in every camp. Because most of the men had never been exposed to large groups of people, various diseases—particularly those traditionally labeled "childhood" illnesses such as measles or chicken pox—took their toll on the men. Epidemics swept through many camps, killing some men, incapacitating others, and creating a great demand for nurses to tend the sick. Once the war began in earnest, and there were wounded men to be tended by the thousands, the sparse supply of Confederate nurses was quickly overwhelmed.

Some women contributed to the war effort in less dramatic but still very important ways. From the war's outset, Mississippi was short on supplies for its volunteers. State authorities could not meet the demands of its troops, and the flow of supplies from the Confederacy would be inadequate for the war's duration. Illustrating one of the many ironies of the Confederate war effort, the South was awash in cotton, but was not able to adequately clothe its armies. As a result, women in all parts of Mississippi worked feverishly producing clothing for the men in the field. Sewing circles formed in most counties and "ladies aid societies" held rallies to solicit funds. Some efforts were more organized than others and many were, to one extent or another, class-based in nature. In a given community, the more socially prominent women who had the time and resources usually participated in fund-raising concerns while women in poorer families did their part by sending home-made clothing or other personal items to relatives and friends on an individual basis. Regardless of whether they were organized, the women of Mississippi's communities produced significant amounts of clothing for the soldiers, particularly during the first stages of the war. A typical report came from Tunica County, where by August 1861 the women "having completed the uniforms to the present comfort of their fathers, husbands, brothers, and friends who have joined the Confederate service, now tender their services to knit socks, make flannel shirts, drawers, and all other wearing apparel for winter use."[9]

While Mississippians on the battlefield were exposed to the dangers of war, others from the state who were in the North or who traveled there as sectional tensions bubbled over also placed themselves at risk. In the free states, particularly after the Battle of First Bull Run, the authorities were obsessed with civil and military security. Abraham Lincoln suspended habeas corpus and, due to the confused nature of the conflict and the inherent difficulty in distinguishing friend from foe in many quarters, government officials ordered many unnecessary arrests (Jefferson Davis and Confederate authorities acted in the same manner). Anyone who exhibited even a hint of infidelity to the United States might find himself imprisoned, awaiting a hearing with only a vague knowledge of the charges that he or she faced.

Such was the situation with Charles Kopperl. Kopperl, who by most accounts was a decent man but occasionally loud and boastful, was a New York native who had moved to Carroll County, Mississippi, and had established himself through the years as a successful merchant. Though he put down roots in the South, Kopperl still had

---

[9] *Memphis Daily Appeal*, August 24, 1861, 4.

relatives in New York and Pennsylvania and he visited them annually. Normally his excursions to the North were routine and uneventful, but nothing was normal for anyone in the United States during summer 1861. In late 1860, as Mississippi's secession convention met, the Carroll County store owner apparently was very vocal in his support for his state leaving the Union, and later claimed that he was going to finance a local cavalry troop for which he would serve as captain. As a merchant whose store attracted much foot traffic on a daily basis, many of Kopperl's neighbors heard his plans, as did any strangers who visited the store as they passed through the area. While Kopperl continued his vocal support of secession, he did not form his own Confederate unit nor did he serve in the Confederate army. Several months after Mississippi left the United States, and despite the state of affairs in the country, he made plans to visit his family in the North. Kopperl arrived in New York City on August 13 with plans to stay for several days. While he was there, a local man, Jeremiah Wardwell, who was acquainted with Kopperl and had visited with him in Carroll County several months earlier, saw the Mississippian and alerted authorities to his presence in the city. Wardwell signed an affidavit stating that when he had been in Mississippi several months earlier, he saw Kopperl and in talking with the merchant had "learned that he was then engaged in raising a cavalry company and that he was captain thereof." A local newspaper picked up the story and published a false account stating that Kopperl was a Confederate cavalry commander who had participated in the Battle of Bull Run, and therefore his presence behind enemy lines made him a spy. All the information pertaining to Kopperl was forwarded to Washington where it made its way to Secretary of State William H. Seward, who ordered the Mississippian's arrest.

Federal authorities took Kopperl into custody and confined him to Fort Lafayette in New York Harbor with others who were suspected of being disloyal. He was eventually transferred to Fort Warren in Boston Harbor during a confinement that lasted almost six months. After his arrest Kopperl produced a frantic stream of correspondence to Seward and others in hopes of gaining a release. In one letter, the man who once boasted of forming his own

Confederate cavalry company in Carroll County assured the secretary of state that he was "a Union man, always opposed to secession," and that he had never said or done anything detrimental to the United States.[10] Through his family connections in New York, Kopperl was able to enlist others to plead his case and vouch for his character. Ultimately, federal authorities concluded that while the store-owner from Mississippi was indeed a secessionist in spirit, he was not a member of the Confederate army nor had he come North with any nefarious intent. In February 1862, federal and Confederate authorities arranged a trade. An Indiana soldier being held in North Carolina was exchanged for Kopperl, who upon his release made his way as quickly as possible back to Carroll County.

As 1861 drew to a close, the war effort continued to generate a great deal of excitement in Mississippi, and most of the state's citizens still predicted victory. At that point it was easy for them to do so. The state still had adequate supplies and stores of food for its citizens. Mississippians in Virginia had experienced success, and had written letters home that included glowing reports of their battlefield exploits. Casualties were relatively low, particularly when compared to what would occur over the next three years. More importantly, the state had not yet been invaded. The blood of Mississippians had not been spilled on Mississippi soil. Towns had not been captured and buildings had not been burned. Fields had not been stripped and livestock had not been confiscated or driven away. As 1861 turned into 1862, most Mississippians were still confident. They still believed in the Cause, and in the Confederacy, but their faith was about to be tested.

---

[10] *OR*, ser. 2, vol. 2, p. 487.

3

IN DEFENSE OF THE STATE: 1862

The train was filled with wounded. All told terrible tales of
the scenes at Corinth.[1]
Kate Cumming
Okolona, Mississippi, April 9, 1862

From the war's outset, the Confederacy struggled with strategies for
protecting the Deep South, and particularly the lower Mississippi
Valley. In the early stages of the war, authorities viewed Kentucky as
the gateway to the region, and they feared that losing the border state
would leave the heart of the Confederacy vulnerable. At the time,
strong pro-Union sentiment in eastern Kentucky and Tennessee also
concerned Southern leaders. As a result, the Confederate high
command established its first line of defense in 1861, which was
designed to keep the Cotton South secure. The left flank of the line
was anchored at Columbus, Kentucky, on the Mississippi River while
the center was established at Bowling Green. The right flank
concentrated in the east around the Cumberland Gap. In Tennessee,
the Confederates established Fort Henry on the Tennessee River and

---

[1] Richard Harwell, ed., *The Journal of Kate Cumming, Confederate Nurse,*
1862–1865 (Savannah GA: Beehive Press, 1975) 3.

Fort Donelson on the Cumberland to meet the threat of amphibious assault. Albert Sidney Johnston, a veteran of the United States Army, took overall command of Confederate forces west of the Appalachian Mountains.

The year 1862 began with a series of sweeping federal victories in the Upper South as Union forces breached the Confederate defenses with relative ease. On January 19, United States troops under George H. Thomas pushed back the Confederate right by defeating a force commanded by Tennessean Felix K. Zollicoffer at Mill Springs, Kentucky. While Zollicoffer's command was made up primarily of Tennessee units, the 15th Mississippi Infantry also participated in the battle and suffered it's first major casualties of the war. Zollicoffer was killed during the fight and his men quickly retreated from the area. The following month the federals launched a successful assault on Confederate river installations in a cooperative effort involving a land-based force under Ulysses S. Grant and naval forces under Andrew Foote. On February 6, Fort Henry on the Tennessee River fell, and ten days later the Confederates surrendered the Cumberland River's Fort Donelson, whose defenders included several Mississippi infantry regiments. Finally on March 6–7, federals under Samuel R. Curtis defeated Mississippian Earl Van Dorn's command at Pea Ridge, Arkansas. The Confederate defense line in Kentucky collapsed for good as Albert Sidney Johnston abandoned its outflanked center at Bowling Green, falling back through Tennessee. With Kentucky and much of Tennessee gone, the Confederates scrambled to establish a new line of defense, and to protect one of the most strategically important points on the Southern map.

As the Civil War began, Corinth, Mississippi was a boomtown. First settled in the 1850s, it grew quickly because of its location in the northeast corner of the state at the crossroads of two major rail lines. The Mobile and Ohio ran north and south through the town and the Memphis and Charleston—called by many the backbone of the Confederacy—ran east and west. The town boasted 1500 residents, a number of thriving businesses, several churches, a small women's college, and three hotels, the most notable being the imposing three-story Tishomingo Hotel located near the intersection of the two rail lines. Because of the railroads, Corinth in just a few years had emerged as an important center of commerce in Mississippi. With the outbreak of hostilities it also became, from a military standpoint, one of the most important towns in the South. Many of the trains that had once generated business for Corinth now ferried soldiers and supplies to points throughout the Confederacy. The lines that met at Corinth connected the Upper South with the cotton states and the Mississippi River with the Atlantic Ocean. Confederate authorities recognized the importance of holding the town just as United States officials recognized the importance of capturing it. "The occupation of this point," one Confederate wrote of the town, "was of vital importance, and will appear [so] to any intelligent reader who glances at a map."[2]

With the collapse of Southern defenses in Kentucky, the Confederates made plans to concentrate as many troops as possible around Corinth to protect the town and hopefully launch an offensive that would turn back the federal invasion. Troops came into Northeast Mississippi from various commands around the South. Johnston's army, which had fallen back from Bowling Green through Nashville, was joined there by troops from the Gulf Coast commanded by generals Braxton Bragg and Daniel Runnels. Generals Leonidas Polk and Pierre Gustave Toutant Beauregard also brought in soldiers from Columbus, Kentucky. After all the troops arrived, the Confederates under Johnston had a sizeable force around Corinth numbering just over 40,000 men. Meanwhile, as rebel troops poured into Mississippi, Ulysses S. Grant and his force of more than 40,000 Union troops moved freely through Tennessee, finally halting at Pittsburg Landing on the Tennessee River about 20 miles north of Corinth across the Tennessee state line. There he waited for the arrival of Don Carlos Buell's 20,000 man Army of the Ohio. Once Buell arrived, Grant planned to march the combined Union force south and capture Corinth, then plunge into the heart of Mississippi.

---

[2] An English Combatant, *Battlefields of the South, From Bull Run to Fredericksburg; with Sketches of Confederate Commanders, and Gossip of the Camps* (New York: John Bradburn, 1864) 10.

When Johnston arrived at Corinth in late March 1862, members of his staff quickly looked for a place to set up the general's headquarters. William H. Inge, an attorney and Confederate cavalry officer who was on furlough at the time, offered to host the Confederate commander. Townspeople called Inge's well-kept home, located on the corner of Filmore and Bunch Streets, "Rose Cottage" because it was painted pink. Johnston moved in and immediately called a series of meetings with his generals to discuss strategy.

By early April, the Confederate high command in Richmond was desperate to stop the federal advance in the West. After studying reconnaissance reports of Grant's and Buell's movements, Confederate President Jefferson Davis wrote Johnston instructing him to move quickly against the Union forces. Davis and his military advisors, including Robert E. Lee, believed that if Buell successfully united with Grant, their combined force would be difficult to fend off. "If you can meet the division of the enemy before it can make a juncture," Davis wrote in one dispatch, "the future will be brighter. If this cannot be done, our only hope is that the people of the Southwest will rally en masse...to oppose the vast army which will threaten the destruction of our country."[3]

---

[3] Quoted in Wiley Sword, *Shiloh: Bloody April* (New York: William Morrow and Company, Inc., 1974) 91.

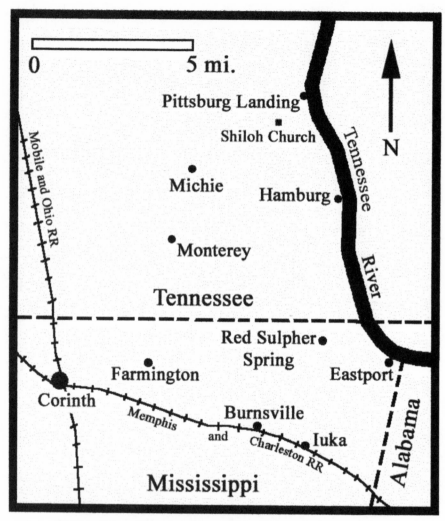

Map 2 Corinth -Pittsburg Landing Vicinity, April 1862

With their objective clearly defined, Johnston's army, with Beauregard installed as second in command, moved north to face Grant. Three corps commanded respectively by generals Polk, Bragg, and William J. Hardee left Corinth on the afternoon of April 3, with John C. Breckinridge's reserve corps following the next day. While troops had been gathered from all over the South, the Confederate force included around 4,700 Mississippians, mostly infantry distributed in various brigades. The two-day approach was difficult. The Confederates advanced over heavily wooded terrain broken by creeks, ravines, swamps and a confusing scramble of simple dirt roads. Most of the Confederate army finally assembled in the vicinity of Pittsburg Landing on the evening of April 5. They camped within earshot of the federal force near a small Methodist meeting house called Shiloh, a church that would give the next day's battle its name. Johnston once again called in his subordinate commanders and announced to them that the attack on Grant's army would commence the next morning at daybreak.

The Battle of Shiloh, fought on April 6–7, 1862, was among the first major bloodbaths that steered the course of the Civil War. The two-day struggle produced a staggering number of casualties and many survivors would forever refer to the battle as the most frightening of their military careers. About 13,000 Union troops fell along with a like number of Confederates. It was a savage, confused battle involving many men who were barely soldiers and who had never discharged a weapon at anything capable of returning fire. For the North, Shiloh was evidence that the United States Army would not easily defeat the Confederates. For the South, it served painful notice that long-winded rhetoric about ideals and honor had little effect on rifles, cannons, and bayonets. After the battle, it was apparent to all that the Civil War would be an exceedingly bloody affair driven by resources, casualty counts, and the collective will of the participants. "Up to the battle of Shiloh," Grant later wrote, "I, as well as thousands of other citizens, believed that the rebellion against the government would collapse suddenly and soon if a decisive victory could be gained over any of its armies...but [afterwards] I gave up all ideas of saving the Union except by complete conquest."[1]

On the morning of April 6, as Grant waited for Buell's arrival, Johnston attacked. Although Grant and his subordinate commanders knew that Johnston's army was close by, the Confederates caught the Union army by surprise and eventually overran the poorly chosen federal positions. After several hours of particularly fierce combat near the center of a 3 mile front—a spot forever after known as the "Hornet's Nest"—the Southerners retired claiming victory and holding the field. While the Confederates had success during the first day, however, there were few celebrations during the evening. Albert Sidney Johnston was killed during the battle and while his men drove Grant's army back to the river, they had not conquered the federals. Buell's formidable army arrived during the night and suddenly the Union possessed a far superior force that included thousands of fresh troops.

The Confederates paid a heavy price for their success, suffering heavy casualties during the fight. The sounds of wounded men screaming for water or for home could be heard through the night across the darkened battlefield. Daybreak found the Confederates, now commanded by Beauregard, disorganized and generally "fought out." First light again revealed to the men the true cost of their previous day's victory. "Wherever I turned," one Mississippi survivor stated, "I saw men pale in death, saw pale faces upturned and besmeared with mud and water, hair matted with gore." Another wrote that the wounded were so numerous that "a person could not move without stepping on them.[2] On the morning of April 7, the reinforced federals launched a massive counterattack, driving the disheveled Southerners back in confusion to their original camps and eventually into full retreat toward Corinth. Men from Breckinridge's corps covered the retreat, exchanging a few final shots with the

---

[1] Ulysses Simpson Grant, *Personal Memoirs of U.S. Grant* (Mineola NY: Dover Publications, Inc., 1995) 142–43.

[2] Augustus Hervey Mecklin, diary, April 6, 1862, Augustus Hervey Mecklin Papers, Mississippi Department of Archives and History, Jackson, Mississippi.

enemy before retiring. Weakened from the fight, the federals did not immediately pursue, and it would be nearly a month before they moved again on their original objective. In the meantime, Major General Henry W. Halleck replaced Grant as commander of the Union troops that had taken part in the battle.

While the Confederate army fell back toward Corinth in reasonably good order, the men were battered and bloodied as they moved across the state line into Mississippi. In two days, the Confederate army had suffered a casualty rate of almost 25 percent. Many of the survivors were ashen and glassy-eyed, in shock as a result of what they had just experienced. Going into the battle, many of the young volunteers had never before seen a dead body, then suddenly they saw thousands, including the mangled corpses of friends and relatives with whom they had enthusiastically enlisted. Wounded soldiers made the trip south in wagons, or limped along with the help of their comrades. The simple farmer's sons who had put down their hoes to pick up rifles in 1861 were now combat veterans painfully aware that the old adage "one rebel can whip a dozen yankees" was a lie.

One of the first Confederates to arrive back at Corinth, in body at least, was Albert Sidney Johnston. The evening of Johnston's death Dr. Samuel Choppin examined the general and injected whiskey into the corpse to serve as a preservative. He then helped members of Johnston's staff wrap the body in a blanket for transport. The entourage left the battlefield the next morning bound for Corinth, where they made their way back to Rose Cottage. Rebecca Inge, the owner's wife who had fed Johnston before bidding him goodbye just a few days earlier, and neighbor Ellen Polk cleaned the body and cut off several locks of his hair as keepsakes for his loved ones. Johnston's body lay in state in a simple white pine coffin at Rose Cottage for a short time before being shipped by rail to New Orleans.

The men under Johnston's command who survived the battle witnessed agony and chaos at Corinth. After the first day at Shiloh, word of the Confederate success reached the town, touching off celebrations. However, after the battle's conclusion, excitement quickly waned as Corinth became one giant field hospital, pathetically understaffed and under-supplied. When the soldiers began to arrive, authorities posted yellow hospital flags on every available structure including public buildings, churches, and many private homes, but the effort was not enough. As the smoke cleared from the Shiloh battlefield, more than 8,000 wounded men overwhelmed Corinth's peacetime population of 1,500. Military and civilian physicians along with volunteer nurses cared for as many soldiers as possible but could offer little comfort to most of the men. "Mrs. Ogden tried to prepare me for the scenes which I should witness upon entering the wards," one nurse wrote after her first day tending the soldiers, "But Alas! Nothing that I have ever heard or read had given me the faintest idea of the horrors witnessed here."[3]

Two of Corinth's largest buildings, the Tishomingo Hotel and Corona Female College, were crowded with hundreds of wounded Confederates and many federal prisoners who were "mutilated in every imaginable way." The steps outside the college were slick with blood and gore. Inside, amputated limbs filled buckets in the corners of makeshift surgery suites that just a few days before had been classrooms. Kate Cumming, a volunteer nurse who looked after many of the wounded in the Tishomingo Hotel, wrote in her diary on April 12 that "The men are lying all over the house, on their blankets, just as they were brought in from the battlefield. They are in the hall, on the gallery, and crowded in very small rooms. The foul air from this mass of human beings at first made me giddy and sick."[4] The streets and alleys of Corinth echoed with the screams and moans of the wounded, and the wailing of relatives who had come to the town searching for brothers, husbands, and sons, many of whom they found dead or maimed for life. According to one Confederate officer who witnessed the scene, wounded Confederates languishing in and around the railroad depot were "in many instances accompanied by their distressed wives or female relatives who had sought and found

---

[3] Harwell, ed., *The Journal of Kate Cumming*, 5.
[4] Harwell, ed., *The Journal of Kate Cumming*, 4–6.

them in mangled helplessness or on the bare earth in ruined health from exposure.... The scene was pitiable."[5]

As Corinth filled with wounded, the authorities sent many men elsewhere to hastily constructed hospitals up and down the rail lines. Seventy miles south of Corinth on the Mobile and Ohio, the town of Okolona accepted almost 2,000 wounded soldiers. As in Corinth, the army commandeered public buildings and some private homes and also constructed temporary shelters for the men. Still further south, citizens in Macon, Lauderdale Springs, Meridian, and elsewhere tended the wounded. Some men were moved west to Oxford, home of the University of Mississippi, where the state had already organized an official military hospital on the campus in anticipation of action in North Mississippi. Around $100,000 from the state's coffers funded the hospital, which had a capacity of 1000. Fifteen doctors, including Thomas D. Isom and Henry B. Branham of Oxford, served as staff and several dozen Oxford women tended the sick as nurses. Local slaveholders also contributed 100 slaves as orderlies. Following Shiloh, the hospital overflowed with wounded men, causing authorities to commandeer other university buildings and set up tents across the campus.

At Corinth, burial details worked overtime for weeks after Shiloh as men continued to succumb to their wounds and to the diseases that were rampant in the town. Poor food and egregiously improper sanitation bred sickness and more Confederates eventually died of disease at Corinth than were killed on the Shiloh battlefield. Simple amenities such as clean drinking water were in short supply. According to one soldier, "The water we had to drink was the most abominable stuff that was ever forced down men's throats. It was obtained from wells and holes around the camps and was of a bluish color and greasy taste."[6] To make matters worse, the Confederate government, desperate to hold the railroad juncture at Corinth,

---

[5] St. John R. Liddell, "Liddell's Record of the Civil War," *The Southern Bivouac* 1/9 (February 1896): 533–34.

[6] Arthur W. Bergeron, Jr., ed., *The Civil War Reminiscences of Major Silas T. Grisamore, C.S.A.* (Baton Rouge: Louisiana State University Press, 1993) 51.

ordered thousands of additional soldiers to the town in hopes of assembling a major force to once again try and fend off federal invasion. With Beauregard in command, the Confederates assembled about 80,000 men around Corinth, but disease quickly took its toll on the force and at any given time as many as a quarter of the men were incapacitated.

While in Northeast Mississippi, the army also sustained another blow to morale when word reached the men that in mid-April the Confederate Congress and Jefferson Davis had approved a national draft law. The controversial legislation called for the conscription of every able-bodied white male between the ages of eighteen and thirty-five for three years service. The mandate caused great controversy throughout the South, where many viewed it as a grievous violation of individual rights and of states' rights principles that had been a large part of the rhetorical foundation for secession. From a practical standpoint, the act obligated most of the men at Corinth to an additional two years in the Confederate army. This was unwelcome news to soldiers who had originally volunteered for one year of service and who were less than two weeks removed from Shiloh. The law was particularly offensive to many because it included a number of exemptions that favored the wealthy. Government officials were not required to serve, nor were men who owned twenty or more slaves. Anyone with the means could also hire a substitute, usually for $300 to $500, to serve in his place.

As the Confederates waited, Halleck assembled a force of about 120,000 men in the vicinity of Pittsburg Landing and, on April 30, 1862, began a slow advance toward Corinth. Plagued by bad weather and disease problems of their own, the federals took almost a month to cover 30 miles. Meanwhile, Beauregard took advantage of the slow approach to strengthen his defenses, flanking Corinth with a semi-circle of entrenchments. The Confederates twice sent out detachments to skirmish with Union pickets, but accomplished little. By May 25, Halleck was establishing a 5-mile battle line facing Corinth, complete with siege guns, and sporadic firing began around the town's perimeter. That same day Beauregard, realizing that his army was in an untenable position, called together his subordinate commanders to discuss the prospect of abandoning the town. The need to evacuate Corinth in the face of a significantly larger and better-equipped Union army was apparent to everyone and that evening Beauregard issued the necessary orders.

The Confederates conducted the four-day evacuation with considerable skill and under the utmost secrecy. As some troops moved south, Beauregard ordered others to the front as if he planned to move on federal positions. Supplies moved south via the railroad. During the evenings, as empty trains returned to Corinth for reloading, Confederate commanders instructed their men to cheer loudly as if the cars carried reinforcements. "We had orders to yell as each train load of reinforcements came in," one soldier remembered, "We yelled and in about ten minutes another came in and we yelled again as we did for six or eight empty trains."

The federals were completely deceived. At one point during the evacuation, the Union's Brigadier General John Pope sent word to Halleck that "The enemy are reinforcing heavily in my front and on the left. The cars are running constantly, and the cheering is immense every time that they unload in front of me. I have no doubt that I shall be attacked in heavy force by daylight." By dawn on May 30, however, the entire Confederate force, with the exception of some cavalry, had withdrawn. The federals briefly pursued before Halleck settled in Corinth and became "engaged in the congenial business of reorganizing and disciplining" his troops. While Beauregard had skillfully orchestrated the evacuation of Corinth and therefore avoided a major confrontation with a superior federal force, he earned the ire of Confederate President Jefferson Davis. Davis, who did not care for the general to begin with, was furious at the loss of the important rail town and placed Braxton Bragg in command of the force that had fought at Shiloh.[7]

---

[7] W. E. Preston, "Memories of the War," quoted in vol. 14 of *Confederate Reminiscences and Letters, 1861–1865* (Atlanta: Georgia Division United Daughters of the Confederacy, 2000) 148; Robert Underwood Johnson and Clarence Clough Buel, eds., *Battles and Leaders of the Civil War*, 4 vols. (New York: Century Company, 1887) 2:720.

Shiloh and the evacuation of Corinth marked a critical turning point in the service of many of the Mississippians who had fought under Johnston and Beauregard. They were no longer volunteer farm boys in search of adventure or glory. Regardless of their expectations of what army life had in store for them when they entered Confederate service, they had become realists who had taken part in a battle that would be remembered as one of the fiercest of the war. The deaths of friends and relatives had proven that the soldiers had entered the service under a host of false and fatal misconceptions. Northern men would indeed fight and kill if pressed, and the war was turning into a protracted struggle that would keep survivors away from their homes for an extended period of time. The dangers of war had become painfully clear to the men as they came face to face with their own mortality. With each passing day, the invading federal armies crept closer to their homes and supplies were becoming more difficult to obtain. The Southern volunteers of 1776 and the Mexican War had emerged victorious from their struggles, and their deeds had passed into legend. However, for many Mississippians the revolution of 1861 was not going as planned.

The nature of the war also changed the nature of the men's service and effectively voided their original mission. They were no longer volunteers charged with protecting their communities. The Conscription Act forced the men into longer service and at the same time favored the wealthy, therefore turning the struggle in the minds of many into "a rich man's war and a poor man's fight." The men had been told again and again that they were going to war to protect their communities and the native soil of their home state, but as part of the Confederate army their mission involved protecting all the Southern states as a single political entity. They had in essence become what they were fighting to avoid, subordinates to a central government that held sway over the individual states. The men were now forced to follow the commands of officers that they did not know, and depend on the actions of men in regiments from other parts of the country. The original community commitment remained, but it could no longer be practically applied. For many of the men, their new situation fostered second thoughts about their service, and the war effort in general.

Growing dissatisfaction in the ranks as a result of battlefield experiences, the Conscription Act, homesickness, and poor field conditions increased desertion rates in the army. After Shiloh, many of the men believed that they had done their share for the Southern rebellion as their original one-year enlistments expired. Their units had been organized as local undertakings, and as the soldiers' original enthusiasm for the war effort waned, many refused to accept the concept of Confederate nationalism as a reason to continue fighting. As a result, some soldiers responded to their condition by walking away. During the week before Shiloh, Johnston's army reported 1,334 enlisted men absent without leave. After the battle, that number quickly doubled to almost 2,700, or roughly 5 percent of the total. Many who remained still considered themselves, for the time being at least, honor-bound to do their duty, but they no longer held visions of the war as a romantic adventure. "Corinth!" one Confederate soldier later lamented, "The mere mention of the name to this day depresses my soul as no other name on this earth! Why? Because it was here that the first dart of doubt pierced my soul as to the ultimate success of the Confederate cause."[8]

From a military standpoint the fall of Corinth further destabilized the Confederate West. To make matters worse for the Southerners, the Union navy, under the command of Admiral David G. Farragut, steamed up the Mississippi River as the Confederates evacuated the Northeast Mississippi railroad center. The federals had captured New Orleans in late April, and soon afterwards Baton Rouge and Natchez surrendered. By late June, the Union fleet threatened Vicksburg, the most coveted point along the river. Strategists on both sides knew that the capture of Vicksburg would split the Confederacy, disrupt Southern supply lines and allow federal ships safe passage up and down the river. As early as November 1861,

---

[8] T. J. Walker, "Reminiscences of the Civil War," quoted in vol. 10 of *Confederate Reminiscences and Letters, 1861–1865* (Atlanta: Georgia Division United Daughters of the Confederacy, 69–70).

Lincoln had stated emphatically "Vicksburg is the key. The war can never be brought to a close until that key is in our pocket." As Farragut's ships approached during summer 1862, however, the city was well fortified and defiant. In response to demands for surrender, both civilian and military authorities were emphatic. The mayor sent word to the Union fleet that "neither the municipal authorities nor the citizens will ever consent to the surrender of the city." Colonel James L. Autry, commander of the Confederate post in Vicksburg, was even more combative. "Mississippians don't know, and refuse to learn how to surrender," he scribbled in a dispatch to the federals on the river, "If Commodore Farragut...can teach them, let [him] come and try."[9]

Confederate authorities eventually broke up the army that fought at Shiloh, reassigning various commands to locations throughout the South. As Farragut moved up the river, John C. Breckinridge's corps moved to Vicksburg where it became part of a 10,000-man force commanded by Major General Earl Van Dorn. The flamboyant and egotistical Van Dorn had recently taken charge of the District of Mississippi lying along the eastern bank of the Mississippi River.

Although they held New Orleans, Baton Rouge, and Natchez, the federals would have to wait another year for the capitulation of Vicksburg. Farragut moved his ships into position and, as the end of June approached, began furiously shelling the city. One witness to the scene reported that on July 28 "The roar of the cannon was continuous and deafening; loud explosions shook the city to its foundations...men, women and children rushed into the streets and amid the crash of falling houses commenced their hasty flight to the country for safety." While the city sustained some damage, Vicksburg rested on a 200-foot bluff and the batteries that defended the city opened fire and would not be silenced. With each passing day it became more apparent to Farragut that his attempt to capture Vicksburg was ill-timed. Trading blows with the Confederate guns

---

[9] Quoted in James M. McPherson, *Battle Cry of Freedom: Civil War Era* (New York: Ballantine Books, 1988) 420–21.

accomplished little, and Union commanders deemed an infantry assault from the river without support from a significant land-based force suicidal. In addition, the river itself refused to cooperate. Due to a summer drought, the Mississippi dropped several inches each day and soon threatened to strand several of Farragut's larger ships.

Toward the middle of July, the federals gave up their initial attempt to capture Vicksburg, but not before the Confederates delivered a parting blow from upstream. In the early morning on July 15, the CSS *Arkansas*, an ironclad operating above Vicksburg on the Yazoo River, steamed down river to harass the federal fleet. Isaac N. Brown, a veteran of the US Navy before the war, commanded the unusual Confederate vessel that some described as looking "more like a monster turtle swimming along down the river than a gunboat." As it neared Vicksburg, the ironclad first encountered and crippled the USS *Carondelet*, forcing the ship to run aground. It then moved in among the federal fleet and began "firing rapidly at every point on the circumference." Recovering from the shock of such a sudden action, the Union navy fired on the *Arkansas*, inflicting heavy damage. "A flash of a report," one witness to the federal barrage later wrote, "and then another and another. Now all joined the chorus, making the very earth tremble for miles around by the rapid explosions of the huge guns. Everything was dire and confused. We could not discern friend from foe for a while." Despite the massive counterattack, the Confederate ship was still able to sink a federal ram before finally drifting into port under the protection of the Vicksburg guns. Thousands of Confederate soldiers along with many citizens witnessed the spectacle from the heights and greeted the *Arkansas* with cheers as it tied up on the waterfront. Regimental bands began to play as Brown, stunned and bloodied from two wounds, stumbled off the vessel to a hero's welcome. The excitement of the moment was soon tempered as spectators descended on the dock to get a closer look at the Arkansas. There they saw the badly damaged ship as well as the bodies, blood, and brains of Confederate casualties. According to George W. Gift, an officer on the *Arkansas*, "A great heap of mangled and ghastly slain lay on the gun deck, with rivulets of blood running away from them....brains, hair and blood were all about." Official reports listed 22 casualties from the *Arkansas*, though the actual number was probably closer to half of the 120-man crew. Official reports from the Union navy listed forty-two killed and sixty-nine wounded. Soon after the battle with the *Arkansas*, the federal fleet withdrew.[10]

The federals failed in their first attempt to capture Vicksburg, but the successful Confederate defense of the river port was far from the last major military action in Mississippi during the calendar year 1862. Despite the reconfiguration and redeployment of the armies that had fought at Shiloh, the northeastern part of the state remained a focal point. Braxton Bragg took part of the Confederate force into Tennessee and Kentucky, and Don Carlos Buell pursued Bragg to meet the threat. Union general William Rosecrans and his army of 9,000 remained in Corinth to protect the railroad lines and cut off any Confederate reinforcements that might be sent to aid Bragg's army. For the Confederates, Sterling Price remained at Tupelo with orders to distract Rosecrans's attention so that he could not move into Tennessee to help Buell. Bragg also ordered Van Dorn and his 10,000 men from the Vicksburg area into northeast Mississippi to combine with Price. These movements set the stage for more bloodshed in northeastern Mississippi.

---

[10] "History of the Water Valley Rifles, Company F, Fifteenth Mississippi Infantry," 31–34, supplement to the WPA Historical Research Project, Yalobusha County, February 16, 1937, Special Collections Department, J. D. Williams Library, University of Mississippi, Oxford; quoted in Richard Wheeler, *The Siege of Vicksburg* (New York: Thomas Y. Crowell Company, 1978) 58–64; quoted in J. Thomas Scharf, *History of the Confederate States Navy from Its Organization to the Surrender of Its Last Vessel* (New York: Gramercy Books, 1996) 320.

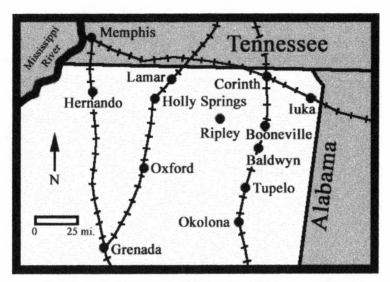

Map 3 North Mississippi, 1862

After Henry Halleck received a promotion to command all federal forces, he moved to Washington DC, leaving Grant once again in command in the west. Noting the military situation in the region, Grant took an aggressive tact, planning an assault against Price before his Confederates could combine with Van Dorn's men. To be more accessible for a potential move into Tennessee or Kentucky, Price moved his men from Tupelo to Iuka, Mississippi, 20 miles east of Corinth on the Memphis and Charleston rail line. Grant ordered a two-pronged assault on Price. Rosecrans moved out with about 9,000 men while General Edward Ord, with Grant riding along, moved west with about 6,000 troops. The federals planned to position themselves so that Rosecrans could attack Price from the south while Ord attacked from the north. Poor coordination plagued the federal effort and on September 19 Rosecrans reached Iuka, where he faced Price alone. The Battle of Iuka began just after 2:00 in the afternoon in the shadow of Woodall Mountain, the peak of which was the highest point in Mississippi. With Ord just a few miles away and unaware of what was taking place, the fighting raged for several hours until just after dark. Confederate casualties numbered

86 killed and 408 wounded while the federals reported 141 killed and 613 wounded. Initially, Price planned to continue the struggle the following day but his subordinates convinced him that withdrawing from Iuka was the best course of action. Rather than fight, they argued, the Confederates should move west and complete their rendezvous with Van Dorn. Rosecrans failed to cover the roads out of town, allowing Price to move out unmolested during the night. After discovering that the Confederates had fled, the federals took up a half-hearted pursuit but accomplished little. Some of the Union soldiers, agitated and angry that they would not immediately have the opportunity to finish off Price's force, took their frustrations out on the civilian property as they moved west on the evening of September 20. "I will never forget that night march," a Minnesota man wrote in a letter home, "The soldiers, infuriated at the escape of Price, fired every rebel house on the road that was unoccupied, which was the case with nearly all.... Flames crackled and roared and threw their light far into the deep woods that surrounded them."[11] Price fell back to the west eventually concentrating his force with Van Dorn's at Ripley on September 28. Van Dorn, as senior officer, took command of the entire army and immediately planned a counter offensive toward Corinth.

Van Dorn's decision to attack Corinth would later be called into question. He claimed that from a military standpoint the attack was justified because any delay would allow the federals to further fortify the town. The strategic importance of Corinth was beyond question, and the brash Van Dorn also knew that whoever reacquired the railroad center for the Confederacy would be hailed across the South as a military savior. He hoped to drive the Union army out of Corinth and then move into Tennessee where he could eventually provide assistance to Braxton Bragg. "It was clear in my mind," Van Dorn wrote, "that if a successful attack could be made on Corinth.... West Tennessee would soon be in our possession and communication with General Bragg effected through Middle

---

[11] T. D. Christie to "My Dear Sister," September 21, 1862, Minnesota Historical Society, St. Paul MN.

Tennessee." Unfortunately for Van Dorn, the federals were already
heavily invested at Corinth. Following the Battle of Iuka, Rosecrans
occupied the town with around 22,000 men and quickly employed
several detachments of "colored engineer troops" to dig a network of
breastworks inside the old breastworks that were abandoned by the
Confederates in May. By the first of October, Corinth was heavily
fortified. "I knew that the enemy intended a strong movement,"
Rosecrans later remembered, "and I thought that they must have the
impression that our defensive works at Corinth would be pretty
formidable."[12]

Van Dorn's force also totaled around 22,000 men, including
Major General Mansfield Lovell's division and two divisions under
Price commanded respectively by brigadier generals Louis Hebert
and Dabney H. Maury. On October 2, the army crossed the
Tuscumbia River bridge and moved over difficult terrain to
Chewalla, where the men camped for the night. The next day the
Confederates moved into position and attacked Corinth from the
north. Lovell's division occupied the Confederate right with Maury
in the center and Hebert on the left. The army included a significant
number of Mississippians who were trying to drive the federals from
their home state. Eleven Mississippi infantry regiments along with
two cavalry units and scattered artillery prepared to make the assault
on Corinth.

---

[12] Johnson and Buel, eds., *Battles and Leaders*, 2:740–43. United States War
Department, comp., *The War of Rebellion: Official Records of the Union and Confederate
Armies*, 130 vols. (Washington, DC: Government Printing Office, 1880–1901) ser. 1,
vol. 17, n. 1, p. 377.

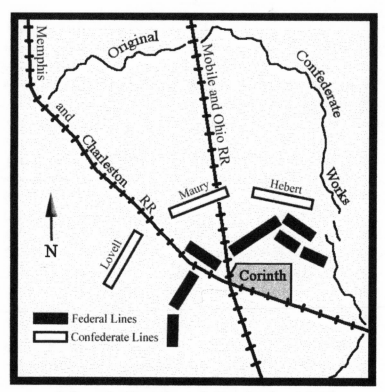

Map 4 Battle of Corinth, 1862
(Troop Positions 4 October)

The Confederate attack began on October 3 at 10:00 A.M. Van Dorn's men moved forward and clashed with federal troops stationed along the town's outer defenses. The Southerners were initially successful, and despite sharp resistance drove the federals back to their inner works. By the end of the day Van Dorn could claim victory but many of the Confederates were completely exhausted. As the sun set, he reported to Richmond that "We have driven the enemy back from every position. We are within three-quarters of a mile of Corinth. The enemy are huddled together about the town trying to hold the position. So far all is glorious and our men behaved nobly."[13] Van Dorn then assembled his commanders and made plans to finish off Rosecrans's force.

Though the federals were driven back, they were far from demoralized. They had inflicted heavy casualties on the Confederates and were well positioned in the works. As they tended their wounded and regrouped, one observer reported, "Our troops, conscious of a strong position; of their well-tried bravery; of the justice of their cause, and the great interest at stake, were determined to stand to their colors."[14] The next morning, for reasons never adequately explained, confusion reigned along the Confederate lines. Van Dorn planned an assault for daybreak but poor coordination hindered the effectiveness of his troops. On the left, Hebert fell ill, delaying his division's movements. On the right, Lovell's men skirmished with the federals but the general withheld orders to advance, supposedly following a directive from Van Dorn to "move cautiously." Despite the disorganized effort, the Confederates pressed the federals and at one point briefly broke the Union defenses. Sharp hand-to-hand combat took place on the streets of Corinth around the railroad depot and in front of the Tishomingo Hotel before federal reserves closed the breach and killed or captured most of the Southerners who had crossed their defenses.

Some of the most savage fighting of the day took place near the center of the battle lines on high ground around a well-placed fort called Battery Robinette. The federals outfitted the formidable three-sided enclosure with three large cannons and manned it with an infantry unit commanded by Lieutenant Henry C. Robinette, for whom the fort was named. With a harsh "rebel yell," Brigadier General John C. Moore's brigade in Maury's Division led the Confederate assault on the position. Union soldiers who witnessed the scene later described the advance on Battery Robinette as one of the bravest and deadliest charges that they had ever seen. Bullets and

---

[13] Quoted in Albert Castel, *General Sterling Price and the Civil War in the West* (Baton Rouge: Louisiana State University Press, 1968) 114.

[14] "Attack on Corinth, Full Particulars of the Fight," *Davenport* (IA) *Daily Gazette*, 13 October, 1862, 1–3.

Bravery

canister shot rained down on the Confederates, tearing men to bits as they approached the battery. "Oh! God! I never saw the like," one of Moore's Confederates wrote in his diary later that night. "The men fell like grass.... I saw men running full speed stop suddenly and fall on their faces with their brains scattered all around; others with legs and arms cut off. The ground was literally strewn with mangled corpses.... Oh! We were butchered like dogs."[15]

In a Texas unit, a former Mississippian passed into legend when he was killed at the height of the attack on Battery Robinette. The son of a well-to-do lawyer and political activist, William Peleg Rogers was born in Georgia in 1819. When he was a child his family moved to Monroe County, Mississippi, and established a plantation near the town of Aberdeen. Rogers showed great promise as a young man, and proved to be a hard-working and intelligent scholar. He studied medicine and law and eventually practiced both professions in North Mississippi. He also acquired a newspaper in Aberdeen, through which he was able to wield significant political influence in the region. In 1846, Rogers volunteered to fight in the Mexican War, serving as the captain of Company K in Jefferson Davis's 1st Mississippi Infantry Regiment. After the war, President Zachary Taylor appointed him United States consul at the port of Vera Cruz. Eventually leaving that post, Rogers settled with his wife and children in Texas where he practiced law and became a professor at the newly established law department of Baylor University. Always active in politics, he was a delegate to the Texas secession convention where he signed the state's secession ordinance. After Texas left the Union, Rogers secured a position as colonel in the 2nd Texas Infantry, which eventually led him to Corinth of the morning of October 4, 1862. As part of Moore's brigade, Rogers led his Texans in the assault on Battery Robinette and was a conspicuous figure at the front of the Confederate columns as they made the charge. With sword drawn, Rogers spurred his horse toward the fort, waving his men on in the face of withering fire. After federal bullets killed his

[15] Quoted in Wiley Sword, *Southern Invincibility: A History of the Confederate Heart* (New York: St. Martin's Griffin, 1999) 203.

horse, the colonel continued leading the charge on foot. He reached the top of the parapet before being shot and tumbling down into the ditch in front of the federal works. He was later buried, along with the bodies of many of his men, in a hastily dug grave just a few yards from Battery Robinette, and in future years those discussing the bloody Battle of Corinth would never do so without praising Rogers's conduct and sacrifice.

All along the lines, the Confederates were repulsed and by two o'clock that afternoon Van Dorn's army had disengaged and was retreating to the west. The general initially planned to reform and attack Corinth again, but his subordinate commanders convinced him that nothing could be gained, and much would be lost, in another assault. The retreat took the Confederates first back to Ripley, and then to Holly Springs, where the army regrouped. The Battle of Corinth was over, but both sides suffered heavy casualties. Because they were charging well-fortified positions, the Confederate casualty count was especially high, over 20 percent as opposed to just over 10 percent for the federals. Because his division did not take part in the second day's assault, Lovell's casualties for the two-day conflict were relatively light—77 killed, 285 wounded, and 208 missing out of around 7,000 men engaged. Losses in Price's two divisions were far greater—428 killed, 1,865 wounded and 1,449 missing out of almost 14,000 men engaged. federal casualties totaled 355 killed, 1,841 wounded and 324 missing.

Following the defeat there was a great deal of finger-pointing in the Confederate officer corps. While some saw Lovell's inaction as the reason that the assault on Corinth failed, Confederate authorities in Richmond and much of the Southern press placed the blame solidly with Van Dorn. To make matters worse, Brigadier General John S. Bowen, a brigade commander in Lovell's division, leveled official charges against Van Dorn, accusing him of incompetence, misconduct, and cruelty with regard to his treatment of the men under his command. Soon after the battle a court of inquiry, chaired by Price, convened in Abbeville, Mississippi to study the charges. After hearing the evidence and a lengthy testimonial by the accused, the court dismissed the charges as groundless, but the episode tarnished Van Dorn's reputation. He was relieved of command and transferred to the cavalry where he would ultimately achieve success and a great deal of notoriety. In his final report Van Dorn vaguely recognized his failure at Corinth, but was far from apologetic: "The attempt at Corinth has failed, and in consequence I am condemned and have been superceded in command. In my zeal for my country I may have ventured too far with inadequate means, and I bow to the opinion of the people whom I serve. Yet I feel that if the gallant dead who now lie beneath the batteries at Corinth see and judge the motives of men they do not rebuke me, for there is no sting in my conscience."[16]

Coupled with Bragg's defeat at Perryville, which ended his invasion of Kentucky, the Battle of Corinth was a severe setback for the Confederacy in the western theater of the war. Once Van Dorn was driven away from Corinth, Ulysses S. Grant, with the blessing of Halleck in Washington, received permission to put together a significant western force with which to begin a major offensive into Mississippi, the ultimate goal being Vicksburg. Grant assembled more than 36,000 men around Grand Junction, Tennessee, near the Mississippi state line. He planned to move south with the army, sweeping aside any resistance that he encountered until he captured the state capital at Jackson. This would effectively isolate Vicksburg and allow him to move on the port city from the east. Meanwhile, the Confederates in Mississippi were still feeling the effects of defeat. Van Dorn remained with the force that had fought at Corinth, but on October 14, 1862, General John C. Pemberton superceded him as commander. Pemberton established his headquarters at Jackson, leaving Van Dorn in temporary physical charge of the troops. Pemberton then ordered the army to evacuate Holly Springs and the Confederates moved south through Oxford and Water Valley to Grenada. As planned, Grant also moved south in pursuit. He occupied Holly Springs and there established a major supply depot designed to fuel his move into central Mississippi. The bulk of the federals then moved south and went into camp around Oxford. Not

---

[16] *OR*, ser. 1, vol. 17, n. 1, pp. 381–82.

long afterwards, Grant ordered General William Tecumseh Sherman to move south on the Mississippi River toward Vicksburg with a force of around 30,000 from Memphis, effectively making the Mississippi invasion a two-pronged effort

Creeks and rivers swollen by recent rains slowed the federal columns as they moved out of Oxford in pursuit of Pemberton's men, but a great deal of skirmishing, mostly between various cavalry detachments, took place in North Mississippi as the two armies lumbered through the region. On December 5, a significant encounter took place in Coffeeville, just north of Grenada, between Union cavalry that was far in advance of the main body of troops, and the rear guard of Pemberton's force. The Southerners drove the federal cavalry away and afterwards Grant halted his advance to re-deploy some of his men. The federal delay proved significant, and made Holly Springs the focal point of what would be remembered as the greatest Confederate victory in Mississippi during the war years.

In 1862, Holly Springs was one of Mississippi's most vibrant towns. Settled since the 1820s, it became Marshall County's seat of government when the state organized the old Chickasaw holdings in 1836. Just two years later the town boasted fourteen law offices, six doctors' offices, five churches, three hotels, and nine dry goods stores. Almost from the time it was officially founded until the war broke out, Holly Springs was a boomtown and a major hub of North Mississippi's cotton economy. By 1850, Marshall County's population was larger than that of any other county in the state, and Holly Springs and the surrounding area produced huge quantities of cotton. Mansions sprung up in Holly Springs, seemingly overnight, and the town's streets bustled with activity, so much so that Marshall County was known as the "Empire County" because of its great prosperity. "Holly Springs is a nice place," one Union soldier wrote soon after passing through the town in 1862, "and was without a doubt before the war a considerable place of business.... In fact, everything that displayed taste was visible."[17]

---

[17] Samuel Zinser to "Friend," Private Samuel Zinser letters, Cullom Davis Library, Bradley University, Peoria IL.

Confederate commerce ceased after Grant occupied the town, but Holly Springs remained a hub of activity. The federals commandeered the stately Marshall County courthouse, the railroad depot, and just about every other public building capable of holding supply stores. According to one observer "The depot buildings, the round-house, and every available place was packed full to overflowing. Scores of houses uptown were likewise filled. The courthouse was filled.... A large livery stable was packed with unopened cases of carbines and Colt's army six-shooters."[18] Some citizens of Holly Springs who had not sought refuge elsewhere ambled around the courthouse square on a daily basis looking on in curious indignation as Union soldiers went about their business. Others simply stayed inside and out of sight in hopes that no harm would come to them while still others could not avoid contact with the Yankees. Federal officers stayed in private homes and enlisted men pitched tents in the private yards. Some of the local gentry quietly accepted the intrusion and some even developed amiable relationship with the invaders. Still, one angry local woman called the federals "cowardly rascals" and wrote in a letter to a friend that "The day the army came to Holly Springs...thirty or forty Yankees would rush in at a time, take everything to eat they could lay their hands on, and break and destroy and steal everything they wanted to."[19]

When most of Grant's force left Holly Springs in pursuit of Pemberton's Confederates, an occupying garrison remained behind under the command of Colonel Robert C. Murphy of the 8th Wisconsin Infantry. Murphy had several hundred men at his disposal but from all accounts they were poorly positioned and relaxed in the belief that they would see no combat as long as they remained in the town. Unfortunately for the federals, the assumption was incorrect. On December 17, Earl Van Dorn, discredited army commander but

---

[18] J. G. Deupree, "The Capture of Holly Springs, Mississippi, Dec. 20, 1862," in Franklin L. Riley, ed., *Publications of the Mississippi Historical Society*, vol. 4 (Oxford: Mississippi Historical Society, 1901) 57.

[19] Cordelia Lewis Scales to "Mt Dear Sweet Little Friend," quoted in Katherine M. Jones, *Heroines of Dixie: Confederate Women Tell Their Story of the War* (Indianapolis: Bobbs-Merrill Company, Inc., 1955) 204.

veteran horsemen, was ordered by Pemberton to break away with 3,500 cavalry, work his way around the pursuing federal columns, and disrupt Grant's supply lines by attacking the supply depot at Holly Springs. By the night of December 19, the Confederates were closing in on their target, and although Murphy had been warned that rebel cavalry was in the area, the garrison was taken completely by surprise.

The next morning at dawn Van Dorn's men swept into Holly Springs, captured Murphy and routed his unprepared infantry. According to one Confederate participant, "the scene might well have been described as wild and exciting: Federals running, Confederates pursuing, tents and houses burning, torches flaming, guns popping, sabres clanking... a mass of frantic and frightened human beings." Union cavalry camped just outside of town at the fair grounds and unaware that danger was imminent formed a battle line when they heard the first shots. They attempted to offer resistance before the Confederates overwhelmed them and forced a hasty retreat. As Van Dorn's men in town rounded up stunned federal soldiers, many citizens cheered the effort from their front porches and yards. "Oh how I did shout when Van Dorn came to Holly Springs," one resident wrote, "I was so glad I had the chance to see Mr. Yankee run."

Aware that Grant had sent reinforcements to Holly Springs, and that the fresh Union troops would arrive soon, the Confederates loaded as many supplies as they could take with them and then set fire to the rest. As the Confederates left, seemingly as quickly as the arrived, many buildings were in flames but one structure that was untouched during the raid was the spacious mansion of Harvey W. Walter, a wealth planter and politician. Walter had opposed secession and was handily defeated by John Jones Pettus in the 1859 race for governor. It was not Walter's politics, however, that made his home interesting in the context of Van Dorn's raid. The previous night Mrs. Ulysses S. Grant was a guest in the home. She was staying at the Walter mansion as she made her way south to Oxford to visit her husband at his headquarters. Once word reached Holly Springs that a large force of Confederate cavalry was in the area, Mrs. Grant barely had time to escape by train. She rode 20 miles south to the

Union headquarters at Oxford where, according to her account, there was so much activity that her husband was unable to meet her train at the depot.

His wife's visit was not the only family concern that Grant had while in Oxford. As if he did not have enough on his mind, by the time Mrs. Grant reached the town an unseemly situation had developed there involving the general's father, Jesse Grant. Unlike his son, the elder Grant was a shrewd businessman, and always scheming. Earlier in the year he entered into a partnership with a firm called Mack and Brothers, run by a family who happened to be Jewish. Together the partners came South with the idea of purchasing large quantities of contraband cotton at reduced prices and selling it in the North at a significant profit, a practice that was fairly common at the time. However, as the father of the commanding general in north Mississippi, Jesse was obviously not the average cotton agent. He brought his partners to Oxford where he asked his son to assist them in obtaining the proper permits and credentials to procure as much cotton in the area as they could ship out. The general was livid. He wanted no part in war profiteering and was embarrassed by the conduct of his father, with whom he already had a strained relationship. In what was probably an emotional response by a man under a great deal of pressure, the younger Grant lashed out. Not wanting to publicly admonish (or draw attention to) his father, Grant issued an official directive, General Order Number 11, that banned all Jews from the region. The order stated that "Jews, as a class, violating every regulation of trade established by the Treasury Department...are hereby expelled from [Grant's] Department," and that "No permits will be given these people to visit headquarters for the purpose of making personal application for trade permits." The controversial order caused an immediate stir in Washington and Grant was ordered to rescind it, which he did. However, the incident led some to accuse Grant of anti-Semitism, although his future conduct seemed to indicate otherwise.

While the raid on Holly Springs was a stirring victory for the Confederates, it represented an embarrassing defeat for the federals, and a critical loss from a strategic standpoint. Grant was incensed that a better effort had not been made to hold the town, as was Major John J. Mudd, who was in command of the federal cavalry there. Both Grant and Mudd believed that if the town had been properly fortified, and the infantry properly prepared, the Union could have repulsed Van Dorm's attack. As commander of the post, Robert Murphy was held accountable for the fiasco, though he tried to deflect the blame. Murphy questioned the actions of his cavalry, claiming that they had run away at the first sign of trouble when in fact they had not. He also made a career-ending mistake in placing veiled blame on Grant, who he claimed failed to provide Holly Springs with adequate resources. "I have done all in my power," Murphy wrote in his report of the events soon after receiving a parole from the Confederates, "in truth my force was inadequate. I have foreseen this and so advised…. I have obeyed orders and have been unfortunate in so doing." Mudd's report accused Murphy of incompetence, and was especially scathing once he realized that Murphy was trying to blame the cavalry. "I cannot close this report," Mudd wrote, "without expressing the opinion that this disaster is another added to the long list occasioned by the drunkeness and inefficiency of commanding officers. I cannot doubt but that the place could have been successfully defended by even half the force here had suitable precautions been taken." Grant's response to the charges and countercharges was swift and to the point. He dismissed Murphy from the United States Army for cowardice.

While the Holly Springs raid ended Murphy's military career, it made Van Dorn a hero in Mississippi. The memory of his defeat at Corinth seemed to disappear as Southern newspapers and the Confederate high command in Richmond celebrated the flamboyant cavalry officer's victory. As word of the raid spread, many viewed Van Dorn as the western theater's correlary to Confederate cavalry commander J. E. B. Stuart of Virginia, and the comparison had merit. Both men were considered dashing by those who saw them in the saddle, and both were charismatic, brash, egotistical, and somewhat reckless. Regardless of their shortcomings, Stuart and Van Dorn both fit the mold of a brave, aggressive horse soldier that

Southerners readily accepted without question. Ultimately neither man would survive to see the war's end. Stuart died at the Battle of Yellow Tavern, Virginia, in 1864 and passed into legend, but Van Dorn's ultimate demise hurt his lasting image.

As a result of his victory in north Mississippi, Van Dorn was assigned a cavalry corps in middle Tennessee, where he proved himself as an able commander of mounted troops. In the early months of 1863, he achieved a number of successes, including a stirring defeat of the federals at Thompson's Station on March 5. Soon afterwards he established his headquarters and settled into a local home at Spring Hill, Tennessee, just south of Nashville. There Van Dorn reportedly engaged in an active social life and was seen in the company of a number of local women. This would prove to be his downfall. On May 7 an angry and resolute civilian, Dr. George B. Peters, marched boldly into Van Dorn's headquarters and shot and killed the general for allegedly carrying on an affair with his wife. Van Dorn's death was officially reported throughout the Confederate armies with the circumstances behind it discreetly omitted. Thus perished one of Mississippi's first heroes of the Civil War.

Though Van Dorn was gone, other Mississippians continued to serve in high-ranking positions in the Confederate army, including West Pointers Samuel Gibbs French and William Henry Chase Whiting and cavalryman William Thompson Martin. Born in New Jersey in 1818, French graduated fourteenth in the class of 1843 at the United States Military Academy. He served as a lieutenant of light artillery during the Mexican War and sustained a serious leg wound at the Battle of Buena Vista. French relocated to Mississippi where he married into a prominent family, lived on a large, profitable plantation, and became an adopted and devout son of the South. With the outbreak of the war he commanded artillery in the state forces and entered the Confederate army as a brigadier general in 1861. He served with Longstreet in Virginia and under Joseph Johnston and Leonidas Polk in Mississippi and Georgia before commanding a division as a major general during John Bell Hood's 1864 invasion of Tennessee. He finished the war in Mobile, Alabama.

A native Mississippian, William H. C. Whiting was born on the Gulf Coast at Biloxi in 1825. He graduated first in his class at West Point in 1845 and served in the United States Army with the engineers corps until resigning with the outbreak of the war. As Joseph Johnston's chief engineer, Whiting distinguished himself at the first Battle of Bull Run and, after an appointment to brigadier general, in Stonewall Jackson's command in the Seven Days battles. The object of political friction between Johnston and Jefferson Davis, Whiting was appointed to major general and commander of the district surrounding Wilmington, North Carolina, where he made Fort Fisher one of the most formidable installations of the Confederacy. He was mortally wounded when the fort finally fell in January 1865 and died as a prisoner of war.

William T. Martin was another Mississippi transplant who made a name for himself in his adopted state. Born in Kentucky, he studied law and moved to Mississippi where he established a lucrative practice. When the war began his political connections led him to command a cavalry unit, the Jeff Davis Legion, from Adams County. He served with J. E. B. Stuart in Virginia, was promoted to brigadier general in Joseph Wheeler's cavalry in 1862, and eventually commanded his own division. Martin distinguished himself in some of the bloodiest campaigns of the war, taking part in the battles of Antietam and Chickamauga. He served with Johnston, leading his division during the Atlanta campaign before briefly commanding the Department of Alabama, Mississippi, and East Louisiana in 1865. He survived the war and parlayed his service into a successful political career and a seat in the state legislature.

By the final months of 1862, the number of Confederate casualties from the Mississippi theater had grown significantly. However, not every Confederate soldier who lost his life in Mississippi succumbed to combat wounds or disease. Accidents of various types were frequent, and sometimes deadly. In the aftermath of the Battle of Corinth, men and supplies were transported around the state at a frantic pace via the railroads. Overloaded trains sped from one location to another on a rickety rail system that routinely ran off schedule even under the best of circumstances. Not long after the Corinth engagement, a major accident occurred on the Mississippi Central Railroad near Duck Hill, a sleepy little community just south of Grenada. The well-traveled Mississippi Central was a significant transportation artery that ran north and south through the middle of the state from the Gulf Coast to the capital at Jackson and on into Tennessee. As night settled over the state on October 18, Peter Kirby, a veteran engineer on the line, was at his usual post driving a southbound steam engine, the *James Brown*, as it pulled eleven cars through the central counties of North Mississippi. Not long after midnight, the train pulled into the Duck Hill station to pick up fuel and additional passengers and then, around 2:30 A.M., slowly pulled out of the station to continue its trip through the pitch-black Mississippi countryside.

As the *James Brown* began to move, a northbound train on the same tracks barreled toward the Duck Hill station at great speed. It was a troop train, and though it was under the command of Colonel Horace Miller of the 20th Mississippi Infantry, its twelve cars were crowded with Confederate soldiers from several states. The engine was the *A. M. West*, named for Absalom M. West, a Confederate general and one-time president of the Mississippi Central. About a quarter of a mile south of Duck Hill, Peter Kirby spotted a lantern on the northbound train and instantly realized that danger was imminent. He blew his engine's whistle, applied his brakes, and ultimately jumped to safety seconds before the two trains crashed into one another. The sound of the collision echoed for miles as damaged cars and the bodies of dead and injured men littered the area around the wreck site. A soldier who survived the crash compared the mangled bodies of some of his fellow passengers to those they had seen in combat. In short, though no engagement had taken place, the area around the site had suddenly taken on the appearance of a battlefield.

Within minutes of the crash, citizens of Duck Hill woke up and stumbled out of their homes into the darkness to render aid. Women tended the injured while men help remove bodies from the wreckage and formed burial details. Around eighty soldiers, mostly from the northbound train, were killed or injured in the incident.

Townspeople wrapped the dead bodies individually in blankets and laid them to rest side by side in a long burial trench. As dawn crept over the eastern horizon on October 19, strangers recited prayers and sang hymns as part of a hastily arranged mass funeral service. Word of the accident quickly drew railroad and military officials from around the state to Duck Hill. In a reflection of the times, the officials came not to mourn the dead, but to make sure that the important rail line was not long out of service. Within two days of the crash a temporary line was built around the wreck site, reopening the Mississippi Central for wartime traffic.

December 1862 marked the high water mark of the Civil War in Confederate Mississippi. After Van Dorn's Holly Springs raid, Grant withdrew his invasion force and moved his headquarters to Memphis to reorganize and reassess his options. As Grant left the state, well-entrenched Confederate defenders turned back the right wing of the federal invasion force under Sherman just north of Vicksburg. Sherman's task had been from the beginning a difficult one. He was charged with driving back Confederates under General Stephen D. Lee who were defending some of the most formidable terrain in the South. Chickasaw Bayou, named for the native tribe that once occupied the area, was a large, low-lying piece of ground just north of Vicksburg. It was dark, muddy swampland of almost impenetrable vines, brush, and trees. The swamp led up to the Chickasaw Bluffs, also called the Walnut Hills, on which Vicksburg rested and on which the Confederates had placed artillery and dug numerous rifle pits. Anyone who emerged from the swamp to approach the bluffs—if they emerged at all—would find themselves under heavy fire every step of the way.

Sherman moved his force of just over 30,000 men down the Mississippi to Milliken's Bend, and then to the mouth of the Yazoo River just north of Vicksburg, where they landed on the day after Christmas. For the next two days the federals picked their way through the swamp, exchanging shots with Confederate pickets while searching for the best place to launch a full-scale assault on the bluffs. Finally on December 29, Sherman attacked. All along the lines, "a flaming hell of shot, shell, shrapnel, canister and minie balls" rained down from the Walnut Hills, staggering the federal troops and driving them back toward the swamp. A group of federal soldiers from the 6th Missouri made it to the foot of the bluffs but then found that they could go no further. With their retreat also blocked by Confederate fire, the men dug into the side of the hill, scooping away the dirt with their hands to create shallow caves. They huddled there until nightfall, when they made their escape. The Battle of Chickasaw Bayou, as the engagement became known, was a significant setback for the federals. Sherman eventually withdrew after suffering almost 2,000 casualties compared to around 200 for the Confederates. "Our losses had been pretty heavy," the general later recalled, "and we had accomplished nothing."[20]

As 1862 ended, Confederate forces in Mississippi, it seemed, had successfully fought off the Northern invaders, but this was not enough to completely placate the general public in the state. Grumbling could be heard from many quarters. Families had lost loved ones, property had been destroyed, and while Grant had been driven away, most Mississippians realized that the war was far from over. Knowing this, Jefferson Davis came back to his home state for Christmas and took the opportunity to address the Mississippi legislature at Jackson on December 26. Davis aimed the speech not only at his old Mississippi constituents, but at the South in general since the president knew that Southern editors would reprint his words. With the address, he tried to allay the fears of Southerners and motivate them through patriotic rhetoric about commitment and ideals. He exaggerated Confederate victories of the past year and downplayed, or simply ignored, Confederate defeats. He spoke of heroism, sacrifice, and chivalry as he urged Mississippi and the South to look to a bright future.

Davis also took great pains to try and soothe class-based apprehensions about the war effort. Since the Confederate Congress

---

[20] Captain William W. Olds of the 42nd Ohio is quoted in Jerry Korn, *War on the Mississippi: Grant's Vicksburg Campaign* (Alexandria VA: Time-Life Books, 1985) 63; William T. Sherman, *Memoirs of General William T. Sherman, by Himself* (Bloomington: Indiana University Press, 1957) 292.

passed, and Davis signed, the Conscription Act with its "twenty-negro exemption," many in the working classes had howled that the sectional conflict was "a rich man's war but a poor man's fight." This perception was a great concern to the Confederate leadership in that it was indeed young men from the poorer classes that did most of the actual fighting and dying. In his speech, Davis was quick to cite examples of wealthy families who had contributed members to the effort as he praised the patriotism of the rank-in-file, both male and female. "I never meet a woman dressed in home spun [clothing] that I do not feel like taking my hat off to her," he said. "I never meet a man dressed in home spun but I feel like saluting him." As for the exemption for large slaveholders, the president of the Confederacy played on the race-based fears of the white public, explaining that it was actually a safety measure. The exemption was not designed to favor the wealthy, he insisted, but "simply to provide a force, in the nature of a police force, sufficient to keep our negroes in control. This was the sole object of the clause. Had it been otherwise, it would never have received my signature." This explanation, or perhaps rationalization, seemed to placate some of the state's small slaveholders or non-slaveholders. Since the outbreak of war slave insurrections had been a major concern among whites in lonely communities that had contributed a significant portion of their male populations to the Confederate army. Davis at once was justifying a measure that favored the wealthy and reassuring anxious whites that a "police force" was in place to keep the slave population in check.

Jefferson Davis's speech to the Mississippi legislature on the day after Christmas in 1862 was in part designed to lift the spirits of a people who had developed misgivings about the Confederate war effort. The address contained carefully chosen language, much of which was genuine. It also was peppered throughout with misrepresentations and downright falsehoods in an attempt to convince the public that the war effort up to that point was a success, and that peace, independence, and prosperity soon would be at hand if the South remained resolute. Still, despite the high tone and flowery language of the occasion, one fact could not be ignored and Davis addressed it directly. "I was among those who from the beginning predicted war as a consequence of secession," he told his audience, "although I must admit that the contest has assumed proportions more gigantic than I ever anticipated."[21]

The president of the Confederacy was not the only Mississippian who noticed that the war effort had assumed "gigantic" proportions. As the year drew to a close, secessionist sentiment began to wane as a result of the state witnessing a frightening amount of death and destruction. In 1861, few expected that the war would last more than a few weeks, if that, and despite the dangers involved in leaving the Union, for most Mississippians the idea of federal troops moving through their state had been unthinkable. After twenty months of war, however, many notions that were beyond comprehension when the conflict began had become painfully real, and there was no end in sight. While there was still a great deal of patriotic spirit in Mississippi at the end of 1862, and an even greater amount of support for the troops in the field, the Confederate experience in many quarters was wearing thin.

---

[21] Full text of Jefferson Davis' speech to the Mississippi legislature was printed in the 29 December 1862 edition of the Memphis *Appeal* which, at the time, was being printed in Jackson, Mississippi.

4

THE TURNING POINT, 1863

I rode into Vicksburg with the troops and went to the river to exchange congratulations with the navy upon our joint victory. At that time I found that many of the citizens had been living underground.[1]

Ulysses S. Grant

As the calendar year 1863 began, Vicksburg was still safely in Confederate hands. The rebels had turned back Grant, but the Union commander was determined to capture the "Confederate Gibraltar" and open up the Mississippi River for federal traffic. He continued to issue orders as he sent expeditions into the field to search for Confederate weaknesses. Grant's tenacity was such that he never lacked ideas or opinions on strategic matters. He and his lieutenants formulated a number of plans to take Vicksburg and acted on many of them with varying degrees of success. Though the federal advances on the city during late 1862 and early 1863 did not result in the capture of the major river port, they did succeed in spreading thin the Confederate troops in Mississippi, making the situation

---

[1] Ulysses Simpson Grant, *Personal Memoirs of U.S. Grant* (Mineola NY: Dover Publications, Inc., 1995) 225.

increasingly difficult for John Clifford Pemberton, the man whose job it was to protect the area from federal encroachers.

At first glance, Pemberton seemed out of place as the commander charged with defending the Confederate stronghold at Vicksburg. Born in 1814 on free ground in Philadelphia, Pennsylvania, Pemberton had served with distinction as a career soldier in the United States Army. A member of the West Point graduating class of 1837, he took part in the Seminole War and received two brevets for bravery during the war with Mexico. Despite his Northern heritage, Pemberton was sympathetic to the cause of states' rights, and his Southern proclivities only increased after he married Martha Thompson of Norfolk, Virginia, in 1848. When the Civil War began, he resigned from the United States Army, in which two of his brothers continued to serve, and cast his lot with the Confederacy. Jefferson Davis appointed Pemberton as a brigadier general in the Confederate army in June 1861 and placed him in command of the Department of South Carolina, Georgia, and Florida. Within a year he was raised to the rank of lieutenant general and given a new command, the critical Department of Mississippi and East Louisiana, which included Vicksburg as a focal point.

Pemberton's task was unenviable from the beginning. Like those commanding other Confederate forces in the field, he would never have enough men at his disposal to adequately defend his department. He would spend much of his time in Mississippi franticly ordering weary soldiers to locations around the state in response to federal troop movements both real and rumored. As a result, Pemberton's resources never were completely concentrated for maximum effect, and over time he could not conceal his weaknesses. The Confederate chain of command also worked against him. Joseph Johnston was the overall commander of the troops in Mississippi and Pemberton's immediate superior, but Confederate President Jefferson Davis also took an active interest in the region (to say the least). Davis and Johnston did not care for each other and their squabbles produced a consistent flow of conflicting ideas, suggestions, and orders to Pemberton as well as a frustratingly inconsistent flow of reliable intelligence. In the end, Pemberton's

Northern birth was also a handicap in that many Mississippians would never accept the Pennsylvanian as a true Confederate. Despite the fact that he had arguably given up more to support the Confederate cause than most native Southerners, he operated in Mississippi under a constant cloud of suspicion. This would make Pemberton a convenient scapegoat when Mississippi's fortunes began to decline.

One of Grant's ideas for solving the Vicksburg problem involved a major engineering project. While the city lay on a high bluff, it was also located on a severe bend in the Mississippi River. The position was such that it might be possible, in theory at least, to cut a canal that would change the river's course so that it would bypass Vicksburg completely. This would allow federal gunboats to float unmolested past the city's batteries. It would also literally leave Vicksburg's docks and warehouses high and dry and render the city irrelevant as a war aim. A similar project was begun and abandoned the previous year, but Grant still thought the idea had merit, as did President Abraham Lincoln. As a riverman during his younger years, Lincoln knew the twists and turns of the Mississippi and also knew that natural changes in the river's course were far from rare. He approved Grant's plan with enthusiasm in hopes that a properly constructed canal might coax the Mississippi into a new channel. Unfortunately for the federals, the river refused to cooperate. During the first weeks of 1863, Grant used as many as 4,000 men to cut the 1-mile canal, but in March rising water flooded the work camps and trenches and the project came to a permanent halt.

As the men tried to dig the canal opposite Vicksburg, more involved plans were also placed in motion. Fifty miles upriver federal engineers attempted to create another bypass by breaching a levee and flooding a significant body of water known as Lake Providence, on the Louisiana side of the river. Once the water level in the lake rose, the federals hoped that it would spill into local swamps and streams to create a navigable waterway. This plan ended in failure as the trees and thickets in local swamps proved to be impenetrable. Even further up the river, about 200 miles from Vicksburg, plans took shape for a water-based invasion via a tangled network of North

Mississippi rivers including the Coldwater, Tallahatchie, Yalobusha, and Yazoo. This effort also involved breaching a levee on the Mississippi and allowing the water to flow into an area of swampy streams called the Yazoo Pass, hopefully creating a navigable water system that included the larger rivers. In late February, federal engineers exploded a mine at the base of a levee and the water poured through. The streams and rivers began to rise and soon two ironclads, a number of smaller vessels, and troop transports loaded with soldiers were slowly moving south.

While the federals had successfully created a navigable waterway that they hoped could deliver significant numbers of troops to the Vicksburg vicinity, flaws in the strategy quickly developed. The fleet descending the rivers was vulnerable in a number of ways. The slow moving boats were easy targets for snipers and Confederate soldiers felled trees along the route to impede the federals' progress. Large tree branches also hung low over many of the narrow river passages, damaging the ships as they passed. Soon after the slow-moving expedition began, Pemberton made his own plans to meet the threat. He sent his ranking subordinate, General William Wing Loring, to Greenwood near the point where the Tallahatchie and Yazoo Rivers met. There Loring organized some of his troops along with black work gangs to construct breastworks of dirt and cotton bales which he armed and named Fort Pemberton. The Confederates then scuttled a ship in front of the fort to further obstruct the river. When the federals reached Fort Pemberton during the second week of March, the ironclads *Baron de Kalb* and *Chillicothe* exchanged heavy fire with the Confederates but were held in check. Unable to pass the fort and afraid that they would be trapped by further obstructions behind them, the ships retreated back up the Tallahatchie, effectively ending the invasion.

While Grant, who was headquartered on the river at Milliken's Bend, accepted these setbacks with a calm determination to press on, others were more apprehensive. Grant's critics in the federal command structure increased the volume of their carping, as did many members of the Northern press. "They pronounced me idle and incompetent," Grant later remembered, "and unfit to command men in an emergency, and clamored for my removal." Despite mounting pressures, Abraham Lincoln retained his confidence in Grant as the general began what would prove to be "a final move which was to crown the long, tedious and discouraging labors with success."[2]

Giving up on the demolition of levees and attempts to invade from the north, Grant proposed a bold new plan. He would move a large force down the western side of the Mississippi River to a point south of Vicksburg, ferry the men across the river into Mississippi, and launch a major offensive from below. As part of the campaign, the federal fleet operating on the Mississippi above Vicksburg, with its guns and transports, would also move south, run the Vicksburg batteries, and move into position to support the army. Grant's plan was met with skepticism from a number of quarters. Lincoln questioned the logistics of such a campaign and Sherman believed it would be more prudent to concentrate a large force around Union-occupied Memphis and make another much larger movement through north Mississippi. However, Grant's plan prevailed and in April he launched a campaign that in less than six months would make him a national hero.

Part of Grant's strategy included diversions designed to divide Pemberton's forces in Mississippi and draw the Confederates' attention away from the main body of federal troops on the Louisiana side of the river. Grant sent General Frederick Steele with his division to the vicinity of Greenville, where they wreaked havoc on local plantations and confiscated a great deal of "hogs and hominy" bound for Confederate consumption. Another diversion was more involved, and far more destructive. On April 17, Union Colonel Benjamin H. Grierson began what would in later years be remembered as a legendary cavalry raid through east and south Mississippi. Grierson's raid was designed to disrupt Confederate supply and communication lines that serviced Vicksburg and siphon off Confederate troops that could be used in Vicksburg's defense.

---

[2] Grant, *Personal Memoirs*, 179.

Among other things, Grant charged the colonel with "destroying all telegraph wires, burning provisions, and doing all mischief possible."[3]

Map 5 Grierson's Raid, 1863

[3] William T. Blain, "Banner Unionism in Choctaw County," *Mississippi Quarterly* 29/2 (Spring 1976): 213; D. Alexander Brown, *Grierson's Raid* (Urbana: University of Illinois Press, 1954) 5; Samuel Carter III, *The Final Fortress: Campaign for Vicksburg, 1862–1863* (New York: St. Martin's Press, 1980) 164–65.

Born in Pittsburgh, Pennsylvania, in 1826, Benjamin Henry Grierson seemed miscast as a daring cavalry officer. A talented musician, he composed and arranged songs, taught music, and played a variety of instruments including the guitar, piano, and flute. He also was frightened of horses as the result of a childhood accident during which he was kicked in the head by a pony and nearly killed. Such was the confused nature of the times in 1861 that once the war began Grierson, who also had political connections, enlisted in the army and ended up as a cavalry officer. Despite his background, the former music teacher had a knack for the job, and distinguished himself as a leader of horsemen. He was well known in Union command circles by the time Grant called on him to lead almost 2,000 cavalry through Mississippi.

The raid commenced on April 17, at LaGrange, Tennessee, just north of the Mississippi state line. The federal cavalry, which included men from the 2nd Iowa and 6th and 7th Illinois, plunged into Mississippi with Grierson in the lead. Soon all of north Mississippi buzzed with reports that the federal cavalry had invaded, and the Confederates scrambled for intelligence as to when and where Grierson might strike. Meanwhile, the raiders moved south, cutting a wide path through Ripley, Pontotoc, and Houston. They skirmished with small, isolated Confederate detachments and sometimes a few local civilians who usually fled when they saw the size of the federal force. Grierson's men destroyed or carried away anything they found that might be of aid to the Confederate effort. The plunder continued as the cavalry reached Starkville on April 21. There, according to one report, the men "robbed the inhabitants of horses, mules, negroes, jewelry and money; went into the stores and threw their contents into the street, or gave it to the negroes."[4]

As the federals had hoped, Pemberton hurried troops from one place to another as he heard reports of the Union advance. Although Confederate cavalry under Clark R. Barteau at one point skirmished with a detachment of Grierson's men at Palo Alto, near West Point,

---

[4] Quoted in Edwin C. Bearss, *Grant Strikes a Blow*, vol. 2 of *The Campaign for Vicksburg* (Dayton OH: Morningside Press, 1986) 201.

Robbing Civilians

most of the Confederates sent to stop the federal horsemen could never find or catch up with the main body of swift-moving raiders. The federals did considerable damage when they reached Newton Station between Jackson and Meridian on the Southern Mississippi Railroad. They swept into the town and captured the railroad depot and two trains fully loaded with provisions and ammunition. They then destroyed everything they could not use or carry away. "Twenty freight cars were burned," according to one observer, "and the depot buildings, and two commissaries. The telegraph wire was taken down for miles and cut to pieces."[5] After enjoying themselves through the benefits of some confiscated whiskey, the raiders again mounted up and set out into the Mississippi countryside. The men rode south to Garlandville and Montrose and then turned west. They arrived at Hazelhurst, 30 miles south of Jackson on the New Orleans, Jackson & Great Northern Railroad. A small group of armed citizens met the party but quickly scattered after the federals fired a few shots. Grierson's men destroyed another train and some public buildings before moving out once again. After avoiding a Confederate ambush at Union Church, the federals rode south through Summit and Brookhaven before leaving the state. Grierson's raid officially ended on May 2 when his dusty and haggard men arrived in federally-occupied Baton Rouge. Their arrival created a sensation and officials organized a parade to celebrate what many in the federal command viewed as a great achievement. Three days later Grierson summed up the events of the past two and a half weeks:

> During the expedition we killed and wounded about 100 of the enemy, captured and paroled over 500 prisoners, many of them officers, destroyed between 50 and 60 miles of railroad and telegraph, captured and destroyed over 3,000 stands of arms and other army stores and government property to an immense amount; we also captured 1,000 horses and mules. Our loss during

---

[5] Quoted in Bearss, *Grant Strikes a Blow*, 206n18.

the entire journey was 3 killed, 7 wounded, 5 left on the route sick....We marched over 600 miles in less than sixteen days.[6]

Grant had not remained idle during Grierson's raid. With much of Pemberton's attention diverted, the Union commander moved down the western side of the Mississippi toward a point below Vicksburg, where he planned to ferry his troops across to river. He needed to coordinate his efforts with the navy and, as a result, the federal ships operating above Vicksburg were also active during the period. On April 15, as Grierson prepared to launch his raid, Rear Admiral David Porter's federal fleet prepared to run the Vicksburg batteries and proceed south. Among the federal gunboats and steamer transports were Porter's flagship, the *Benton*, as well as the *Carondolet, LaFayette, Louisville, Mound City, Pittsburg, Price, Tuscumbia, Forest Queen, Henry Clay* and *Silver Wave*. Engines on several of the ships were modified in hopes of increasing their stealth as crewmen stacked cotton bales, hay bales, and grain sacks on the decks to absorb at least some of the enemy's fire. The next night the ships moved out, and in a very short time Confederate sentries in Vicksburg sounded the alarm. At the time many of the city's military officers, including Pemberton, were guests at a large party, which quickly ended as the Confederate defenses came alive. On the Louisiana side of the river, several houses were set on fire and men ignited barrels of pitch on the Vicksburg docks until the river was illuminated and the ships exposed. "The river," one observer later recalled, "was lighted up as if by sunlight." The city's batteries then opened fire, as did Union gunboats. As the ships passed, federal soldiers could see the bustle of activity on Vicksburg's streets. "We see the people in the streets running and gesticulating as if all were mad," one man wrote, "Their men at the batteries load and fire and yell.... The sky above is black, lighted only by sparks from the burning houses. Down on the river is a sheet of flames.... It was as if

---

[6] United States War Department, comp., *The War of Rebellion: Official Records of the Union and Confederate Armies*, 130 vols. (Washington, DC: Government Printing Office, 1880–1901) ser. 1, vol. 24, pt. 1, p. 528.

hell itself were loose that night on the Mississippi River."[7] It took just over two hours, but the federal fleet passed Vicksburg and continued down the river. By 2:30 A.M. the ships were safely anchored several miles south of the city and out of harm's way.

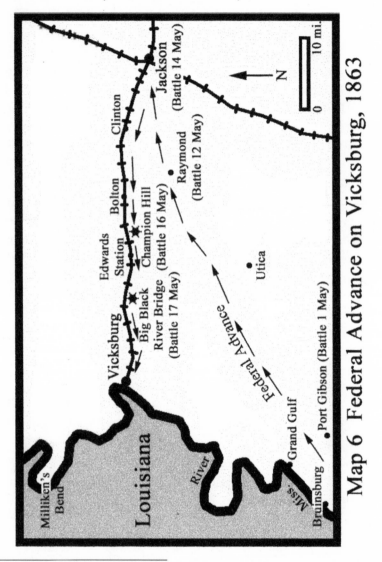

Map 6 Federal Advance on Vicksburg, 1863

---

[7] Quoted in Jerry Korn, *War on the Mississippi: Grant's Vicksburg Campaign* (Alexandria VA: Time-Life Books, 1985) 85.

Over the next few days Grant's men continued moving down the Louisiana side of the river. They were buoyed by news of the successful passage of Porter's fleet but poor roads still hampered their progress. On a daily basis a great deal of cursing was heard up and down the federal columns as the men struggled to free their wagons and heavy guns from the mud. "I thought I had seen bad roads in Virginia," one Ohio veteran lamented, "but these were worse. Sometimes the wheels were nearly buried in ruts.... Teamsters swore and whipped their mules. Some wagons were broken down and left. The scene was terrible." As they moved south the federal columns also grew in size as the region's runaway slaves, who viewed the federal invaders as a liberation force, flocked to the army. "Slaves from the plantations," one man reported, "were seen flocking off in the direction of the federal forces. They went by the hundreds, each carrying a bundle of some description. Old and young—men, women, and children."[8]

Toward the end of April, the army moved into position to ford the river. Grant planned to cross at the Grand Gulf landing, but before this could be accomplished he needed the help of Porter's gun ships. Grand Gulf was situated on a 50-foot bluff that overlooked the river, and on which the Confederates had placed sixteen artillery pieces. The federal fleet moved into position to clear the bluff so that Grant's men could land safely, but found that the rebel batteries were stronger than anticipated. After exchanging heavy fire for several hours the battered and bruised Union fleet retired with the Confederate batteries still in place. The federals decided to find another point to cross. Grant chose Bruinsburg, an old, undefended town site several miles south of Grand Gulf. On April 30, in what was one of the largest amphibious operations in American military history prior to World War II, Grant began moving 24,000 troops and 60 artillery pieces across the river into Mississippi. By the early morning hours of May 1, the Union campaign for Vicksburg had begun, and the first blood of the campaign would soon be spilled.

---

[8] Quoted in Bearss, *Grant Strikes a Blow*, 300; and Richard Wheeler, *The Siege of Vicksburg* (New York: Thomas Y. Crowell Company, 1978) 115.

As Grant advanced during the last days of April, General Pemberton in Vicksburg was confused, apparently believing that the federals had at least temporarily given up their efforts to capture the city. His troops were also scattered around the state chasing Grierson's dust and fortifying various positions in anticipation of federal troop movements. At the same time, Sherman created yet another diversion with his men, who were still operating north of Vicksburg. For two days federal artillery and a few small gunboats shelled the bluffs as the infantry deployed as if they were planning to attack. As Grant's men crossed the river downstream unmolested, it seemed that there was only one Confederate officer in Mississippi, John S. Bowen, who recognized that danger was imminent, and that the federals were launching a major campaign.

Bowen was born in Georgia in 1829 and graduated from the United States Military Academy in the class of 1853. After serving as a lieutenant of mounted rifles on the frontier, he resigned his commission and moved to Savannah. There he began an architecture firm and, due to his military experience, was commissioned as a lieutenant colonel in the state militia. In 1857 he moved his office to St. Louis where he was U. S. Grant's neighbor and a captain in the Missouri militia. After the war began, he raised the first Missouri Infantry and was promoted to brigade commander before sustaining serious wounds at Shiloh. Bowen recovered with his reputation enhanced and was the commander at Grand Gulf as Grant and Porter moved south. Bowen could never quite get the distracted Pemberton's attention to warn him that a major federal offensive was underway. Finally, on April 30, Bowen sent a series of frantic messages to Vicksburg, letting Pemberton know that Grant's army was crossing the river in force. "Hurry up re-enforcement," he scribbled in one hasty dispatch, "my lines are very much extended."[9]

Pemberton got the message, but it was too late. Grant's men crossed the river and moved into position to overwhelm the only Confederates in the area, Bowen's 6,000 defenders. The next day, the first of May, Bowen's force met more than 20,000 federal soldiers at

---

[9] *OR*, ser. 1, vol. 24, pt. 1, p. 657.

the Battle of Port Gibson, fought several miles inland from the river. Skirmishing started before dawn, and around daybreak the battle began in earnest. Bowen's men fought gamely, but they faced an impossible task with little hope of significant reinforcements. "We have been engaged in a furious battle ever since daybreak," Bowen wrote to Pemberton in the early afternoon, "My whole force is engaged.... The men act nobly, but the odds are overpowering."[10] At 5:30 P.M., after fighting an effective delaying action for most of the day, the Confederates fell back. Both sides suffered around 800 casualties during the course of day, though from a strategic standpoint the Southerners had suffered a significant setback. The Union victory at Port Gibson forced the Confederates to evacuate Grand Gulf and firmly established Grant's army on Mississippi soil. Once the smoke from the engagement cleared, Grant called for Sherman and his troops, who were still operating north of Vicksburg, bringing Grant's total strength to more than 40,000 men. Meanwhile, Pemberton's had around 30,000 troops at his disposal in Mississippi, but most were scattered in various detachments, making it difficult for them to impede federal progress.

Grant moved northeast toward Jackson, where he planned to capture the capitol and then destroy the rail lines through which Confederate reinforcements and supplies might pass. This move would isolate Vicksburg against the river, allowing the federals to move on the city from the east. Grant organized his troops into three corps. Major General John A. McClernand's corps took up a position on the left with Sherman's corps in the center and Major General James B. McPherson's corps on the right. As the federals moved through the countryside, they sent out foraging parties that commandeered a significant amount of food from local residents in a relatively affluent region that as yet had not been touched by the war. The men stripped every plantation that they came across, and according to Grant, "Beef, mutton, poultry and forage were found in abundance. Quite a quantity of bacon and molasses was also secured from the country." Bread and coffee were in short supply, but most

---

[10] *OR*, ser. 1, vol. 24, pt. 1, p. 659.

of the plantations "had a run of stone, propelled by mule power, to grind corn for the owners of the plantation and their slaves. All these were kept running...day and night."[11]

As the federals moved north, Pemberton was frantic. Finally well aware that a major Union advance was underway, he was not sure if Grant planned to move on Jackson or directly on Vicksburg. Grant added to the confusion by ordering a series of diversionary movements by his three corps. Believing that the federals would probably move on Vicksburg first, Pemberton sent a force of 3,000 men under Brigadier General John Gregg to the town of Raymond, about 15 miles south of Jackson. There he hoped Gregg would be in position to threaten Grant from the rear once the federals turned toward Vicksburg. Instead, Gregg would meet an entire federal corps under McPherson's command.

Established in the 1820s, Raymond was the seat of government for Hinds County and, as such, a hub of local commerce and politics.[12] The town boasted a courthouse, jail, and a number of hotels and other businesses. Gregg's Confederates arrived at Raymond early on the morning of May 12, apparently unaware that an entire federal corps was approaching the town. At the most, one Tennessean wrote, "We were expecting nothing but cavalry, which we felt we could whip."[13] Nor did the townspeople believe that they were in imminent danger. They welcomed Gregg as a hero, and prepared food for a grand picnic later in the day to honor his men. Gregg deployed his Confederates just outside of town, where they soon met the advanced guard from McPherson's 10,000–man army. Still unaware that they were outnumbered by more than three to one, the Confederates attacked around noon. The contest raged for more than two hours with both sides exchanging shot and shell and, at times, engaging in hand to hand combat. As more of McPherson's men appeared, however, Gregg finally realized that he was facing a

---

[11] Grant, *Personal Memoirs*, 194.

[12] In an unusual arrangement, Hinds County actually had two county seats, Jackson being the other.

[13] Quoted in Wheeler, *The Siege of Vicksburg*, 139.

far superior force. The federals drove the Confederates back and Gregg ordered a hasty retreat, abandoning Raymond completely. "It would have been folly," one rebel private wrote, "to have attempted a defense against such superior numbers. We retreated slowly and in good order to a camping ground seven miles north." Both sides sustained around 500 casualties, but once again the Confederates had been effectively brushed aside by the advancing federals.

When the Union soldiers entered Raymond they seized the town's public buildings to serve as hospitals where both federal and Confederate wounded received care. Blood stained the courthouse floor as wounded men took up all available space in the building. Local churches and hotels were also filled to capacity and many of Raymond's women served as volunteer nurses. For the Confederate citizens the defeat was particularly painful when, upon their arrival in the town, the cheering federals ran an American flag up the courthouse flagpole. According to one Union soldier, "we enjoyed our victory amazingly and marched through and beyond the town singing the 'Union Forever.'" McPherson's corps continued to forage, seizing anything of value that they came across as spoils of war. One bitter Raymond resident later recalled that the soldiers "camped around us, burned all the fences for their cooking pots and emptied the hen houses and the smokehouses. I saw them drive off a cow and calf while my mother begged in vain to spare them."[14] News of the federal victory at Raymond spread quickly, with one result being yet another wave of area slaves rushing into the Union lines seeking protection. Some came on foot while others came in wagons or carriages pilfered from the plantations on which they worked.

The Confederate high command also reacted to the alarming state of affairs in Mississippi, sending Joseph Johnston from Tullahoma, Tennessee, to take personal charge of the Mississippi theater. Johnston was a veteran commander and many considered

[14] W. J. Davidson, "The Diary of Private W.J. Davidson," in vol. 1 of *The Annals of the Army of Tennessee and Early Western History* (Jackson TN: Guild Bindery Press, 1878) 57–58; Letitia Dabney Miller, *The Recollections of Letitia Dabney Miller*, Mrs. Cade Drew Gillespie Collection, Department of Archives and Special Collections, J. D. Williams Library, University of Mississippi, Oxford.

him the South's best general. A native Virginian, he was a member of West Point's graduating class of 1829, had fought against the Seminoles in Florida, and was twice wounded during the Mexican War. Johnston resigned his federal commission on April 22, 1861, to join Virginia's state forces. He shared credit with P. G. T. Beauregard for the Confederate victory at First Manassas and was one of five men to achieve the rank of full general in the Confederate army, though he had a poor relationship with Confederate President Jefferson Davis. Wounded outside Richmond, he recovered and was reassigned to the West to oversee Braxton Bragg's Army of Tennessee. As Mississippi began to slip from the Confederate's grasp, many thought that Johnston was the only man that could salvage the situation. Johnston arrived in Jackson on May 13 and moved into the Bowman House near the capital building. The situation was bleak. While reinforcements were on the way from points around the South, Johnston had only a few thousand men at his disposal as the federals approached.

When Johnston arrived in Jackson he found a city gripped in fear. Governor John Jones Pettus had left the capitol under the pretext of moving the state's seat of government to Enterprise, and his departure dealt a severe blow to the city's morale. Civilians hurriedly packed as much as they could carry and fled the city in what one observer described as a "terror-stricken flight of thousands." Charles H. Manship, the city's mayor, issued a proclamation imploring the citizens to remain calm, but his pleadings fell on deaf ears. As horses, mules, and human beings crowded Jackson's streets a Northern newspaper correspondent described the chaos as "a panic of the most decided kind," that "existed among all classes of society."[15] Many who remained in the city closed up their homes and cowered behind locked doors in hopes that the crisis would pass quickly. In one respect, the crisis did indeed pass quickly. On May 14, Grant ordered McPherson's and Sherman's corps to attack Johnston at Jackson. After a five-hour battle during which the

---

[15] Quoted in Robert W. Dubay, *John Jones Pettus, Mississippi Fire-Eater: His Life and Times, 1813–1867* (Jackson: University Press of Mississippi, 1975) 173.

federals suffered around 250 casualties to just over 800 for the Confederates, Johnston ordered his troops to evacuate the state capital and retire to the north toward Canton. Before leaving, the Confederates burned countless bales of cotton and a number of engines and cars belonging to the Mississippi Central Railroad so that they would not fall into Union hands.

The federals entered Jackson and several officers went to inspect the Mississippi state house. They noted the scattered papers in the hastily evacuated governor's office before raising an American flag over the building. One block over, in the Bowman House, Grant settled into the room that Johnston had occupied the night before. The Confederate evacuation had touched off looting in parts of the city. Poor whites, newly liberated slaves, and convicts that were freed from the local penitentiary roamed the streets breaking into shops and carrying away anything of value. The federals eventually sent out patrols that restored order, but not before the looters had done significant damage. Sherman then ordered men from his command to destroy everything of military value in the city, and the soldiers set fire to a number of structures including arsenal buildings, the government foundry, a gun-carriage factory, the railroad depot, and the state penitentiary building that housed a cotton-processing operation. As fires spread, a number of private buildings were engulfed as their owners watched helplessly from the street. The federals also destroyed the railroad lines that serviced the city, and to insure that the track could not be reused, they placed many short sections of the rails over fires, heating their middles until they were red-hot and pliable. The soldiers then twisted them around the nearest tree, creating what the men referred to as "Sherman's neckties."

As Grant and Sherman made their own inspection of the city, they came across a textile factory owned by local merchants Joshua and Thomas Green. The generals entered the establishment and found 500 employees, most of whom were young girls, busily working at their jobs and apparently oblivious to the fact that Union troops had occupied Jackson. Grant and Sherman watched for some time as the women produced rolls of tent cloth that included a neatly monogrammed "C.S.A." on each bolt. Grant later recalled that "I finally told Sherman that I believed they had done work enough. The operatives were told they could leave and take with them what cloth they could carry."[16]

Before the federals put the torch to the building and equipment, one of the Green brothers arrived to plead his case for saving the factory. The federal commanders were not sympathetic and soon the building was in flames. Several years after the war ended, when Grant was in the White House, the Greens petitioned the president for payment for their property, claiming that the factory had been a private concern not involved with the Confederate war effort. Predictably, Grant denied the request.

During his brief stay at the Bowman House in Jackson, Grant received an important piece of intelligence from an unconventional but effective source. Earlier, federal General Stephen A. Hurlbut had, with a great deal of publicity, exiled a Southern sympathizer from Union-occupied Memphis, Tennessee, officially charging the man with disloyalty. Hurlbut made sure that the regional press carried an account of the event and took great pains in stating that any other citizens charged with disloyalty to the United States would receive the same treatment. The accused man moved south into Mississippi where he was welcomed by Confederate authorities and given a job as courier for the army. Unbeknownst to the Confederates, however, the man had been willingly thrown out of Memphis as part of an elaborate ruse. He was actually a federal agent, and he ended up as a courier for Joseph Johnston. Upon arriving in Jackson, Johnston gave the man a message to carry to Pemberton, whose headquarters was just outside Vicksburg. The message instructed Pemberton to take the offensive, move east, and attack Grant with the help of Johnston's men who were stationed around Jackson. By combining their forces, Johnston surmised, they could drive Grant away. The courier took the message to Grant, who adjusted his strategy accordingly. Once Johnston was driven in confusion from Jackson, Grant ordered most of his men out of the

---

[16] Grant, *Personal Memoirs*, 200.

city to face Pemberton before the Confederates could regroup and coordinate a joint effort.

What resulted was the decisive battle of the Vicksburg Campaign. Grant left Jackson on the afternoon of May 15 and moved west toward Vicksburg with McClernand and McPherson's corps. Sherman's corps, which was the most involved in the destruction of Confederate war supplies in Jackson, soon followed. Meanwhile Pemberton moved east toward the state capital. Grant spent the night in Clinton and the next morning concentrated around 29,000 troops near Edwards Station, where they met Pemberton's force of about 23,000 men at a rise known as Champion Hill. The Confederates were organized into three divisions commanded by John S. Bowen, Carter L. Stevenson and William W. Loring. Early on the morning of May 16, Pemberton deployed his men and at 10:30 A.M. Grant launched an all-out assault on the Confederate positions. During several hours of vicious fighting, Champion Hill changed hands three times. "The battle here raged fearfully," one Confederate participant wrote, "One unbroken, deafening roar of musketry was all that could be heard.... The ground was fought over three times and as the wave of battle rolled to and fro, the scene became bloody and terrific."[17] The outnumbered Confederates eventually lost the field and by five o'clock that evening were retreating to the west, leaving behind twenty-seven cannons and hundreds of prisoners. Casualty counts were high. The Confederates lost almost 4,000 men at the Battle of Champion Hill to just over 2,400 casualties for the federals.

During the battle, Grant was at times close to the front lines issuing orders and observing the action. The general's conduct impressed Samuel H. M. Byers, a corporal from Iowa:

> A good many men were falling, and the wounded were being borne to the rear.... On looking round, I saw immediately behind us Grant, the commander-in-chief.... It was Grant under fire. The rattling musketry increased on our front, and grew louder, too, on our left flank.... He now stood leaning complacently

---

[17] Quoted in Wheeler, *The Siege of Vicksburg*, 153.

against his favorite steed, smoking—as seemed habitual with him—the stump of a cigar. His was the only horse near the line, and must, naturally, have attracted some of the enemy's fire. What if he should be killed, I thought to myself, and the army be left without its commander?... I am sure everyone who recognized him wished him away, but there he stood—clear, calm and immovable.[18]

Following the battle, the federal soldiers cheered and threw their hats in the air as Grant passed through the lines. All concerned realized that the United States had won a major victory. In contrast, the Confederates were in disarray, retreating in confusion toward Vicksburg. From Pemberton down to the rank-in-file, morale was abysmal. In the officers corps, squabbling and finger-pointing was the rule. "There was no harmony, no unity of action," one observer reported, "and instead of there existing mutual confidence on the part of the Commanding General and his subordinates—there was just the opposite." As he rode west Pemberton was depressed, believing that the defeat would cost him his command, and probably his military career. Unable to trust any of his officers, the general confided in Samuel Lockett, one of his staff: "Just thirty years ago I began my military career by receiving my appointment to a cadetship at the U.S. Military Academy; and today—the same date—that career is ended in disaster and disgrace."[19] Lockett tried to encourage the general, but Pemberton was inconsolable.

In addition to casualties at the Battle of Champion Hill, Pemberton also lost an entire division under the command of William W. Loring. Charged with covering the Confederate retreat, Loring's men were cut off from the rest of Pemberton's force that would eventually fall back into Vicksburg. Unable to reunite with Pemberton, the men retreated haphazardly to the southeast toward Crystal Springs. Enlisting the aid of a local farmer as a guide, Loring's force marched all night through dense woods. In the

---

[18] Quoted in Wheeler, *The Siege of Vicksburg.*, 150–51.
[19] Robert Underwood Johnson and Clarence Clough Buel, eds., *Battles and Leaders of the Civil War*, 4 vols. (New York: Century Company, 1887) 3:477–78.

process, they abandoned their artillery and other equipment in the darkness. The next morning, the men crossed the road leading from Jackson to Raymond, at which time local citizens warned them that federal forces were still in the area. Not looking for a fight, Loring kept his soldiers on the march, finally stopping to set up camp near Crystal Springs. The men had been marching steadily for nearly twenty-four hours without food or rest, and a number of stragglers never returned to the ranks. From Crystal Springs Loring's division marched north, arriving in Jackson on May 19 where they united with General Joseph Johnston. After pillaging the state's capital, Sherman's corps had abandoned the city, leaving it free for occupation by the Confederates. Johnston began organizing an "Army of Relief" there during the following week, ostensibly to come to Pemberton's aid in Vicksburg.

Immediately after the Battle of Champion Hill, and as yet unaware that Loring had been cut off, Pemberton ordered a division under the always dependable John S. Bowen and a fresh brigade under John Vaughn to hold the bridges at the Big Black River until the rest of the retreating Confederate army could cross. Waiting in vain for Loring's men to come in sight, Bowen and Vaughn soon found themselves face to face with McClernand's pursuing corps. Bowen's division, exhausted from the previous day's fight, and Vaughn's brigade were no match for the advancing Union columns. The federals quickly drove back the Confederates in what became known as the Battle of Big Black River Bridge. Bowen's men retreated in haste, leaving behind eighteen cannons. Some soldiers ran for the bridges while others drowned as they tried to swim the Big Black River. The federals lost 279 men during the engagement but collected almost 1,800 rebel prisoners. The Confederates who escaped joined the rest of Pemberton's force and fell back into Vicksburg.

As the retreating Confederates exchanged a few final shots with McClernand's men, the federals suffered a rather unusual casualty. U. S. Grant's young son, twelve-year-old Fred Grant, who accompanied his father on the Vicksburg campaign, was on hand for the Confederate retreat and at one point strayed too close to the Big

Black River. "Following the retreating Confederates to the Big Black," the younger Grant later remembered, "I was watching some of them swim the river when a sharpshooter on the opposite bank fired at me and hit me in the leg." The wound was painful but not serious, although at the time seeing his own blood led Grant's son to believe that his fate was sealed. After watching Fred fall to the ground, a federal colonel ran up to him and asked what happened, to which the stunned boy replied simply "I am killed."[20] After examining the leg and seeing that the wound was only slight, the colonel helped Fred to safer ground.

As his corps advanced toward Vicksburg, Sherman rode through Bolton, a small settlement near Edwards Station, where he came across a unique keepsake. Some of his men had gathered there around a well in front of a modest log building that appeared to be servants quarters. As the men drew water from the well Sherman rode toward them for a drink and, as he took his first sip, noticed a book lying on the ground nearby. He asked one of his men to hand him the volume and found that it was a copy of the United States Constitution. Incredibly, upon closer inspection Sherman found the name Jefferson Davis written across the title page. "On inquiry of a Negro," Sherman later recalled, "I learned that the place belonged to the President of the Southern Confederation." Furthermore, Sherman learned that the Confederate president's brother Joseph also had property nearby. The general sent a staff officer and small party of soldiers to investigate, and the men "found Joe Davis at home, an old man, attended by a young and affectionate niece. But they were overwhelmed with grief to see their country overrun and swarming with Federal troops."[21] Sherman's men stayed at the property for only a short time before leaving with two of Joseph Davis's horses.

On May 17, the first Confederates began straggling into Vicksburg, and the city's normal population of around 4,000

---

[20] Fred Grant quoted in Wheeler, *The Siege of Vicksburg*, 158.

[21] William T. Sherman, *Memoirs of General William T. Sherman, by Himself* (Bloomington: Indiana University Press, 1957) 323.

residents soon swelled to more than 30,000 civilians and soldiers. After experiencing a series of crushing defeats, most of the men were despondent, as were local citizens who had heard reports of the defeat at Champion Hill. "The spirit of our troops had undergone great change," one Confederate soldier reported, "Instead of the high hopes that animated us last week, a feeling of demoralization seemed to permeate the rank and file, and none of us were hopeful as to the result of the campaign." Many of the soldiers cursed Pemberton, blaming the Pennsylvanian for the army's poor fortunes. Some of the men declared to anyone that would listen that they would rather desert than serve under Pemberton any longer. Others were too tired and beaten up to place blame. One woman who watched the procession was heartbroken as she described the scene. "I shall never forget that woeful sight," she wrote," humanity in the throws of endurance. Wan, hollow-eyed, ragged, footsore, bloody men limped along.... followed by siege guns, ambulances, gun carriages, and wagons in aimless confusion."[22] Later that evening, bands assembled near the Vicksburg courthouse and played "Dixie" and "Bonnie Blue Flag" in an attempt to rally the troops.

Despite low morale among many of the soldiers, Vicksburg's defenses were still formidable. Pemberton's men held high ground on the bluffs, and several miles of works anchored at each end by the Mississippi River circled the city. In places, felled trees and tangled bales of telegraph wire further obstructed the approaches. One federal soldier, a member of McPherson's staff, described the Confederate positions as an intimidating line "of high, rugged irregular bluffs, clearly cut against the sky, crowned with cannon which peered ominously from embrasures to the right and left as far as the eye can see. Lines of heavy rifle pits...filled with veteran infantry.... The approaches to this position were frightful—enough to appall the stoutest heart." The Confederates also burned a number of buildings, including some private homes, in front of the rifle pits

---

[22] William Pitt Chambers, *Journal of William Pitt Chambers* (Jackson: Mississippi Historical Society, 1925) 269–70; Richard Wheeler, *Voices of the Civil War* (New York: Thomas Y. Crowell Company, 1976) 337.

and canons to give them a better view of the approaching enemy. Witnesses reported fires all along the Confederate lines and the destruction of a number of stately houses that had only recently been constructed.[23]

Grant recognized the strength of the Confederate positions, but he also had every reason to believe that his enemy's spirit was broken. In less than three weeks, the federals had marched through the heart of the Deep South and recorded a series of sweeping victories that had driven Pemberton's reeling Confederates into Vicksburg with their backs against the Mississippi River. Grant surmised that one more show of force would lead the Confederates to give up. "The enemy had been much demoralized by his defeats at Champion's Hill and Big Black," he later remembered, "and I believed he would not make much of an effort to hold Vicksburg."[24] It was one of the few times during the campaign that Grant misjudged his enemy. Flush from recent victories, the federals assumed that the Confederates no longer had the will to resist, and that they would rather surrender the city than suffer more casualties in battles that they could not win. These assumptions were woefully incorrect. Once they were invested in Vicksburg, the Confederates' demeanor changed, at least for a time, to one of grim determination.

In Vicksburg, Pemberton deployed his men in defensive positions around the works. He had received two conflicting dispatches, one from Jefferson Davis and the other from Joseph Johnston. The Confederate president implored Pemberton to hold Vicksburg at all costs while Johnston ordered the general to evacuate Vicksburg and save the army. Pemberton chose to follow the edict of the president. Like Davis, Pemberton believed that the Confederacy might not be able to survive the loss of the port city. The evacuation of Vicksburg, he said, would mean the loss of valuable military stores collected for the city's defense, and in a broader sense it would mean the loss of the Mississippi River, which would effectively split the

[23] Quoted in Alan Hankinson, *Vicksburg 1863: Grant Clears the Mississippi* (London: Ospry, 1993) 62; Wheeler, *The Siege of Vicksburg*, 164.

[24] Grant, *Personal Memoirs*, 209.

Confederacy in two. Pemberton's resolve also sprang, at least in part, from the calumny circulating through the ranks, and through the city, regarding his dedication to the Southern cause. With each battlefield failure, more rumors circulated about the Northern-born general. There was a consensus among some that Pemberton intentionally sacrificed the lives of his men, and that he had served up Vicksburg to the federals as part of a conspiracy that would make him a wealthy man. Outraged, the general lashed out in an address to his men, which made its way into many Mississippi newspapers. "You have heard that I was incompetent and a traitor," he said, "that it was my intention to sell Vicksburg. Follow me and you will see the cost at which I will sell Vicksburg! When... the last man shall perish in the trenches, then and only then will I sell Vicksburg!"[25]

Still believing that a show of force would decide the issue, Grant positioned his men around Vicksburg and made plans for an attack. Hoping for a quick victory, his artillery opened fire on the morning of May 19 and later that afternoon he ordered his men to charge the Vicksburg works. Rather than a demoralized army on the verge of giving up, Grant's men found well-entrenched Confederates determined to drive away the enemy. It was an unsuccessful and exceedingly bloody confrontation during which the federals lost a 1000 men. Over the next two days, Grant licked his wounds and made plans for another assault. He found it hard to believe that the Confederates could resist much longer. He was also concerned about intelligence reports that Joseph Johnston had reoccupied Jackson and was acquiring reinforcements for an army there that would strike the federals from the east. Grant wanted to take Vicksburg and invest his own men on the bluffs before Johnson could organize.

As Grant redeployed his men to strengthen their positions, Porter's gunboats shelled Vicksburg from the river in preparation for another the federal assault. After sunset on May 21, many of the shells crashed into buildings, setting them on fire and illuminating the evening sky. Impressed by the spectacle, a newspaper

---

[25] Quoted in A. A. Hoehling, *Vicksburg: 47 Days of Siege* (New York: Fairfax Press, 1991) 77.

correspondent from the *Chicago Tribune* wrote that "the gunboats and mortars in front of Vicksburg kept up a continual fire and dropped their fiery messengers without distinction." As buildings in the city burned, the flames created an eerie effect that "lighted up the night sky, revealing strange shapes and wonderful outlines standing out in relief of the night sky." In the Union camps, there was a mixture of confidence and trepidation at the thought of another charge the next morning. Some predicted victory but their confidence was tempered somewhat by thoughts of comrades lost during the previous assault. Anticipating the next day's dangers, some men wrote long, emotional letters to loved ones. Others gave watches, rings, photographs, and various keepsakes—along with crumpled pieces of paper on which were scribbled brief notes and the names and addresses of their next of kin—to camp cooks or others not expected to see action. "Who knows who may be living tomorrow night," one soldier wrote in his diary just before going to sleep.[26]

The next morning the federals assembled for a massive attack, preceded for several hours by intense shelling from the gunboats. Then, as the heavy shelling ceased, an equally intense silence settled over the field. Then, according to Confederate General Stephen D. Lee, suddenly "there seemed to spring from the bowels of the earth dense masses of Federal troops, in numerous columns of attack, and with loud cheers and huzzahs, they rushed forward with bayonets fixed." The federals advanced in mass across a 3-mile mile front with many soldiers screaming at the top of their lungs. The Confederates waited as the enemy came within range, then opened fire, pouring volley after volley into the charging ranks. Men began to fall in large numbers, but the blue line continued to advance up hills broken by fallen timbers and underbrush. "Up the hill we pressed," one Union colonel wrote, "through the brambles and brush, over the dead and dying—up up we struggled, over logs, into ditches, clinging here to a bush to keep from falling backwards… Oh! That was a half hour which may God grant we shall never be called upon to experience again." Though some men from McClernand's corps briefly

---

[26] Quoted in Wheeler, *The Siege of Vicksburg*, 172.

breached the Confederate lines, the federals were driven back in what was, for Grant, the worst day of the Vicksburg Campaign. It soon became apparent that the attack was a disaster. The federals pulled back after suffering more than 3,000 casualties to less than 500 for the Confederates. Grant later admitted bluntly in his memoirs that "This last attack only served to increase our casualties without giving any benefit whatever."[27]

Over the next two days, wounded federals languished where they fell outside the rebel trenches as the dead began to decay. Rescue parties and burial details could not reach the men for fear of being picked off by snipers. At night the moans of injured soldiers echoed through the lines, and during the day the hot sun drew an unbearable stench from the corpses. Flies swarmed around the bodies as the Confederates morbidly joked that Grant, after his direct assault failed, had decided to "stink them out" of Vicksburg. On May 25, Pemberton proposed a truce so that the federals could bury their dead. Both armies suspended hostilities for a few hours as the soldiers came out of their trenches. The federals, with the aid of some sympathetic Confederates, buried their dead on the battlefield "by simply throwing a bank of dirt over them." Despite the circumstances, a good deal of fraternization and horseplay between the armies took place during the truce. The men exchanged jibes—some good natured and some not so friendly—and generally "mingled in conversation." Some even sat on the ground and played cards. Burdened with more responsibility, officers on both sides used the truce to examine the lines and the condition of the enemy. Foreshadowing things to come, one Union soldier observed that "From the remarks of some of the rebels, I judged that their supply of provisions was getting low, and they had no source from which to draw more. We gave them from our own rations some fat meat, crackers, coffee and so forth."[28]

After the carnage of the second federal assault, Grant decided to lay siege to the city or, as he put it, to "outcamp" the enemy until

---

[27] Quoted in Korn, *War on the Mississippi*, 130; Grant, *Personal Memoirs*, 210.
[28] Quoted in Wheeler, *The Siege of Vicksburg*, 176.

they ran out of food and supplies. He called on Washington for reinforcements, lengthened his lines and strengthened the works around the city. He also sent raiding parties north of Vicksburg and up the Yazoo River to secure those areas and further isolate Pemberton's men. Part of Grant's strategy also included constant shelling from his siege guns and particularly from Porter's gunboats on the river. As the siege began he also sent out his men to dig approach trenches that zigzagged through the Vicksburg hills. Each night, for the next several weeks, federal soldiers would burrow closer and closer to the Confederate lines. "Every man in the investing line became an army engineer," one federal soldier wrote, "the soldiers got so they bored like gophers and beavers, with a spade in one hand and a rifle in the other." During summer 1863, Grant assembled more than 75,000 troops around Vicksburg, cutting off all traffic in and out of the city.

Before the siege began taking its toll on the soldiers and civilians in the city, the Confederates won another victory that boosted moral. On May 27, Grant ordered Porter to send the *U.S.S. Cincinnati*, an ironclad operating above Vicksburg, downstream to silence one of the city's northernmost forts on the river, hopefully creating a break in the Confederate lines. Again underestimating the enemy, both Grant and Porter believed that the Confederates would be easily cleared from the position. They thought that the heaviest rebel guns had been removed from the fort and placed in other locations, but when the *Cincinnati* came in range it was met by fire from artillery that was still very much in place. The first shot from the bluffs crashed through the ship's hull, creating a gaping hole through which river water rapidly poured. The crew of the *Cincinnati* was stunned and before they could return fire more shells rained down from the battery. The ship's tiller was shot away, then the smokestack. Still taking on water, the doomed vessel drifted toward the shore opposite Vicksburg and the sailors began jumping into the water to swim for safety. The federals suffered thirty-nine casualties, including thirteen men who drowned in the river. When the shelling began many civilians gathered at a safe distance on the bluffs to watch the action, and they cheered wildly as the *Cincinnati* sank. While the spectators may not have realized it at the time, they were experiencing the last high point for their defense of Vicksburg.

While the federals lost the *Cincinnati*, Porter retained the rest of his fleet which, along with Grant's land-based siege guns, furiously shelled Vicksburg day and night, literally driving the civilian population underground. Not long after the siege began many of Vicksburg's residents dug caves in the sides of the numerous hills around the city. They moved in with as much furniture and as many valuables as limited space would allow. "Wherever the passage of a street left the face of a hill exposed," one man wrote, "into it and under it people burrowed, making long ranges and systems of chambers and archways."[29] While these quarters were cramped to say the least, they provided a refuge from the constant shower of shot and shell. For generations, the tales and images of Vicksburg's caves and their civilian occupants would come to define the city's Civil War experience. Mary Loughborough, who left a detailed firsthand account of her Civil War experience in a diary later published under the title *My Cave Life in Vicksburg*, described her new living arrangement:

> And so I went regularly to work, keeping house underground. Our new habitation was an excavation made in the earth, and branching six feet from the entrance, forming a cave in the shape of a 'T.' In one of the wings my bed fitted; the other I used as a kind of a dressing room.... We were safe at least from fragments of shell—and they were flying in all directions; though no one seemed to think our cave any protection should a mortar shell happen to fall directly on top of the ground above us. We had our roof arched and braced, the supports of the bracing taking up much room in our confined quarters. The earth was about five feet thick above, and seemed hard and compact.[30]

By the end of the siege, the Vicksburg hills contained around 500 caves of various shapes and sizes. Some people used them as

---

[29] Quoted in Wheeler, *Voices of the Civil War*, 34.
[30] Quoted in Katherine M. Jones, *Heroines of Dixie: Confederate Women Tell Their Story of the War* (Indianapolis: Bobbs-Merrill Company, Inc., 1955) 229–31.

temporary bomb shelters while others moved in for extended periods. During the heaviest shelling many of the caves were overcrowded with men, women and children alike seeking shelter and spilling out of the entrances. For some the prospect of a night in the cramped, uncomfortable caves was only marginally better than the prospect of wounds from federal shrapnel. "I have stayed at home every night except two," one part-time cave dweller wrote, "I could not stand the mosquitoes and the crowd in the caves. Most people spend their time entirely in them, for there is no safety anywhere else. Indeed, there is no safety there."[31] Rumors circulated on the streets of Vicksburg that certain individuals or entire families had been killed by cave-ins or from federal fire. In truth, while such rumors caused panic among much of the population, less than a dozen civilians were killed during the siege and only about forty suffered injuries.

While the civilians suffered in their caves, the Confederate soldiers suffered in the trenches around the city. They were short on rations and clean clothing, and were constantly exposed to the elements as well as to federal shells and snipers. Many of the men were sick, and the tedious nature of a prolonged siege also took a psychological toll on the army. Boredom and uncertainty gave way to anxiety and depression as the Confederates crouched behind their fortifications, day after day, with little to do other than ponder their bleak circumstances. "No rest for our poor soldiers who have to stay down in the trenches all day in the hot sun," one observer noted. "It is a most discouraging sort of warfare. The enemy shoot from their muskets and Parrott guns all day; if a head, even a hand appears above the works it is fired upon."[32] Not long after the siege began a small but steady stream of deserters began fleeing into the federal lines. This was especially alarming to Pemberton and his officers because, in addition to the drain on manpower, some deserters provided the federals with important intelligence on the condition of Vicksburg and its occupants.

[31] Quoted in Wheeler, *The Siege of Vicksburg*, 178.
[32] Quoted in Hoehling, *47 Days of Siege*, 62.

A notable structure owned by a notable family was situated between the opposing lines at Vicksburg, and it became a focal point of both armies during the siege. In the 1830s, Nicholas Gray, an immigrant from Wexford County, Ireland, came to Vicksburg, purchased land, and built a home that he called "Wexford Lodge" about 2 1/2 miles east of the river city on the main road leading to Jackson. Around 1850, Gray sold the home, which at the time was described as "A most desirable residence.... 40 by 60 feet, containing nine rooms, seven large ones and a wide passage." James Shirley, a New Hampshire native, became the new owner of Wexford Lodge, its outbuildings and an adjacent 16 acres. Shirley was an accomplished man, having studied law at Dartmouth and practiced in New York City before moving south to Georgia, and then to Alabama. His wife Adeline Quincy, who he met while in Georgia, was a native of Boston, Massachusetts and a great niece of John Hancock. When the Shirleys moved to Vicksburg James quickly established a lucrative law practice along with his place in the upper reaches of Vicksburg's social circles.

The Shirleys prospered during the 1850s as James dabbled in real estate and the cotton trade in addition to his legal work. He watched in alarm, however, as the slave states and the non-slaveholding states grew further and further apart. Despite being a slaveholder himself, he disagreed with those who in 1861 said that Mississippi could only protect itself by severing its ties with the United States. Shirley was a Union man of the first order and once the war began his outspoken views made him unpopular with many of Vicksburg's citizens. As a result, the Shirleys kept to themselves as the conflict progressed, though sometimes James met clandestinely with others who shared his views to discuss events of the day. According to Alice, one of the Shirley children, her father "was an old-time Whig, and when secession was broached he was firm in his allegiance to the Union.... no easy matter when neighbors and friends all flocked to secession, and were loud in their denunciation of Union men, calling them traitors." When the Shirley's son Frederick refused to serve in the Confederate army some in

Vicksburg threatened to lynch him, and the young man hastily left town, moving to Indiana.

During the siege the Shirleys occupied their home for a time before moving into a cave to avoid fire from both armies. Shot and shell damaged Wexford Lodge, and Confederate soldiers looted many of the Shirleys' personal possessions, but the house survived the war. As for the Shirleys, they maintained contact with federal officials after the fighting ended. Another son, Quincy, joined the Union army during the siege, an act that impressed U. S. Grant to such an extent that he arranged an appointment for the boy to the United States Military Academy at West Point. A year after the siege ended, the Shirley's daughter Alice married Union chaplain John Eaton, who held the post of superintendent of freedmen and was in charge of establishing camps for the newly-freed slaves in Mississippi. James Shirley died soon after the siege ended and the rest of the Shirley family eventually left Vicksburg, but Wexford Lodge remained in the family. Around the turn of the century, Alice Eaton sold the house to the federal government, which had recently established the Vicksburg Military Park, on the condition that the remains of her parents would be brought to Vicksburg and reburied on the property. The house, which became known as the Shirley House, was restored and became a focal point for visitors to the park, most of whom were unaware that the home's Southern occupants during the siege were actually union sympathizers who developed significant ties to U. S. Grant and other federal officials.[33]

As the siege wore on in June 1863, another significant event related to Grant's campaign took place up river. Twenty miles north of Vicksburg a serious engagement developed on June 7 as Confederate troops attempted to take the federal garrison at Milliken's Bend on the Louisiana side of the Mississippi. There Confederates under Brigadier General Henry E. McCulloch

---

[33] An excellent treatment of the story of Alice Shirley and Wexford Lodge can be found in a short publication titled *Wexford Lodge*. The work is edited with an introduction by Terrence J. Winschel and distributed by the National Parks Service at the Vicksburg National Military Park in Vicksburg, Mississippi.

launched an attack on a small federal force under Colonel Hermann Lieb in hopes of distracting Grant at Vicksburg and cutting at least some of the federal supply lines. Lieb's men eventually drove the Confederates away but what gave the engagement added significance was the makeup of the federal force. Just over 1,400 soldiers defended Milliken's Bend, of whom all but 160 were former slaves, recent recruits from contraband camps in Mississippi and Louisiana. At the time the black soldiers had been in the army for less than three weeks and carried heavy, antiquated muskets that were sometimes difficult to load and fire. The Confederates launched their assault early on the morning of June 7 and the fighting continued for several hours. The Confederates eventually reached the federal lines and vicious hand to hand fighting ensued that included some of the fiercest bayonet combat of the war. While they suffered heavy casualties, the black soldiers held their ground until two federal gunboats, the *Choctaw* and *Lexington*, appeared on the river and began firing on the Southerners. The Confederates eventually withdrew and Milliken's Bend remained in federal hands. The engagement drew praise for the black troops and, in the minds of many, proved the fighting value of former slaves in the federal army. "The bravery of the blacks at Milliken's Bend," Assistant Secretary of War Charles A. Dana wrote, "completely revolutionized the sentiment of the army with regard to the employment of Negro troops." Even Confederate General McCulloch paid grudging if muted tribute to the former slaves from Mississippi and Louisiana when he wrote in his report that his "charge was resisted by the Negro portion of the enemy's force with considerable obstinacy."[34]

As the noose tightened around Vicksburg, Grant had only one major concern. After the last federal troops abandoned Jackson in mid-May, Joseph Johnston entered the city and called in reinforcements in an effort to organize a force large enough to help liberate the port city. Indeed, the idea that Johnston was coming to the rescue was one of the few things that lifted the morale of the

---

[34] Quoted in Benjamin Quarles, *The Negro in the Civil War* (New York: Russell and Russell, 1968) 222–24.

Confederates behind the siege lines. "The firing was continuous day and night," one soldier recalled, "And so the time passed, always the same, except the daily rumor that Gen. Joe Johnston was near and we would soon be relieved."[35] By early June, Johnston had assembled around 23,000 men at Jackson, less than a third of the federal force around Vicksburg. Keeping more than 40,000 troops around the Vicksburg works, Grant sent Sherman to the Big Black River with 35,000 men to secure any approach that Johnston might use. As a result, there would be no relief for Vicksburg. In Johnston's view, he simply had too few men to launch a rescue operation. On June 15, the general informed Confederate Secretary of War James A. Seddon that he believed the situation in Vicksburg was hopeless, to which Seddon frantically replied "Vicksburg must not be lost without a desperate struggle.... You must attack."[36] Johnston's attack never materialized, though in late June and early July he moved his army to the vicinity of the Big Black River, near Sherman's lines. The Confederate general's lack of action would later lead to a great deal of finger-pointing in Confederate command circles. After Vicksburg capitulated, Jefferson Davis and Pemberton blamed Johnston's inaction for the loss while Johnson blamed the debacle on a lack of adequate reinforcements and support from the Confederate government, and on Pemberton's strategic blunders.

Of the many lasting stories generated by the Vicksburg Campaign, one of the most legendary concerned the drinking habits of U. S. Grant during the siege. Rumors of Grant's heavy drinking had circulated for years, and in many cases the stories had been embellished by his enemies. However, in a three-day stretch during the weeks of siege along the Mississippi River, Grant seems to have gone on a true bender. Some historians would later attribute Grant's drinking bouts, which were rare but nevertheless serious, to boredom during times of inactivity, or to the extended periods of separation

[35] "Recollections of Vicksburg during the Siege," *The Southern Bivouac*, 1/1 (September 1882): 9.
[36] Quoted in Craig L. Symonds, *Joseph E. Johnston: A Civil War Biography* (New York: Norton and Company, 1992) 214.

from wife and family that were common in the life of a soldier. Others simply cited the pressures of command as the reason for Grant's "infrequent intoxications." For whatever reason, on the afternoon and evening of June 5 the commander of the Union forces at Vicksburg took to the bottle with a vengeance. Assistant Adjutant General John A. Rawlins, who was Grant's friend, keeper, and apparently the only person allowed to chastise the general about his vices, later that night wrote a terse note to Grant admonishing him that the safety of the federal army depended it's leader's sobriety. Grant either did not read, or did not heed the message the next day as his drinking continued. Despite his condition, Grant and a small party that included Rawlins rode out to a safe point on the nearby Yazoo River and boarded a steamer bound for Satartia, a federal outpost supposedly vulnerable to raids from Johnston's cavalry. Grant wanted to confer with the commander there, Brigadier General Nathan Kimball, and assess the situation. Upon boarding the steamer, Grant settled into the boat's cramped bar car for what turned into an afternoon-long tippling session at the end of which Grant "retired" for the night. Due to security concerns the steamer eventually turned around 25 miles upriver before reaching its destination. On June 7, as his party steamed back down the Yazoo, Grant continued his binge and eventually insisted on being put ashore at the nearest federal outpost on the river. The boat docked near the Chickasaw Bayou and after sunset Grant went ashore. Before anyone could stop him, the inebriated general climbed aboard a horse, ironically named Kangaroo, and galloped off into the night through the campsites of startled federal soldiers. Sylvanus Cadwallader, a friendly journalist who was traveling with Grant, chased him down and brought him back to the river. The discreet Cadwallader did not at the time file a story concerning the incident, but later related that Grant "tore through and over everything in the way. The air was full of dust, ashes and embers from camp fires and shouts and curses of those he rode down in his race."[37] When Grant

---

[37] Quoted in William S. McFeely, *Grant: A Biography* (New York: W. W. Norton & Company, 1981) 134.

and Cadwallader got back to the boat, they faced a livid John Rawlins, who once again admonished Grant for his behavior in no uncertain terms. By the next morning, the binge had passed and a sober, but probably hung-over, Grant turned his attention back to the business at hand.

As the siege continued, Confederate civilians and soldiers in Vicksburg suffered, as did the city's structures. Though Union shells were supposed to be aimed only at the Confederate works, hundreds fell behind the lines, damaging property and causing fires that could wipe out an entire block in an afternoon. The missiles destroyed businesses and damaged homes indiscriminately. One woman who left her cellar to rest in her bedroom during what she thought was a brief pause in the hostilities had, quite literally, a rude awakening on the afternoon of June 21. "I had gone upstairs today during the interregnum to enjoy a rest on my bed," she wrote that night in her diary, "when a shell burst right outside the window in front of me. Pieces flew in, striking all around me, tearing down masses of plaster that came tumbling over me.... I realized my narrow escape. The wood frame began to smoke, and we saw that the house was on fire."

As days turned into weeks, the lack of food in Vicksburg also became a problem. According to one account the cows, pigs, and poultry quickly disappeared, followed by the horses and mules. Eventually the city's dogs and cats began to disappear. "I saw some delicious looking rats boiled one evening," a soldier later recalled, "but they were not numerous enough to be of much use. Our fare upon the whole was very rough, badly prepared, and very scant." By the end of June there was no more meat to be had and soldiers and civilians alike were living on little more than a handful of cornbread and boiled rice per day. As a result, the overall health of the city's occupants deteriorated and problems with disease increased.[38]

By the end of June it was apparent that Vicksburg could not be saved. Pemberton's men were completely demoralized, as was the civilian population. An anonymous letter containing an ultimatum and signed "Many Soldiers" reached the commanding general's tent

---

[38] "Recollections of Vicksburg," 6.

on June 27. "If you can't feed us," it read, "you had better surrender, horrible as the idea is, than have this noble army disgrace themselves by desertion. I tell you plainly, men are not going to lie here and perish." Sensing the inevitable, Pemberton on July 3 called a council of war with his division commanders Carter L. Stevenson, Martin Luther Smith, John H. Forney and John S. Bowen. The men had all given up on Joseph Johnston's relief effort, which left them with only two choices. The undermanned and starving Confederates could try to break through the federal siege lines by force, or they could surrender. Pemberton's subordinates were in unanimous agreement that the men under their command were in no condition to mount an offensive, and even if they were in good health, federal strength made escape impossible. The equation was simple, Pemberton later wrote, his men were "overpowered by numbers, worn down by fatigue."[39]

Meanwhile, Joe Johnston finally made plans to attack the federal siege lines and hopefully save Pemberton's garrison. Unlike Jefferson Davis and others in the Confederate command, Johnston had never been enamoured with the concept of saving the city itself. Geographic locations like Vicksburg, he believed, could always be retaken when better circumstances prevailed. On the other hand, he was very concerned with the prospect of losing Pemberton's army, manpower that the Confederacy could scarcely afford to do without. As Pemberton discussed the bleak situation with his commanders, Johnston prepared a dispatch outlining plans to attack the federal lines on July 7. Johnston began moving his men into position and instructed the Confederates in the city to be ready. However, Johnston's message would not reached Pemberton until July 10, by which time it was several days too late.

On the morning of July 3, Pemberton sent his top subordinate, John S. Bowen, into the federal lines under a flag of truce with a message for General Grant. Bowen and Grant had known one another before the war when both lived in St. Louis, and it seemed logical that Bowen should be the man to open the initial stage of

---

[39] Quoted in Robert Leckie, *None Died in Vain* (New York: Harper Collins Publishers, 1990) 557; Korn, *War on the Mississippi*, 152.

negotiations with the federal commander. Pemberton proposed an armistice to discuss surrender terms in order to "save the further effusion of blood, which must otherwise be shed to a frightful extent, feeling myself fully able to maintain my position for yet an indefinite period." Grant accepted the message but insisted on negotiating personally with Pemberton rather than Bowen. Despite claims to the contrary, Grant knew that the Confederates were near the end of their tether and he sent word back through the lines that Pemberton could himself end the "further infusion of blood" by immediately and unconditionally surrendering Vicksburg. Of the actual ranks inside the city, Grant added that "Men who have shown so much endurance and courage as those now in Vicksburg will always challenge the respect of an adversary, and I can assure you will be treated with all the respect due prisoners of war." Bowen set up a meeting between Pemberton and Grant to take place later in the day. In the mean time, the commanders issued orders for a cease-fire and the men of both armies crawled slowly from their trenches. For the first time in weeks, the men had a chance to access the disposition of their enemy. "Now the two armies stood up and gazed at one another with wondering eyes," one Confederate stated, "They were amazed at the paucity of our numbers; we were astonished at the vastness of theirs." Another Confederate, staggered by the amount of reinforcements that Grant had collected, described the swollen federal lines as "a huge blue snake coiling around our ill-fated city."[40]

As thousands of soldiers from both sides looked on, Pemberton and Grant met at three o'clock that afternoon under a tree between the lines. Pemberton had with him his aid, Colonel L. M. Montgomery, as well as Bowen. Grant's entourage included generals McPherson, Logan, Ord, and Smith. From all accounts Pemberton was somewhat agitated during the meeting, which was natural considering his position. Surrender was his only real option and Grant knew it, leaving Pemberton with almost no leverage in the negotiations. In addition, the Pennsylvanian was still sensitive to the

---

[40] Grant, *Personal Memoirs*, 221; Quoted in Wheeler, *The Siege of Vicksburg*, 230–31.

erroneous charge that "selling out" Vicksburg had been his true intention all along. Regardless of what happened, once the city fell there was little doubt that he would garner the lion's share of blame for the loss. At one point, Pemberton threatened to break off the talks and let the siege continue but Bowen, always the voice of reason, intervened by proposing that negotiations continue. The meeting eventually broke up but both sides exchanged letters through the night until the commanders agreed on final surrender terms.

Ironically, Vicksburg officially surrendered on July 4, 1863, the eight-seventh anniversary of American independence. Pemberton later claimed that he chose the date intentionally in hopes of receiving better surrender terms. "I knew they would attach vast importance to the entrance on the 4th of July into the stronghold on the great river," he wrote, "and that, to gratify their national vanity, they would yield then what could not be extorted from them at any other time." If these were Pemberton's true feelings at the time, they were based on a false assumption that sentimentality was likely to sway any of the federal commanders. Though Grant initially insisted on unconditional surrender, he agreed to a proposition that allowed for the parole of the captured Confederate troops rather than their imprisonment. While this seemingly lenient arrangement drew criticism from some in the North, Grant actually made the decision out of practical concerns. Had he not paroled the Confederates, more than 25,000 prisoners would have to be transported to various locations in the North under heavy guard and at a great expense. On the other hand, Grant knew that as parolees freed after signing a simple loyalty oath to the United States, most of the men would not reenter Confederate service, at least not willingly. He surmised correctly that their ordeal behind the Vicksburg siege lines had destroyed many of the Confederate soldiers' will to fight. "Pemberton's army was composed of many men whose homes were in the South-west," Grant later wrote, "[and] I knew many of them were tired of war and would get home just as soon as they could."[41]

---

[41] Grant, *Personal Memoirs*, 223.

The surrender ceremony began around 10:00 A.M. as the Confederates came out of their trenches, stacked their arms and prepared to sign their parole forms. While there were isolated celebrations at points along the Union lines, the occasion as a whole was solemn as federal soldiers stood fast in mute praise of their enemy. Afterwards many of Grant's men were also quick to share their provisions with the hungry, hollow-eyed Confederates. "The two armies began to fraternize," Grant later noted. "Our men had had full rations since the siege commenced.... I myself saw our men taking bread from their haversacks and giving it to the enemy they had so recently been engaged in starving out." Along the city docks there was a great commotion as part of Admiral Porter's fleet pulled up loaded with provisions for Vicksburg's civilian population. As word spread that the ships had coffee, flour, and other amenities on board, blacks and whites alike quickly lined the wharves. "Truly it was a fine spectacle," one woman wrote, "The townfolks continued to dash through the streets with their arms full, canned goods predominating."[42] Federal troops gathered around the Vicksburg courthouse, which had survived the siege with only minor damage, to bear witness as a color guard hoisted an American flag over the building. A brigade band played "Hail Columbia" as the Stars and Stripes unfurled and the soldiers offered up cheers to the Union. The capitulation was complete, and Vicksburg became an occupied city.

For Grant, the fall of Vicksburg was a great personal victory. It made him forever famous and began a chain of events that would eventually lead to his election as president of the United States. Grant rode into the city as a conquering hero to his men, though during his stay there his demeanor was reserved as usual. One of his first stops was the riverfront, where he met with Porter and his staff. As he moved toward the docks he was mildly startled when he passed a number of caves, slowing his mount to get a better look at the primitive dwellings. After visiting with Porter, Grant rode back through the Vicksburg streets as a growing crowd of newly freed slaves followed. They viewed Grant not just as a military hero, but as the leader of a liberating force, the man who led the army that delivered their freedom. Grant stopped at the courthouse and then rode back to his headquarters outside the siege lines, where he remained until he moved into a private home in town on July 6.

As Vicksburg fell, the Confederacy suffered another devastating setback in Pennsylvania. After three days of fighting at Gettysburg (July 1–3) the federal army under General George Meade drove away Robert E. Lee's Confederate invasion force, inflicting large numbers of casualties including many Mississippians who were part of Lee's Army of Northern Virginia. The state contributed eleven infantry regiments, an artillery battery, and a cavalry unit to the doomed effort at Gettysburg. Prominent among the Mississippians there were former United States congressman William R. Barksdale, who died during the battle while leading a brigade of Mississippi soldiers, and Carnot Posey, a Wilkinson County lawyer who also led a brigade of men from his home state. Scattered among the troops who survived the struggle were many of Mississippi's future political leaders, including regimental commanders and future governors John M. Stone and Benjamin G. Humphreys. At almost the exact moment that Grant's men raised the American flag over the Vicksburg courthouse, Lee's battered army began its retreat out of Pennsylvania. Once word of the Confederate defeat at Gettysburg reached Mississippi, the morale of the state's already depressed Confederate population reached new lows. Although some would not yet admit it, most realized that the twin blows of Vicksburg and Gettysburg were probably the beginning of the end of the Confederacy.

Although Vicksburg was now safely in Union hands, the fighting in Mississippi did not cease. With his primary goal accomplished, Grant turned his attention toward Joseph Johnston's "Army of Relief" that still lurked around the Big Black River. On the day of the surrender, Grant ordered Sherman to cross the Big Black and attack the Confederates. Johnston knew that his force of around 23,000 men was no match for the federals, who were now free to concentrate far superior numbers against him. When he heard the "astonishing news came that Vicksburg had capitulated," he immediately ordered his army to fall back eastward toward Jackson, with Sherman and more than 40,000 federal troops in hot pursuit. As they marched, Johnston's men poisoned all the wells that they came in contact with. Central Mississippi had not seen rain for weeks and the Confederates hoped in vain that a water shortage might hamper Sherman's progress. The Confederates reentered Jackson on July 9 and immediately began preparing more defensive works. While Sherman's larger and better-equipped army approached, the Confederates in the city listened as Johnston made a rare address to the troops, speaking of pride, sacrifice, and victory. Despite the appeals to patriotism, Johnston's men were powerless to halt the Union advance. Sherman's men reached Jackson and laid partial siege to the city for several days as the Confederates languished behind their fortification. Soon federal siege guns opened fire and shells began to fall with authority into the state capital. The federals pressed, and there was heavy skirmishing around the lines. As time wore on the odds against any form of Confederate success grew longer and longer, and it looked as if the rebel army might be trapped in Jackson. "The enemy will not attack, but has entrenched," Johnston wrote to Jefferson Davis in Richmond on July 15, "evidently making a siege that we cannot resist. It would be madness to attack him."[43] The next day Johnston finally ordered the evacuation of Jackson and the Confederates fell back to the east through Brandon and Morton. Sherman did not pursue, allowing his men a respite from marching in the intense summer heat. Instead, he set up his headquarters in Mississippi's governor's mansion and put many of his troops to work destroying any infrastructure—especially rail lines—that the Confederates had put back in place after reoccupying the city. "I do not pursue because of the intense heat, dust and the fatigue of the men, but I will perfect the work of destruction," he reported, "I propose to break railroad 10 miles south, east, and north, and out 40 and 60 miles in spots." Within a week the railroads around Jackson were in ruins along with much of

---

[43] *OR*, ser. 1, vol. 24, pt. 1, p. 207

the city itself. "The inhabitants are subjugated," Sherman told Grant. "They cry aloud for mercy."[44]

The fall of Vicksburg and the destruction of Jackson seemed to break the spirit of Confederate Mississippi. Desertion among Mississippians in the Confederate army reached new highs as many of the men lost the will to fight. The state's original volunteers had signed on for a period of twelve months, firm in the belief that the war would be over before they completed their full tour of duty. They had left communities yet to know the deprivations of war, and had drawn strength from the encouragement that their communities provided. By fall 1863, however, there were no more cheering crowds in their communities. Wartime difficulties had dampened enthusiasm for the war on the homefront, which in turn dampened the spirits of the men. Letters from home that had once provided encouragement told only of deprivations and sorrow. Mississippi's Confederate soldiers had entered the service to defend their communities, but now their communities needed them back, and some of the survivors acted accordingly.

While deprivations at home influenced some to flee Confederate service, many of the men had also grown disillusioned with the general nature of their Confederate experience. The soldiers were originally volunteers, but the Richmond government had forced them into service for an extended period. According to one soldier, the Confederate lawmakers had severely overstepped their bounds "when it comes to pressing the twelve month volunteers into service for two or more years without giving them the privilege of going home as free men." The soldiers had been told that Northern abolitionists were a threat to their independence, yet the Confederate government had stolen their independence through the Conscription Act and through its inability to assist the men's suffering families at home, many of which had become dependent on the charity of neighbors. Some Mississippians were simply tired of fighting a war that already seemed lost. Northern soldiers had defeated them in battle after battle and now the Yankees tread confidently on

---

[44] *OR*, ser. 1, vol. 24, pt. 2, pp. 528–29.

Mississippi soil. For some soldiers who had entered the service as part of a community enterprise, it was the successful federal invasion of their home state in 1863, not the subsequent fall of Richmond or the surrender at Appomattox, that marked the end of the war. As a result, a dramatic wave of desertions took place during the siege of Vicksburg, and for the remainder of the war a steady stream of Mississippians left the army without permission. Even before they could sign their parole forms, many of the Mississippi troops in Vicksburg simply walked away from the city and went home. As Joseph Johnston retreated from the Big Black River to Jackson and subsequently to points further east he reported losing men in large numbers. Many Mississippians from other commands in Tennessee and Virginia had also had enough, and subsequently left for home. Efforts by the Confederate army to round up deserters met with little success. Severely strapped for manpower, the authorities could not commit enough men to the task and local civilians, many of whom had also given up on the rebellion, usually refused to cooperate.

In Mississippi some deserters simply "laid low," waiting for the war's end, while others formed what amounted to outlaw gangs that wreaked havoc in some communities. Citizens in a number of the state's counties petitioned the governor as well as the Confederate authorities for assistance but there was little help available. Mississippi's most famous band of deserters were led by Newton Knight of Jones County. Knight led a group of former Confederate soldiers who protected each other's property and occasionally raided Confederate supply stores. Upset with the "twenty-negro exemption" in the Confederate draft law and with alleged atrocities committed by Confederate cavalry detachments, the group actually tried to cast their lot with the federals at one point, but Union conscription officers never made it into Jones County. The deserters called the territory over which they roamed the "Free State of Jones" and after the war the story of Newt Knight and Jones County became popular with journalists, who exaggerated the activities of Knight and his followers. Several different versions of the story emerged, all of which revolved around the claim that during the war Jones County seceded from Mississippi and the Confederacy and formed its own government. Knight was usually portrayed as a backwoods Robin Hood of sorts who led a group of men who wanted nothing more than the rights and liberties that they deserved as citizens. In truth, there was actually a great deal of support for the Confederacy in Jones County, and Knight and his followers could best be described as a violent band of renegades who resisted all forms of authority, be it Confederate or federal.

By the final months of 1863, the Confederacy's severe military setbacks and the general state of economic affairs in the South had demoralized Mississippi's civilian population. The economic noose had begun to tighten around the South from the first shots at Fort Sumter and after two years of fighting, desperate families populated much of the Southern countryside. From an economic standpoint, the Confederacy had entered the war woefully unprepared. The South for years had looked to European imports for many of its commodities, and the federal blockade left the region dependent on its own meager resources. At the war's outset the rebellious states as a whole had few manufacturing enterprises and an underdeveloped railroad system, and since 1861 speculators had hoarded many important items in hopes of selling them at enormous profits as demand grew. The South relied on agriculture, with cotton being the primary cash crop, yet the Confederate cause had depleted much of the region's agricultural labor force. Thousands of non-slaveholding yeomen farmers, many of whom had been the sole family breadwinner at home, were in the army or dead. Thousands of slaves had run away as federal troops moved through the Confederacy. Many fields that had flourished in 1860 grew little but weeds in 1863. Meanwhile, neither the Richmond government nor the state governments could significantly alleviate the suffering. They lacked the resources to feed all of the soldiers in the field, much less their destitute families at home. Programs to aid the poor had little widespread effect due to poor administration and a general deterioration of the South's fiscal infrastructure. At depots throughout the Confederacy, perishable foodstuffs rotted as workmen waited to load them onto freight cars that would never arrive over the South's fragile railroad network.

Mississippi suffered these conditions along with the other Southern states. Efforts by state officials to increase food production during the war met with only limited success. From 1861, state leaders had encouraged farmers to plant less cotton and devote more acreage to cereal grains, which initially increased the production of corn and wheat. However, a severe draught in 1862 ruined much of Mississippi's corn crop and the general disorder produced by the war resulted in many crops being left in the field unharvested. Meat was relatively plentiful in the state during the war's first year, but shortages of salt hampered meat production, and as the conflict wore on, the supply of domestic livestock dwindled. Eventually most families learned to improvise, producing homemade coffee from parched corn or okra, tea from dried raspberry leaves, and consuming on a regular basis a variety of boiled roots, berries, and foliage previously considered of little culinary value. Because of the war, one Mississippian conceded in 1863, "Our civilized conventionalities must once more give place to primitive necessities and simplicities."[45]

By the midpoint of the war, the state's economy was already in a downward spiral from which it would never recover. With most of Mississippi's wealth tied up in land, slaves, and cotton, the government and the public in general operated largely on constantly deflating paper. The state legislature tried to solve the state's fiscal problems by simply printing more money, which ultimately drove the value of the state's notes and bonds down and greatly inflated the prices of most goods. After the fall of the state capital, records were so confused that it was impossible for a full accounting of the state's finances. Apparently stricken by the pressures of his job, state treasurer M. D. Haynes actually committed suicide during the period. To make matters worse, as Mississippi's economy deteriorated so did the rule of law in many parts of the state. Vigilantes policed some communities and local courts met on an irregular basis, if at all. In addition to anxieties brought on by hunger

---

[45] Quoted in John K. Bettersworth, "The Home Front, 1861–1865," in Richard Aubrey McLemore, ed., *A History of Mississippi*, 2 vols. (Hattiesburg: University and College Press of Mississippi, 1973) 1:504–508.

and poverty, many Mississippi whites lived in constant fear of slave insurrections, particularly after federal troops entered the state. Slaves made up a majority of the state's population and rumors of rebellion caused alarm even in those regions where slaves were in the minority.

Of course, the war greatly affected the lives of Mississippi's slaves. At the beginning of the conflict, many nervous slaveholders took steps to safeguard their slaves, and themselves, by moving with their bondsmen to locations that, at the time, seemed to be out of harm's way. Others placed harsher restrictions on the activities of their slaves, and in many communities slave patrols increased. Some slaves remained loyal to their master's family during the course of the war, and some even went to war with their masters as servants. The annals of the Confederacy contain many stories of the loyal slave who dutifully served his master during the conflict, even tending his master's wounds or recovering his master's body from the battlefield so that it could be sent home to his family for burial. After the war, a slave who could prove that he had given loyal service to his master during the conflict might be eligible for a small pension, if and only if the former master or other whites were willing to vouch for him.

Such cases were the exception rather than the rule. From the time that the war began, slaves throughout Mississippi and the rest of the South had a growing awareness of the stakes of the conflict. This was particularly true after Lincoln issued the Emancipation Proclamation at the end of 1862. Far from what Jefferson Davis described as "an inferior race [of] peaceful and contented laborers," the slaves took the prospect of their freedom very seriously. Many of the servants who followed their Mississippi masters into the war ran away at the first opportunity and thousands left their plantations to follow Union armies as they moved through the state. Crowds of cheering blacks greeted victorious federal forces as they rode through Mississippi, and Vicksburg and Natchez in particular became havens for newly freed slaves. More than 17,000 former Mississippi bondsmen also joined the Union army, serving in a variety of capacities. During the first year of the conflict, federal authorities confined black troops to non-combat positions such as teamsters, orderlies, or scouts, but as the war progressed black units saw significant combat. The presence of black federal soldiers in Mississippi also had a tremendous psychological impact on the state's white population. For former slaveholders and non-slaveholders alike, the presence of armed blacks in their state represented the manifestation of their worst fears. Two month after the Emancipation Proclamation, Lincoln wrote that, if it could be accomplished, "The bare sight of fifty thousand armed and drilled black soldiers on the banks of the Mississippi would end the rebellion at once." From a more practical military standpoint, Grant also recognized the benefits of recruiting the former slaves. Not long after the fall of Vicksburg, he wrote the president on the subject, stating that "By arming the Negro, we have added a powerful ally. They will make good soldiers and taking them away from the enemy weakens him in the same proportion that it strengthens us."[46]

As Grant's army moved through Mississippi in 1863, the sheer number of freedmen flocking into the federal lines created a host of problems. Even though many were employed to perform auxiliary functions for the army, thousands were left with no means of support. Grant appointed Chaplain John Eaton as superintendent of contrabands for the Mississippi Valley and the two men struggled to find a solution to the problem. After exploring a variety of options, federal authorities eventually organized "home farms" on which the freedmen could work for wages. These farms were located on plantations that had been seized by the army and leased, in many cases, to Northern businessmen looking to make profits from cotton production. The system was ripe for abuse and some Northerners made large profits from the enterprise at the expense of the freedmen.

Federal authorities also began distributing some lands to the freedmen themselves, and from this policy sprang one of the unique experiments of the Civil War period. Davis Bend was a 10,000-acre

---

[46] Quoted in James M. McPherson, *Battle Cry of Freedom: Civil War Era* (New York: Ballantine Books, 1988) 565; and in James W. Loewen and Charles Sallis, eds., *Mississippi: Conflict and Change* (New York: Pantheon Books, 1974) 134.

strip of land surrounded on three sides by the Mississippi River about 30 miles south of Vicksburg. Though it was called Palmyra on some maps, the peninsula was named for two of its principle owners, Confederate President Jefferson Davis and his older brother Joseph. Before the war, the Davis brothers built large plantations there, complete with a work force of several hundred slaves. Ironically, Grant had the land seized and, with Eaton, planned to transform the acreage into a "negro paradise" that would alleviate the suffering of at least some of Mississippi's freedmen and perhaps provide a model for similar efforts in the future. Eventually the federals settled 1,800 freedmen at Davis Bend where they cultivated individual plots of their own land with a great deal of success. A system of self-government was put in place including a sheriff, a court system, and a regiment of black soldiers sent to protect the area from Confederate guerrillas or abuses by white stragglers from the Union army. The colony at Davis Bend astounded federal authorities by ultimately producing hundreds of thousands of dollars worth of cotton. Despite its initial success, however, time was against the "grand experiment" along the Mississippi River. Following the war and the death of Abraham Lincoln, President Andrew Johnson, with little concern for the rights of the freedmen living there, allowed Joseph Davis to regain ownership of the old Davis plantations. With the loss of the land on which it had prospered, the Davis Bend colony collapsed.

By late 1863, military defeat and economic chaos had eroded Mississippi's political structure significantly. Federal forces occupied Vicksburg, and Jackson had been pillaged. The transient state capital was little more than sealed boxes of hastily filed papers and a loose collection of public officials who were prepared to take flight at a moment's notice. During the course of the war the state's seat of government moved from Jackson to Enterprise, to Meridian and back to Jackson, to Meridian again and then to Columbus, Macon, and finally back to what was left of Jackson. Governor Pettus at one point even had to briefly flee into Alabama to avoid federal patrols. While Sherman was in Jackson during July, he reported meeting with a number of prominent residents of the city who seemed interested in ending the war, and who were angry at those they blamed for taking

Mississippi out of the Union in the first place. Sherman reported to Grant that during the discussions with these men "They admit themselves beaten, and charge their rulers and agitators with bringing ruin and misery on the state." Just as the federals had done in Vicksburg, Sherman distributed supplies to Jackson's hungry citizens. "I am satisfied a change of feeling is now going on in this state," he wrote to one of his cavalry commanders, "and we should encourage it."[47]

Reports similar to Sherman's came in from other parts of the state as well. At the federal headquarters in Memphis, desperate, frightened citizens from a number of communities in the northern part of Mississippi requested an audience with General Stephen A. Hurlbut to discuss peace. In August 1863, Hurlbut wrote to Abraham Lincoln that "The days of chivalry are gone in the South as elsewhere. The Emancipation Proclamation and the arming of negroes is a bugbear in Mississippi. I have now an application from some fifty men of mark and position in Mississippi, asking if they may hold a meeting to consider the possibilities of recognition by the United States." In the southern part of the state, Union General T. E. G. Ransom led a three-day cavalry raid during which he heard rumblings that many Mississippians were tired of fighting. His men moved from Natchez through Kingston, Liberty, and Woodville, destroying war supplies and public buildings. They reported that wherever they went they found citizens who were "discouraged with the rebellion, and anxious for peace."[48]

Still, Mississippi's state government continued to function, at least to such an extent that it was able to hold elections in 1863. Under state law, Pettus could not seek another term, and it was unlikely that he could have been reelected even if he was able to run. The severe downturn in Mississippi's fortunes had discredited the governor and his radical allies. In 1861, they had promised the state a short war that would end in a glorious victory, but they had not delivered. Mississippi voters went to the polls in October and chose

---

[47] *OR*, ser. 1, vol. 24, pt. 2, pp. 530–31.
[48] Ibid., 685; *OR*, ser. 1, vol. 24, pt. 3, p. 588.

Charles Clark as their new governor by a wide margin. Though certainly not willing to give up the fight, Clark was seen as a moderate, level-headed alternative to more radical candidates. He also had been wounded in the service of the Confederacy, which gave him instant credibility. Clark received 16,428 votes, far outdistancing two of Pettus's close associates, Absalom W. West and Reuben Davis, who split around 7,000 votes between them. When the regular session of the legislature met in Macon in November, Pettus gave his final address to the body. Defiant to the end, he railed against the Yankees and appealed to Mississippi's white population to continue the struggle. After leaving office, Pettus toured the state making patriotic speeches in hopes of rallying the people and served for a time as an officer in the 1st Mississippi Infantry, but in truth the overbearing fire-eater who confidently led his state out of the Union in 1861 was a spent man. When Mississippi surrendered in 1865 he signed a loyalty oath to the United States and, his health failing, moved to Arkansas where a number of his family and friends lived. He died there of pneumonia in early 1867 at the age of fifty-four, outliving the Confederacy by a little less than two years.

In Mississippi, Charles Clark took over a government that was barely functioning. It could offer its people little relief from the ravages of war, and many of its citizens lived under enemy occupation. The state's major cities were damaged, railroad lines destroyed, and families permanently disrupted by the loss of loved ones. The dreams of Southern independence had faded, only to be replaced by an unending nightmare of death and deprivation. Clark governed a state filled with thousands of men, women, and children who had lost hope by the end of 1863. In his inaugural address, the new governor railed against Northern tyranny and emancipation as he urged his people to fight on. Believing that he needed to put on strong front despite his moderate reputation, Clark used themes familiar to the day. He told his white constituents that surrender was not an option for to do so would lead to "the confiscation of your property, the immediate emancipation of your slaves and the elevation of the black race to a position of equality—aye, of superiority, that will make them masters and rulers."[49] Such rhetoric served only to further frighten an already battered and dispirited people. While the war would not end for more than a year, and Mississippi would see more fighting, much of the state already felt the sting of defeat, and a sense of deep regret over the events of the past two years. Not long after the fall of Vicksburg, Matilda Champion, whose family owned the property that gave the Battle of Champion Hill its name, wrote a few lines that likely expressed the prevailing sentiment of many of those who lived in her state: "Our own Mississippi is now invaded and what is to become of us? We must suffer as others have done long since, our property destroyed and our negroes taken away. I am willing to work, but oh God, when will this war end."[50]

[49] Quoted in Dunbar Rowland, *History of Mississippi: Heart of the South*, 4 vols. (Jackson MS: S. J. Clarke Publishing Company, 1925) 1:815.
[50] Quoted in Hoehling, *47 Days of Siege*, vii.

5

THE END, 1864–1865

And so the war is over. When I consider all that I have seen and heard, all that I have learned of men and motives, I am constrained to ask myself "What is it all for?"
William Pitt Chambers,
46th Mississippi Infantry,
May 16, 1865

Charles Clark had little time to savor his electoral victory. He had to work with the barely functioning state legislature to help feed and protect the citizens of those parts of Mississippi not under federal occupation. Clark had few resources to work with and his calls for more men to serve in state militia units were met with little enthusiasm. Most men eligible for state service were either already in the Confederate army or hiding out to avoid military service all together, state or Confederate. In some areas, recruiting officers were beaten and their lives threatened if they did not immediately leave the vicinity. As time wore on, many enterprising Mississippians thought of creative ways to legally avoid service. Men from different parts of the state petitioned the government to organize local cavalry companies to continue the fight, and once the government accepted these petitions, the men involved were exempt from the draft. Intentional delays in recruiting and organizing the new units kept the men out of harm's way indefinitely.

The Confederate military situation in the state was also bleak and chaotic. After the fall of Vicksburg, Mississippi was no longer a primary focal point for major federal offensives, but United States troops still clashed with outnumbered Confederates in the state, and men continued to die. In December 1863, Joseph Johnston left Mississippi to take command of the Army of Tennessee and Episcopal-bishop-turned-Confederate-lieutenant-general Leonidas Polk took over the Department of Alabama, Mississippi, and East Louisiana. He arrived in Mississippi around Christmas and established his headquarters at Meridian, the most strategically important point in the state still held by the Confederates. One of Polk's first tasks was to organize his cavalry to defend the state. Though the Confederate infantry in the state was battered, the cavalry remained formidable, as did the men who led the horsemen. Polk's cavalry was organized under two commanders, Stephen Dill Lee and Nathan Bedford Forrest.

Stephen D. Lee, who would be a prominent member of Mississippi's political community after the war, was born in Charleston, South Carolina, and graduated seventeenth in a class of forty-six at the United States Military Academy in 1854. Secretary of War Jefferson Davis signed Lee's commission and he served for seven years in the United States Army in artillery and administrative posts. When South Carolina seceded, he entered state service as a captain and became a member of General Pierre Gustave Toutant Beauregard's staff in April 1861. Lee was with Beauregard at Fort Sumter and delivered the general's terms of surrender to Major Robert Anderson inside the fort. Lee distinguished himself as an artillery officer in Virginia during the first year of the war, rising to the rank of brigadier general, and was eventually assigned to the western theater where he became commander of Pemberton's artillery at Vicksburg. He helped drive away the federals at Chickasaw Bayou but surrendered with the rest of the Vicksburg garrison in July 1863. Recently paroled and an able horsemen, he received a promotion to major general and a cavalry command. Polk placed him in charge of rebel cavalry in the southern part of Mississippi.

The irascible Nathan Bedford Forrest commanded the cavalry in the northern part of the state. Forrest was born in Bedford County, Tennessee, in 1821 and moved as a young boy with his family to Tippah County, Mississippi. With little formal education, he worked farm jobs and as a blacksmith before marrying and moving to Memphis. A self-made man of the first order, Forrest accumulated a small fortune before the war trading cotton, land, and slaves. He moved back into North Mississippi and established a large plantation in Coahoma County. When the war broke out he initially enlisted as private, but his status afforded him the opportunity to raise a cavalry company at his own expense. He distinguished himself at Fort Donelson and was wounded during the Battle of Shiloh as he helped cover the Confederate retreat. In July 1862, he received a promotion to brigadier general and made a name for himself conducting surprise raids on federal supply lines and isolated federal garrisons. The model of the colorful, swashbuckling cavalry hero, Forrest was a constant thorn in the side of Union commanders who tried unsuccessfully to contain or capture him. Forrest was said to be the only Confederate general who William Tecumseh Sherman feared.

Outwardly at least, Sherman seemed to fear no one. After Vicksburg, he planned, with Grant's blessing, to organize a force that would sweep the remaining Confederate forces out of Mississippi and eliminate Meridian in the eastern part of the state as a railroad and supply center. His plans were delayed by actions outside the state, which took him to Chattanooga where he helped Grant defeat Braxton Bragg. Soon afterwards, however, Sherman was back in Vicksburg with a force of more than 20,000 men that he planned to lead across the middle of the state, through Jackson yet again, and on to Meridian. At the same time, he would send Brigadier General William Sooy Smith into Mississippi from Memphis with a cavalry force of 7,000 men. They would move southeast to Okolona, brushing aside any Confederate cavalry that they came across, and then follow the Mobile and Ohio Railroad lines due south to rendezvous with Sherman's men in Meridian. In addition to his own cavalry, Polk could counter with only two infantry divisions, one camped at Canton under the command of William W. Loring and another at Brandon under Samuel French.

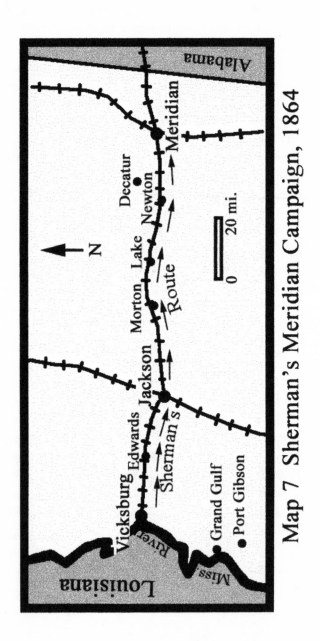

Map 7 Sherman's Meridian Campaign, 1864

Sherman moved out of Vicksburg on February 3 with his army organized in two columns under Generals McPherson and Hurlbut and accompanied by a small force of cavalry under Colonel E. F. Winslow. They crossed the Big Black River and passed the Champion Hill battlefield near Edwards Station. Two of Stephen Lee's cavalry brigades, commanded by Wirt Adams and Peter Stark, harassed the Union columns along the way but did little to stop their progress. Sherman's men occupied Jackson yet again on February 5 and the next day crossed the Pearl River. Rumors were rife that Loring and French's divisions might unite for an attack, but instead both divisions fell back to the east, through Morton and eventually through Meridian and into Alabama. Polk knew that he was outnumbered and outgunned and, as a result, Confederate resistance to the great blue tide sweeping toward Meridian was minimal. From Jackson to Meridian Sherman did a great deal of damage in what amounted to a rehearsal for the total war strategy that he would employ during his famous "march to the sea" in Georgia. "Sherman's army left fire and famine in its track," one federal participant wrote of the Meridian campaign. "The country was one lurid blaze of fire; burning cotton gins and deserted buildings were seen on every hand. I regret to say it but oft times habitations were burned down over the heads of occupants."[1] On February 9, the federals entered Morton where they remained long enough to tear up the railroads and raze a number of buildings. Further east they virtually destroyed the small town of Lake. For the Confederates, the high point of the campaign took place at Decatur, where rebel cavalry under Wirt Adams struck the still advancing Union lines. Catching the federals temporarily off guard, Adams's men destroyed forty wagons and came close to capturing Sherman himself, who was staying at a house nearby. Federal troops quickly came up to reinforce the weak point in their columns and the rebel cavalry was forced to retire. The episode did

---

[1] Quoted in Laura Nan Fairley and James T. Dawson, *Paths to the Past: An Overview History of Lauderdale County, Mississippi* (Meridian MS: Lauderdale County Department of Archives and History, 1988) 65.

not slow Sherman down to any great extent, but it did help make Adams's reputation.

Next to Forrest, William Wirt Adams emerged from the Civil War as Mississippi's most notable cavalry commander. The son of a judge, Adams was born in Kentucky in 1819 and moved to Mississippi with his family as a small boy. After attending college he left home for Texas where in 1839 he fought for the new republic in campaigns against the Native Americans. He later lived in Louisiana, establishing a successful sugar plantation at Iberville before returning to Mississippi in 1850 and making his home in Jackson. Adams established plantations near Jackson and Vicksburg, entered the banking business, and won election to the state legislature. After Mississippi, left the Union he was appointed commissioner to Louisiana and Jefferson Davis offered Adams a cabinet position as postmaster general in the Confederate government. After turning down the office, Adams recruited his own cavalry unit and entered the Confederate army as a colonel. Much of his service during the war involved defending his home state. He took part in the battles of Iuka and Corinth as well as the Vicksburg campaign, and eventually received a promotion to brigadier general. After harassing federal troops during Sherman's Meridian expedition, Adams remained active in various commands in North Mississippi and Tennessee and concluded the war riding with Forrest's cavalry.

On February 13, Polk's infantry completed their evacuation of Meridian. While much would be made in future years of abuses by Sherman's "thieving Yankees" as they crossed Mississippi, the Confederates stripped Meridian of everything that could be carried away, regardless of who it belonged to, as they left the city. In comparing the behavior of the federal troops to that of the retreating Confederates, one local plantation owner bitterly complained that "our army was nearly as bad, in seizing upon anything wanted, as was the enemy, with the exception of burning up houses, etc. They took nearly all the provisions of corn and meat, stock, oats, potatoes, in fact everything they could find for supplies."[2] The Confederates

---

[2] Fairley and Dawson, *Paths to the Past*, 63.

moved out to the east, across that Alabama state line where Polk established a new headquarters at Demopolis. On February 14, Sherman's men marched into Meridian unmolested.

Upon his arrival, Sherman established his headquarters at the same house Polk had used during his stay, and he immediately issued orders that called for the destruction of the city. "Meridian, the great railway center of the southwest, is now in our possession," he told his troops, "and by industry and hard work can be rendered useless to the enemy." For five days, Sherman's men dedicated themselves to destroying the city with "axes, crowbars, sledges, clawbars, and with fire" until the general finally reported that "Meridian, with its depots, warehouses, arsenals, hospitals, offices, hotels, and cantonments no longer exists." During the course of the expedition across central Mississippi, Sherman's force destroyed 115 miles of railroad, sixty-one bridges, twenty locomotives, and countless other businesses and homes. In addition to the property loss, the Confederates in Mississippi sustained another deep psychological blow as Sherman moved across the middle of their state. While Confederate cavalry harassed the federal columns as they moved toward Meridian, the horsemen were, in the end, little more than an annoyance and Polk's infantry was outnumbered to such an extent that it could offer no resistance. To all concerned, Mississippi seemed almost helpless, a shell of its former self, unable to defend its borders or govern itself effectively. "We lived off the country," Sherman reported on February 29, "and made a swath of desolation 50 miles broad across the State of Mississippi that the present generation will not forget."[3] Sherman also sent word that a number of Meridian's more prominent residents had approached him expressing a desire to end the war and rejoin the Union immediately.

Nathan Bedford Forrest and the horse soldiers that he led were not ready to admit defeat, nor was there anyone, it seemed, who

---

[3] Fairley and Dawson, *Paths to the Past*, 65; United States War Department, comp., *The War of Rebellion: Official Records of the Union and Confederate Armies*, 130 vols. (Washington, DC: Government Printing Office, 1880–1901) ser. 1, vol. 32, pt. 2, p. 498.

could make them do so. During the final year of the war in a destitute Confederacy, Forrest's successes in North Mississippi kept federal commanders frustrated and made the rebel general a legend. One of his victories took place during Sherman's march across Mississippi, though he did not attack the federal columns directly. Part of Sherman's plan had included a cavalry raid through the northern part of the state by William Sooy Smith's cavalry. Smith left Memphis on February 11, several days late, and moved his men through New Albany, Pontotoc, and Houston, where they skirmished briefly with state militia. The federals made poor time, which Smith blamed on the weather, poor roads, large numbers of captured stock, and in general the "peculiar formation of the country." Along the way, liberated slaves flocked into the federal lines, and by the time he reached the Mobile and Ohio Railroad at Okolona, Smith had a thousand freedmen traveling with his command. As they moved south, Smith's men skirmished at Prairie Station and Aberdeen with detachments from Forrest's cavalry, including troops under the command of the general's brother, Colonel Jeffrey Forrest. After another skirmish near West Point, Smith suddenly decided to retreat. Later, Smith claimed that he was concerned for the safety of the freedmen that were traveling with him, and that intelligence reports suggested that Forrest had concentrated a well-equipped and numerically superior force near Starkville. Instead of meeting Sherman in Meridian as planned, the federal cavalry backtracked and Forrest assembled the bulk of his force in pursuit. A major engagement took place at Okolona, where the Confederates drove the federals into a full retreat. Jeffrey Forrest was killed during the battle and his brother, probably fueled by grief, followed Smith for 11 miles, skirmishing with the rear guard until his ammunition ran low. By February 26, Smith was back in the vicinity of Memphis preparing to write a report for Sherman that justified the cavalry's actions. Sherman was livid, and later chastised Smith for failing to follow orders despite the cavalry commander's countless apologies and excuses.

After destroying Meridian, Sherman planned to march his men back to Vicksburg with Smith's horsemen leading the way. He waited for several days but finally gave up and began the march back without the cavalry. On his way to Vicksburg, Sherman, like Smith and any other federal commander who moved a significant body of troops through the state, collected a staggering number of refugees, mostly former slaves. "We bring in some 500 prisoners, a good many refugee families, and about 10 miles of negroes," Sherman reported to Washington, "I am afraid to guess the number, but it was a string of ox wagons, negro women, and children behind each brigade that equaled the length of the brigade itself, and I have twelve brigades."[4] By early March, Sherman's men and all of their charges were back in Vicksburg.

Despite Forrest's military success, he could do little to offer material relief to North Mississippi's civilian population. The general reported that while his victory at Okolona had provided a degree of comfort to a section of the state "whose inhabitants anticipated and expected to be overrun, devastated and laid waste," much of the population remained hungry and demoralized. He also reported a general breakdown of law and order in the region and the presence of "roving bands of deserters, stragglers, horse thieves and robbers who consume the substance and appropriate the property of the citizens." Meanwhile, Governor Clark struggled to solve economic problems in Mississippi that were spiraling out of anyone's control. Confederate notes were dramatically devalued, state and local militia had not been paid in months, and there was little money in the state treasury. Along the Mississippi River and in cotton centers like Holly Springs, wily civilians openly (and illegally) traded cotton with the enemy in exchange for gold or federal notes that they hoarded and kept hidden from tax collectors. Clark literally begged the Confederate government for relief but there was little help available. Away from home, Mississippi sons, brothers, cousins, and friends continued to die in large numbers from disease and wounds suffered during great battles in Virginia, Georgia, Tennessee, and elsewhere—Cold Harbor, Petersburg, the Atlanta campaign, Franklin, and Nashville.

---

[4] *OR*, ser. 1, vol. 32, pt. 2, p. 498.

The roll call of the dead grew longer and longer with each passing week.

In addition to material and emotional hardships, many white Mississippians were forced to endure an unfamiliar and, for them, unsettling sight on a frequent basis. Black soldiers in blue uniforms guarded federally occupied cities and traversed Mississippi's roads as battle-ready infantry, cavalry, and artillery. From the time that the Union armies first came to Mississippi, slaves flocked to the lines seeking freedom, and the federals set up contraband camps to meet the needs of the freedmen population. Once the United States government decided to use black troops in 1862, these contraband camps provided a pool of eager recruits, as did the consistent flow of runaways into the federal lines. Former slaves did guard duty in Vicksburg and Natchez, and occupied Ship Island on the Gulf Coast. Black troops at Milliken's Bend in 1863 drew praise and in early 1864 soldiers of African descent from the 1st Mississippi (US) Cavalry and the 8th Louisiana (US) accompanied James Coats on an expedition up the Yazoo River where they took part in heavy action at Liverpool and Yazoo City. As the Confederacy crumbled, black soldiers continued to serve, and many distinguished themselves.

During the first months of 1864, Nathan Bedford Forrest added to his reputation in Northern Mississippi, but he was not the only Confederate general with ties to the region that gained fame as a result of the war. Though Edward Cary Walthall saw little action in his home state, he led troops in many of the western theater's major campaigns and, as a result, became one of the Confederate army's most respected commanders. Walthall was born in Richmond, Virginia, in 1831 and as a child moved with his family to Holly Springs, Mississippi. He received his education at St. Thomas Hall military school in Holly Springs and afterwards studied law. He moved to Coffeeville in Yalobusha County, established his own law practice and in 1856 won election as district attorney for the 10th Judicial District of Mississippi. At the outbreak of the war, Walthall resigned his civil post and enlisted as a lieutenant in the Yalobusha Rifles, a volunteer company that became part of the 15th Mississippi Infantry. Walthall briefly commanded the regiment and made a name for himself at the Battle of Mill Springs, Kentucky. In April 1862, he left the 15th Mississippi to organize and command the 29th Mississippi Infantry. Walthall led the new regiment during the siege of Corinth in May 1862 and later in the year received a promotion to brigadier general. During 1863, he led his brigade through the Tullahoma campaign and at Chickamauga. He helped defend Lookout Mountain at Chattanooga and was severely wounded at Missionary Ridge. Fully recovered, he led his brigade in the Atlanta campaign, during which he received a promotion to major general. Walthall accompanied John Bell Hood on his ill-fated invasion of Tennessee and the Mississippian's career as a Confederate soldier eventually ended in North Carolina, where he surrendered with Joseph Johnston in 1865. After the war, Walthall returned to Mississippi a hero, reestablished his law practice, and eventually parlayed his military notoriety into a successful political career.

Following Sherman's Meridian campaign, both Forrest and Polk sought to keep the morale of their troops high. This was a somewhat easier task for Forrest, whose men could take pride in their success at Okolona. Both commanders treated the victory in North Mississippi as if it were one of the most important of the war. In early March 1864, Forrest issued a congratulatory message to his men, lauding their efforts in a fight during which the enemy "was defeated, routed, demoralized, and driven from the country, his plans frustrated, his ends unaccomplished, and his forces cut to pieces." In praising his soldiers' valor, Forrest failed to mention that before retiring Smith had done a great deal of damage in North Mississippi, and the Union cavalry's departure from the area did not have much of an effect on Sherman's march to Meridian. Likewise, Polk exaggerated the battle's outcome, referring to it as "the brilliant and successful campaign just closed," as he overstated its long-term consequences. He also disparaged the enemy for being overconfident. "Their proclaimed and boasted object," Polk wrote of the federals, "was to overrun and desolate our country, if not to strike a death-blow to our cause. They have been forced to retreat, beaten and distracted."[5]

---

[5] *OR*, ser. 1, vol. 32, pt. 1, p. 356.

Ironically, the general had to issue his congratulations for the "successful campaign" from his headquarters in Demopolis, Alabama, after having been driven from Mississippi by Sherman.

Though Sherman eventually left Mississippi, he still affected events in the state, and Nathan Bedford Forrest continued to be a thorn in the federal commander's side. By March 1864, U. S. Grant was in command of all Union forces and Sherman was in Chattanooga planning his Atlanta campaign. Sherman launched the offensive during the first week of May, moving slowly south while battling Confederate forces under Joseph Johnston, an excellent defensive fighter. Johnston called in reinforcement, including Polk with his two infantry division, which in turn left Stephen D. Lee in command of the Confederates in Mississippi. Lee took charge but wisely gave Forrest the authority to act independently in the northern part of the state and in Tennessee.

During the four-month Atlanta campaign, the federals advanced steadily, but in the process extended their supply lines that stretched back to Nashville. As the campaign progressed, Sherman grew concerned that the brazen Forrest might move his Confederate cavalry out of North Mississippi into Middle Tennessee, strike the supply lines, and perhaps jeopardize the entire federal effort. As a result, Sherman in late May ordered Brigadier General Samuel Sturgis out of Memphis and into North Mississippi with a force of just over 8,000 men. Sturgis's mission was to keep Forrest occupied and if possible destroy the Confederate cavalry force that Forrest commanded. Sherman's orders to Sturgis came just in time, as Forrest's cavalry had just left for Middle Tennessee and was forced to turn back into Mississippi to once again defend the northern part of the state. The federals marched out of Memphis on June 1. In his search for Forrest, Sturgis had a great deal of discretion in his movements, but was generally expected to "proceed to Corinth, Miss., by way of Salem and Ruckersville, capture any force that may be there, then proceed south, destroying the Mobile and Ohio Railroad to Tupelo and Okolona, and as far as possible toward

Macon and Columbus."[6] The federals reached Corinth, but torrential rain that made some roads impassable slowed their progress.

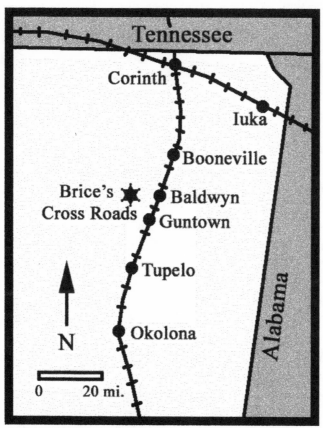

Map 8 Vicinity of Brice's Cross Roads, 1864

---

[6] *OR*, ser. 1, vol. 39, pt. 1, p. 90.

On June 9, Stephen D. Lee and Forrest held a war council at Booneville to discuss the situation, but they did not make specific battle plans. Because Forrest was outnumbered, they determined that his cavalry should harass Sturgis in an attempt to delay him while Lee tried to round up reinforcements. The next day, Forrest's tenacity was such that he did a great deal more than delay the enemy's progress. As Sturgis advanced from the Corinth vicinity, he met Forrest's men at Brice's Cross Roads near Guntown. The Confederates first drove back the federal cavalry under Benjamin Grierson in a ferocious attack the likes of which Forrest was famous for. He then outflanked Sturgis's infantry and the federal lines collapsed in panic. Many Union soldiers abandoned their arms and equipment, literally running for their lives in what many would consider Forrest's finest hour. With the federals in full flight, the Confederates mounted a pursuit and over the next three days the forces skirmished at Ripley, Salem, and Davis' Mill. Exhausted, Forrest's men eventually halted, allowing the federals to limp back into Memphis dazed and bleeding. The Battle of Brice's Cross Roads was a stirring victory for the Confederates. Forrest inflicted more than 600 casualties on the federal cavalry and captured more than 1,600 prisoners, 16 artillery pieces, and wagons loaded with supplies. Sturgis was disgraced and false rumors began to circulate that he was drunk during the battle. Once he reached Memphis, he asked to be relieved of command.

While Brice's Cross Roads was a great victory for Forrest, the battle also won accolades for his immediate superior, Stephen D. Lee. As overall commander of the troops in Mississippi, Lee received a great deal of credit for the victory, which seemed even more significant when compared to the bleak fortunes of Confederate Mississippi up to that point. Not long after the battle, Lee received a promotion to lieutenant general, making him, at the age of thirty, the youngest man in either army to achieve that rank. "He has won distinction on every field," one friendly reporter wrote of the general, "and when the faithful chronicler of the times closes his book, the part played by Stephen D. Lee will be found among the brightest annals of our struggle."[7]

The Battle at Brice's Cross Roads also reopened a controversy over the status of black troops captured by the Confederates. This had been a sensitive issue since troops under Forrest's command captured Fort Pillow in Tennessee earlier in the year. At Fort Pillow, the Confederates executed several dozen black soldiers after they had surrendered, prompting Abraham Lincoln and other government officials to discuss appropriate forms of retaliation. Two regiments of black troops were among Sturgis's federal force in North Mississippi, and rumors reached Major General Cadwallader C. Washburn, the federal commander in western Tennessee, that "the massacre at Fort Pillow had been reproduced at the late affair at Brice's Cross Roads." This prompted a sharp exchange of letters between Washburn and both Lee and Forrest. The Confederate commanders vehemently denied that any atrocities had taken place while restating the Confederacy's official policy concerning captured federal troops of African descent. "With reference to those captured," Lee wrote, "I will state that, unless otherwise ordered by my government, they will not be regarded as prisoners of war, but will be retained and humanely treated." Forrest added that he regarded "captured negroes as I do other captured property and not as captured soldiers…it is not the policy nor the interest of the South to destroy the negro—on the contrary, to preserve and protect him." In a way, these last few words were certainly true in that the Confederacy routinely "preserved" captured black soldiers so that they could be forced into service as laborers, returned to their former master, or sometimes sold to new owners.[8]

After Sturgis's defeat, William Tecumseh Sherman was angry and still concerned about his vulnerable supply lines in Tennessee. Declaring that "there will never be peace in Tennessee until Forrest

---

[7] Quoted in Herman Hattaway, *General Stephen D. Lee* (Jackson: University Press of Mississippi, 1976) 115.

[8] Washburn, Lee and Forrest quoted in Hattaway, *General Stephen D. Lee*, 116–17.

is dead," he quickly ordered another expedition into Northern Mississippi to "follow Forrest to the death, if it cost 10,000 lives and breaks the treasury."[9] Sherman wired Andrew Jackson Smith in Memphis and ordered him to assemble of large force to go after Forrest. Smith, who had served under Sherman during the Meridian campaign, established his headquarters at LaGrange, Tennessee, near the state line, and called in troops from various locations until he had around 14,000 men at his disposal. Covering some of the same territory as Sturgis, but determined not to make the same mistakes, Smith moved cautiously into Mississippi on July 5 and over the next few days took his men through Ripley, New Albany, and Pontotoc in search of their quarry.

From all accounts, Forrest may not have been at his best against this new federal threat. He and his men were beginning to wear down as a result of the constant action that they had been involved in over the past few weeks, turning back two major federal advances with little chance for rest. Forrest's health was also in question as he suffered from a painful case of boils that made riding difficult. The general also may have been out of sorts because Stephen D. Lee had received so much credit for the victory at Brice's Cross Roads. For at least some of these reasons, Forrest requested that Lee take command of the troops in the field for what he assumed would be another major engagement with the federals. Recognizing Forrest's value perhaps better than anyone else, Lee resisted the request and the two men reached a compromise. Forrest remained in the field, with Lee arriving in the area to take overall command of the operation. Lee rode into Forrest's camp with a small number of reinforcements that brought the Confederates total in the region to around 7,500 men.

On July 13, Smith was on the road from Pontotoc moving east. During the march, Confederate detachments moved behind the advancing federal columns and struck at the rear guard with little success, and by the end of the day Smith's men were camped near

---

[9] Quoted in James M. McPherson, *Battle Cry of Freedom: Civil War Era* (New York: Ballantine Books, 1988) 748–49.

Tupelo, where they formed a line of battle. As evening fell, Lee and Forrest moved their army into position to face the federals, and then met to discuss strategy. Despite being outnumbered almost two to one, Lee ordered an attack for early the next morning, and though Forrest did not protest, it seems that he disagreed with his commander. The federals were entrenched on high ground with superior numbers and while Forrest had accomplished what some considered a miracle at Brice's Cross Road, the general was also a realist. When his meeting with Lee broke up, an irritated Forrest, in a moment of sheer bravado, decided to scout the situation himself. He set out with one of his aids and actually rode into the federal lines under cover of darkness as if he belonged there. He rode over the terrain examining the federal positions. At one point sentries challenged the general, who responded by barking out orders to the startled men as if they were under his command. Before anyone knew what was happening, Forrest and his aid disappeared into the night and back into their own lines.

Regardless of the odds against success, the attack began the next morning. The Confederates assaulted well-defended federal positions and, unlike Sturgis's troops, Smith's men did not waver. They cut down the Southerners, whose movements were poorly coordinated. The fighting continued for several hours until Lee disengaged. The rebels suffered around 1,300 casualties to only 648 for the federals. Luckily for the Confederates, the federal troops were short on rations and ammunition, and Smith ordered a withdrawal the next day. He knew that the enemy had sustained high casualties, and as a result was no longer in a position to immediately threaten Sherman's supply lines. Forrest hastily organized a pursuit and skirmishing took place here and there as the federals retired back toward Memphis. When Forrest sustained a painful wound in the foot, the pursuit ended.

The Battle of Tupelo—also called the Battle of Harrisburg after a local town that some years earlier was bypassed by the railroad and abandoned—was a major setback for the Confederacy. The high number of casualties demoralized the rest of Lee's and Forrest's men and it became painfully apparent that Sherman's movements in Georgia would not be checked. Lee downplayed the defeat by claiming victory due to the fact that the federals technically had retreated, leaving the Confederates in control of the field. Lee did not want to absorb the blame for the defeat, nor did he want to tarnish Forrest's reputation as one of the Confederacy's dwindling list of heroes who still retained the public's confidence. Lee submitted no written report of the battle while Forrest also was careful not to affix blame for an engagement that he had been less than enthusiastic about in the first place. Forrest's report emphasized the superior federal numbers and the fact that the enemy had left the area after the fight. "The Battle of Harrisburg," he concluded, "will furnish the historian with a bloody record, but will also stamp with immortality the gallant dead and the living heroes it has made."[10] After the action at Tupelo, Stephen D. Lee, far from discredited by the debacle, received a transfer to Joseph Johnston's Army of Tennessee and eventually took command of a corps in Georgia. After John Bell Hood replaced Johnston, Lee also accompanied the army on its unsuccessful invasion of Tennessee. After Lee's departure, command of the Department of Alabama, Mississippi, and East Louisiana passed to General Richard Taylor, son of former president Zachary Taylor and brother of Jefferson Davis's deceased first wife.

In Georgia, Sherman, who was closing in on Atlanta, was irritated that Smith had not pressed the Confederates at Tupelo, believing that Forrest should not have been allowed to escape alive. As a result, he ordered Smith back into North Mississippi. Smith put the torch to several towns and heavily damaged Oxford on this new advance but never got a chance to kill Forrest. Instead, detachments from Smith's command skirmished occasionally with Forrest's Confederates but accomplished little. Believing it unwise to fully engage Smith again, Forrest instead withdrew and made a daring raid on Memphis that further enhanced his reputation. Afterwards, Smith gave up his pursuit of the wily Confederate cavalry commander, Sherman captured Atlanta, and protecting federal supply lines from Nashville was no longer a major concern. Forrest continued to

---

[10] *OR*, ser. 1, vol., 39, pt. 1, p. 324.

maneuver through Tennessee and Northern Alabama before he also joined Hood's invasion force as it moved toward Nashville.

With the departure of major Confederate armies from Mississippi, the state in many cases was forced to defend itself with home guard or state units recruited locally. During the final months of 1864, severe manpower shortages made this task impossible. federal cavalry moved through the state at will and continued to destroy public and private property as quickly as the Confederates could make repairs. In August, Governor Clark called the legislature into session at Macon to discuss the state's many problems including the need to recruit more men. Clark was especially concerned at the number of exemptions that allowed able bodied men in the state to escape service, one of the most notable being the exemption of those in public service positions that in reality did little to serve the public. "Some counties in this state are entitled to fifteen or twenty justices of the peace," Clark pointed out in his address to the legislature. "The office of constable has suddenly become desirable.... Sheriffs, having by law the power to appoint an unlimited number of deputies, have been besieged by applicants." Clark recommended that exemptions for civil officers be dramatically reduced and that all men "not liable to conscription or enrollment in Confederate service [and] capable of bearing arms, between the ages of 16 and 55 years" should be recruited to protect the state.

Despite Clark's pleadings, recruiting new men for service to the state, or the Confederacy for that matter, was no easy task. Most Mississippians realized that the cause was lost and the small number of eligible men left in the state were not willing to risk their lives for nothing. One correspondent from Leake County observed that in his area there was "a general discontent and loss of confidence in the administration and our success, a disposition among the people to rise up in opposition to the powers that be [and] declare for reconstruction or anything else but the way things are." Conscription officers continued to meet violent opposition in some areas and there was evidence that in some parts of the state physicians were selling medical exemptions to the highest bidder. "I fear that medical boards have in many instances done a disservice to the cause," one knowledgeable observer noted. "The Board of Brookhaven, Miss., from April to October, last, examined 1,125 men, and of these discharged 807 (over 70 percent) as unfit for duty." Even when the state was able to enlist new men, there were few supplies available, certainly not enough to adequately outfit troops for defense. "I have not the means to supply State troops with clothing," Clark wrote. "I cannot even procure a blanket, and I fear I shall not be able to pay them." The need for supplies also brought the desperate state government into direct conflict with the equally desperate national government in Richmond. In a clear violation of states' rights principles that had supposedly taken Mississippi and the other slaveholding states out of the Union, the Confederacy confiscated most of the available supplies, leaving the individual states to fend for themselves. "All manufacturing establishments of both clothing and shoes," Clark complained, "are monopolized by the Confederate States. They impress everything at their own valuation. I can seldom purchase anything." Appeals to Confederate authorities, who had problems of their own, were met with excuses, apologies, and hollow directives to make the best of the present situation.[11]

As if to demonstrate the impotence of Mississippi's civil and military infrastructure, Benjamin Grierson made yet another cavalry raid into the state in December 1864. His mission included destroying as much of the state's remaining railroads as possible and burning anything that could even remotely be used as war supplies. As had been the case with his 1863 raid during Grant's Vicksburg campaign, Grierson's new venture was very effective. He rode out of Memphis with 3,500 troops on December 21 and moved southeast through Lamar and Ripley, burning buildings and "foraging" livestock and other items from the civilian population along the way. At Booneville the expedition turned south and destroyed miles of recently repaired track on the Mobile and Ohio Railroad. Near Okolona, Grierson and his men turned to the west and rode through Houston and Bellefontaine. They burned the Choctaw County

---

[11] *OR*, ser. 1, vol. 45, pt. 1; *OR*, ser. 1, vol. 52, pt. 2, pp. 791–92; *OR*, ser. 4, vol. 3, p. 976.

Courthouse along with a number of other buildings in Greensboro before moving on to Bankston, where they found a legitimate military target that unbelievably was still operating at full capacity: the Bankston Textile Mill.

Founded in 1848 by James M. Wesson, the Bankston Textile Mill—officially chartered as the Mississippi Manufacturing Company—was Mississippi's first successful mechanically powered textile mill and one of the most successful operations of its kind in the antebellum South. Situated on a tributary of the Big Black River, the mill flourished from the moment that it first opened its doors and consistently turned a profit through the 1850s. Wesson and several partners took their profits and expanded the business to include a flour mill, gristmill, tannery, and shoe factory. By 1860, the textile mill operated 1,000 cotton spindles, 500 wool spindles, and 20 power looms and employed around 500 local workers. As a result, Bankston became a model mill village on par with those that "New South" entrepreneurs would create in the decades after the war. Converted to produce cloth and shoes for the Confederacy after Mississippi left the Union, the Bankston mill was by 1864 the only significant textile mill still operating in the state.

Bankston's location in the backwoods of Choctaw County kept it out of harm's way for most of the war, but it would not save the town or the mill from Grierson's men. After receiving information from a scout about "a large manufacturing establishment that was turning out one thousand yards of cloth and two thousand pairs of shoes per day," the federals arrived at Bankston just before midnight on December 30. They found the town quiet and went to work setting fire to the cotton and wool factories, the flour mill, and the shoe factory. Hearing the commotion, weary citizens trickled into the streets to watch the flames as they consumed building after building, and Grierson's men allowed some destitute families to take away as much cloth, flour, and as many shoes as they could carry before burning several warehouses. At first unaware that it was federal soldiers who were burning his factory, James Wesson himself appeared in his night clothes. According to one observer, the mill owner was "swearing, threatening to arrest the guard and night watchers, and wanting to know what in hell they were about that they did not extinguish the fire." An officer from one of Grierson's units sarcastically informed Wesson that "the night was so very cold that he had concluded to have a fire."[12]

After destroying the Bankston mills, Grierson's men moved west toward the Mississippi Central Railroad, which ran north and south through the center of the state. At Lodi they shot almost 800 hogs that had been collected for Confederate consumption and lit yet another large fire to burn the carcasses. Finally reaching central Mississippi, they tore up the railroad lines between Grenada and Durant and, in the process, damaged the towns of Winona, Vaiden, and West. Turning toward Vicksburg, Grierson's men met their only significant challenge but were able to drive away rebel cavalry under Wirt Adams. On January 4, 1865 the raid ended as the federal raiders rode into Vicksburg secure in the knowledge that they had once again done a great deal of damage to Mississippi.

In mid-January 1865, a major Confederate army assembled in Mississippi for the final time, but not to defend the state or launch a major offensive against the federals in the Deep South. It was John Bell Hood's worn out Army of Tennessee, not long removed from its disastrous Tennessee invasion. During Sherman's Atlanta campaign, Jefferson Davis replaced Joseph Johnston with Hood, much to the chagrin of many who knew both men. Hood subsequently evacuated Atlanta and took his army on an ill-conceived offensive into Tennessee with dreams of capturing Nashville and then moving on to Virginia to assist Robert E. Lee. On November 30, 1864, Hood ordered a series of frontal assaults against well-entrenched federal positions at Franklin, Tennessee, that almost destroyed his army. Still, the Confederates pressed on and met defeat again during the two-day Battle of Nashville. Afterwards, the remnants of Hood's once formidable force withdrew from Tennessee and by Christmas were camped at Tuscumbia, Alabama. The army proceeded west

---

[12] Quoted in Harold S. Wilson, *Confederate Industry: Manufacturers and Quartermasters in the Civil War* (Jackson: University Press of Mississippi, 2002) 193–94.

across the Mississippi state line to the vicinity of Corinth, and then turned south. On January 9, 1865, Hood's men began straggling into Tupelo, where the soldiers remained for several weeks. On January 15, Hood resigned his command and Richard Taylor took over the force at Tupelo, which had a total strength of less than 18,000 men. Within a few days petitions circulated among the officers and enlisted men in the Tupelo camps for the reinstatement of Joseph Johnston.

By early 1865, the Confederacy was on the verge of wholesale collapse. On the last day of January, in a move that came at least a year too late, Robert E. Lee was designated commander-in-chief of all Confederate forces. Among Lee's first official acts was the recall of his old friend Joseph Johnston to active duty. On February 25, Johnston took command of the Confederate forces south of Virginia and east of the Mississippi River. His directive from Lee was simple. Johnston was to concentrate all available forces and drive back Sherman, who had followed his march to the sea with an advance into the Carolinas. Although clearly facing long odds, Johnston summoned various commands from around the South to North Carolina, including what remained of the Army of Tennessee. From Tupelo the troops, including many Mississippians, moved sporadically by foot and over a crumbling network of rail lines through the ravaged Deep South. The army continued losing men to desertion through the entire trip to North Carolina. "Many stragglers from the troops of your State belonging to this army are about their homes," Johnston wrote at one point to Mississippi's governor, "I ask your aid to bring them back to the ranks."[13]

By the time Johnston's request reached Mississippi, there were already enough deserters in the state to literally man a small fighting force. By the beginning of 1865, all of Mississippi's counties harbored men who had left Confederate service or had failed to report to the army once conscripted. "The number of deserters is alarmingly large," one official reported. "From a careful examination on this subject I am prepared to say that the number in the state is not less

---

[13] *OR*, ser. 1, vol. 47, pt. 3, p. 707.

than 7,000." Some deserters continued to lay low waiting for the inevitable end of the war while others banded together to take advantage of the chaos of the times. The authorities periodically sent out details to round up soldiers who had left the army but a general lack of manpower hampered the effort. In the countryside deserters were usually able to find safe haven because much of the general public had also given up on the Confederate cause and therefore attached no stigma to those who had escaped the army. Speaking of Mississippi, one Confederate official observed that "The highest military crime, desertion, is committed with impunity. There does not appear on the part of the deserter to be any difficulty in any section of the country."[14] In areas not occupied by the federals, courts rarely met and crude frontier justice usually prevailed, when there was any justice at all. In the southern part of the state looting was commonplace as deserters formed outlaw bands that preyed on the defenseless. Along the river north of Vicksburg, reports reached Confederate authorities that "A large number of persons calling themselves 'scouts' or 'independent companies'" operated in the area who were "nothing less than murderers [and] plunderers." One man described these groups as "principally young men and deserters whose 'cohesive band' is spoils and booty from our own people." Conditions were no better in the northern part of the state where, according to one observer, former Confederates "infest the country, robbing friend and foe indiscriminately." At Holly Springs in Marshall County, dozens of deserters regularly walked the streets without fear of reprisals, condemning the Confederacy and loudly proclaiming that they would never return to the army. Holly Springs was also a hub of significant illegal trade with enemy. There local businessmen James House and William Crump, Jr., openly traded cotton with federal authorities and Northern agents, reaping large profits in direct violation of state and Confederate edicts.[15]

Mississippi's Confederate legislature convened for the final time at Columbus in February and March 1865. Though the body

---

[14] *OR*, ser. 4, vol. 3, p. 690.
[15] *OR*, ser. 1, vol. 45, pt. 2, p. 1247; *OR* ser. 1, vol. 49, pt. 1, p. 950.

discussed a number of issues and passed legislation designed to aid destitute families, their actions had little impact. The state government could no longer protect its citizens and was, in fact, a government in name only. In most of the state, the rule of law had disappeared, there was little food to be had, and much of the public prayed for an end to the conflict. After four years of war many former Confederates who had once railed against the federal government eagerly welcomed the stability that only federal authority could bring, and no longer responded to the commands of Confederate leaders. "The general feeling among the people of Mississippi is that the state is conquered," a Union officer reported, "and the sooner it is occupied by our troops the better."[16]

Still, Governor Clark was defiant. In reality he had no other choice. Like other high-ranking Confederate officials throughout the South, he knew that if the rebellion failed he might be held liable in some way. If the United States triumphed, and the Union remained whole, Confederate leaders might be put on trial for treason, with guilty verdicts potentially resulting in executions. While he certainly put up a brave front, the governor was desperate. On February 20, 1865, Clark addressed the legislature on current affairs in Mississippi and the steps that needed to be taken to improve the state's fiscal and military health. The speech was designed to give the impression that while the state's problems were serious, the situation was far from hopeless. At the gathering, there seemed to be a sense of delusion among the governor and the lawmakers who gathered to hear his speech that they were still in charge of the state, and that their decisions still carried weight. In his address, Clark went down the now tired list of priorities that the state needed to address—destitute families, recruiting new soldiers, crime, disloyalty—before rendering his opinion on what was by far the most controversial military issue facing the Confederacy during its final months: recruiting slaves as soldiers.

Due to severe manpower shortages, Confederate authorities had been for some time wrestling with the idea of recruiting slaves to

---

[16] *OR*, ser. 1, vol. 47, pt. 2, p. 168.

serve in the Confederate army. The subject had been broached periodically since the beginning of the war, but was always met with stifling opposition. However, after setbacks in Virginia and Hood's crushing defeat in Tennessee, the Confederacy was desperate to the point that some of its leaders were willing to dramatically alter their stand on the institution of slavery. Desperation drove many of the South's leaders to subordinate their commitment to the institution of slavery to the rapidly fading hopes for the South's independence. The federals had obviously made good use of black troops, and some in the South believed that the Confederacy should do the same. Others, of course, felt differently.

The arming of slaves was more than just an issue related to the Confederacy's physical need for more soldiers. It struck at the heart of the "Southern way of life" that the slaveholding states originally had mobilized to defend. The Georgian Howell Cobb best summed up the situation in January 1865 when, at the height of the controversy, he wrote, "The day you make soldiers of them (slaves) is the beginning of the end of the revolution. If slaves will make good soldiers our whole theory of slavery is wrong."[17] Some opponents of the plan were less philosophical. They believed that white soldiers would never agree to serve with slaves and would probably desert in even greater numbers if forced to do so. It was one thing to use slaves as manual laborers, they argued, or as servants for officers, or perhaps as cooks, but quite another to arm them for use in combat. Southern whites were brought up to believe that slaves were something less than human, that they were property unable to care for themselves without close supervision. All the Southern states had laws in place that forbid slaves to carry firearms, and for a generation before the war Southern politicians had warned their constituents of the potential for armed slave rebellions promoted by Northern abolitionists. It seemed, however, that by the end of 1864 many of these anxieties had somehow disappeared. Jefferson Davis, who had called the Emancipation Proclamation "the most execrable measure recorded in the

---

[17] Quoted in James M. McPherson, *Marching toward Freedom: Negro in the Civil War, 1861–1865* (New York: Alfred A. Knopf, 1967) 51.

history of guilty man," was suddenly ready and willing to accept slaves into the Confederate army, as was General Robert E. Lee.

In the Confederate Congress, it was a Mississippian, Ethelbert Barksdale, who introduced the "Negro Soldier Law" in November 1864, though the legislation would not pass for several months. The brother of Confederate General William Barksdale who died at Gettysburg, Ethelbert Barksdale had been the editor of the Jackson *Mississippian*, the state's most important Democratic newspaper of the antebellum period. His paper backed John Jones Pettus for governor in 1859 and printed an endless stream of editorials backing Pettus's radical stance on secession and defending the institution of slavery. Four years later, however, the former newspaperman was a lawmaker for a crumbling government that had abandoned one of its foundational principles to promote a desperate military policy. Rather than authoring editorials on Southern rights and the evils of abolitionism, Barksdale had penned a document that would in effect place the Confederacy's faith and future in the hands of slaves. There was no greater irony, or greater hypocrisy, ever associated with the Confederate experience.

The law itself reflected the conflicted nature of the policy. Robert E. Lee and others suggested that slaves who fought for the Confederacy should receive their freedom, but the Barksdale Bill did not address the subject. While it allowed slaves to enter Confederate service as soldiers, with a status that included pay and equipment allotments equal to those of the white soldiers, the law also stated that "nothing in this act shall be construed to authorize a change in the relationship which the said slaves shall bear toward their owners." In other words, according to the law, these new soldiers would be allowed to fight for the freedom of their nation, but they would not be allowed the personal freedom that white citizens in the slaveholding states enjoyed, even if the Confederacy emerged victorious. It was a position that would not reconcile itself.

In his address to the Mississippi legislature, Charles Clark, like many other Southern officials, endorsed the proposal without embracing it. He recognized the need for more men and conveniently ignored the fact that only a desperate and dying Confederacy would accept arming slaves as soldiers. Instead, he referred to the proposal merely as an "experiment" that should be attempted, as if it were progressive in nature, and used a decidedly paternalistic tone when he spoke of the slaves themselves. "With competent officers and firm discipline," he said, "they can be made effective soldiers…. Steady, firm, but kind discipline, such as good masters enforce, is all that it requires." Clark also balked at the idea of offering freedom to those slaves who fought for the Confederacy. Using one of the primary tenets of the haggard pro-slavery argument, he claimed that slavery actually benefited those in bondage and that "Freedom to the slaves, or offering it…would not be a boon to them. Few aspire to this or covet it…. Freedom would be a curse to them and to the country." In the end, after much debate, the Barksdale Bill passed in the Confederate senate by a single vote on March 13, 1865, but it was too late to have any effect. The Confederacy would be in existence for only a few more weeks and there was no time to enlist slaves in significant numbers even if they were willing to fight, which was doubtful. Major A. M. Jackson, a federal officer who was on the scene not long after the law went into effect, reported that in Mississippi "The negroes whom the rebels are conscripting say if they must fight they want to fight for their own side—the Union."[18]

After the legislature adjourned, its members scattered and Charles Clark continued to put on a brave face as if it were only a matter of time until the fortunes of the Confederacy changed for the better. Meanwhile, parts of Mississippi were already being reconstructed. According to one Mississippi newspaper, "Beyond all doubt, the great body of people desire peace, and the failure to conclude an honorable peace is due to moral cowardice." In addition to experiencing more than their share of death and destruction, many in the state were hungry and desperate for peace before the 1865 planting season began in earnest. In Newton, Jefferson and Kemper counties' citizens held public meetings during which they passed

---

[18] Mississippi, *Journal of the House of Representatives of the State of Mississippi, Called Session at Columbus, February and March, 1865* (Meridian MS: J. J. Shannon & Company, 1865) 12–13; *OR*, ser. 1, vol. 48, pt. 2, p. 168.

resolutions declaring their willingness to accept federal authority. In Tishomingo County, where there was a great deal of resistance to secession before the war, federal authorities allowed local leaders to establish their own civil courts. In the occupied cities on the Mississippi River and Gulf Coast, federal and civil authorities began planning for the future.

With little real authority left, Clark looked on helplessly as the Confederacy disintegrated. News of the fall of Richmond reached Mississippi on April 4, and a few days later Confederates in the state were shaken by more alarming dispatches. The governor's daughter later described the scene as she approached the Clark's home after a walk:

> I saw Pa and Brother Tom talking to Ma on the back porch. Both men looked so silent and stern and Pa handed Ma a telegram to read. I could see by their faces that something dreadful had happened and ran to the porch where the telegram was being handed around for all the family to read. Yes, it was all over. Lee had surrendered at Appomattox! Like a thunderbolt it fell upon all of us. We were stunned. I remember feeling astonishment that we were not all dead.[19]

A week later the Clarks and the rest of Mississippi were stunned once again when news of Lincoln's death reached the state.

Although Lee surrendered his army, other Confederate troops were still in the field. Joseph Johnston surrendered his men to William T. Sherman at Bennett House near Durham Station, North Carolina on April 26, leaving Richard Taylor's force around Mobile as the only significant Confederate army remaining east of the Mississippi. At Citronelle, Alabama, on May 4, Taylor, who was in charge of the Department of Alabama, Mississippi, and East Louisiana, surrendered his command, including the entire department, to Richard Springs Canby thus officially ending Confederate military activities in Mississippi. On the same day that Taylor surrendered, skirmishing around Port Gibson marked the

---

[19] Quoted in John K. Bettersworth, *Confederate Mississippi*, 265–66.

final shots fired in the state. Later in the month, when the federals captured Confederate President Jefferson Davis near Irwinville, Georgia, and General Edmund Kirby Smith surrendered the Trans-Mississippi at Galveston, Texas, the Confederacy ceased to exist.

After Taylor surrendered, Charles Clark issued a statement from Meridian, where citizens had been busy rebuilding after Sherman's visit the previous year. On May 6, the governor appealed to the people of Mississippi to "fearlessly adhere to the fortunes of the state, aid the returning soldiers to obtain civil employment, maintain law and order, condemn all twelfth-hour vaporers, and meet the stern facts with fortitude and common sense." Clark seemed to believe that he would lead the state back into the Union as if the end of the war represented nothing more than a return to the status quo. His statement even included instructions regarding the state's slaves. "Masters are responsible," he said "for the protection and conduct of their slaves, and they should be kept home as heretofore." He also made plans to convene the state legislature and send representatives to Washington to inform the new president, Andrew Johnson, that Mississippi was willing to "fully cooperate" in reestablishing ties to the United States. The legislature did convene on May 20 back in Jackson, and in a grand show of arrogance, or detachment from reality, or both, passed a resolution empowering the governor to confer with federal authorities "for restoring the State of Mississippi to the harmonious relations with the Federal government on such a basis as will tend to perpetuate the liberty and prosperity of the American people."[20] The statement assumed that no one would be held accountable for a war that had, over the past four years, led to the deaths of hundreds of thousands Americans. In reality, the legislators likely were very well aware that their pronouncement would not hold up. They had prepared the statement in advance and, because they feared being arrested, met for only an hour before adjourning and fleeing Jackson.

---

[20] Quoted in Dunbar Rowland, *History of Mississippi: Heart of the South*, 4 vols. (Jackson MS: S. J. Clarke Publishing Company, 1925) 2:831–35.

Ignoring the edicts of Clark and the legislature, federal authorities were quick to take charge of the state. General E. D. Osband, who was in command of the Jackson District, notified the governor that federal authorities expected him to turn over all public documents and records, and that the United States did not recognize the present state officials. In the Natchez District, military officials warned citizens not to listen to the "so-called Governor Clark" and reminded them that martial law still prevailed. Having no other choice, Clark delivered the state's papers to Osband on May 22 but insisted that he was doing so under protest. Several days later the federals placed Clark under arrest and sent him Fort Pulaski, near Savannah, Georgia, where he remained until receiving an official parole several weeks later. With the military conflict already over, Confederate Mississippi as a political entity disappeared with the arrest of its governor.

Like the rest of the South, Mississippi would never be the same. Unlike the "Revolution of '76" that Southern secessionists claimed to emulate, the "Revolution of 1861" had ended miserably. Americans traditionally were proud to boast that they had never in their history lost a war, but from 1865 forward the South could no longer make that claim. From the instant the war ended the South was forced to ponder defeat, explain it, and deal with it in a way that no other section of the country would ever have to. "It is all now buried in the graves of the hopes of the Confederacy," one member of the Mississippi Secession Convention wrote in a moment of reflection after the war, "The envies and the jealousies, the hates and the blunders, the victories and the glories, all lie in a common charnel house. God alone knows the very right of it all."[21]

---

[21] Thomas H. Woods, "A Sketch of the Mississippi Secession Convention of 1861,—Its Membership and Work," in *Publications of the Mississippi Historical Society*, vol. 6 (Oxford: Mississippi Historical Society, 1902) 103.

6

RECONSTRUCTION AND REVISION

The past is never dead. It's not even past.
Gavin Stevens in William Faulkner's *Requiem for a Nun*

The Civil War devastated Mississippi, and as the dust and smoke of the conflict settled in 1865, economic and social chaos prevailed. The state's wartime casualties were enormous. Approximately 27,000 of the 78,000 Mississippians who participated in the Confederate fighting did not return from the war, and many of those who did return were crippled for life. One quarter of the white male population of the state who were fifteen years of age or older in 1860 were no longer alive, and for years the ghosts of men who should have still been among the living would haunt the Mississippi countryside. The communities that produced Mississippi's Confederate soldiers were close-knit, and as such few families escaped the loss of a friend, neighbor, or loved one during the struggle. Many of the dead lay in unmarked graves scattered throughout the country, graves that their relatives would never have the opportunity to visit.

The state's economy was also in a shambles. By 1865, many Mississippi farms, large and small, had deteriorated from neglect, hardly any money circulated, and debt was rampant. Five years after the war, the state held more than 2 million acres of land for non-payment of taxes. Property values plummeted. Farmers in post-war Mississippi worked less acreage than they had before the war and yields of both food crops and cotton were limited. The turbulent Reconstruction period offered little relief and once the Democrats wrestled control of the state away from the Republicans in 1875, their conservative fiscal policies made matters even worse. Fifteen years after Appomattox the per capita income in Mississippi was one of the lowest in the country, and it would remain so for generations.

Times were especially tough for Mississippi's newly freed slaves. The war's outcome had given them their freedom but little else. Permanent equality for the former slaves never fully materialized and eventually gave way to social turmoil that would not be dealt with effectively for another century. The freedmen owned no property, had few personal possessions, and slavery had scattered many of their families. After the war, one thing that the former slaves tried to do as quickly as possible was establish some sort of family life, and many freedmen wandered the roads of the state for months searching for lost relatives. Hundreds of slave marriages took place in the months immediately following the war, legally sanctioning unions that had not been recognized during the antebellum period. The federal government created the Freedmen's Bureau to distribute supplies to the needy and settle land claim issues but the agency was never large enough in scope to provide a long-range solution to Mississippi's (and the South's) many problems. For most blacks and whites alike food was scarce, as was adequate medical care. Any sense of hope was almost nonexistent.

Before the war ended, Abraham Lincoln put in place a lenient plan for reconstructing both the Southern states and the nation. His plan involved little more than most white Southerners taking a loyalty oath to the Union and accepting emancipation, with special provisions made for high-ranking officials. Upon Lincoln's death, the presidency passed to Andrew Johnson, who also advocated a lenient plan. While both plans were designed to bring the Union back together as quickly as possible, neither made any concrete provisions for civil rights for the newly freed slaves. Johnson, in fact, was at times openly hostile to the African-American community. As a result, Mississippi and the rest of the Southern states would quickly begin putting together state governments under what their political leadership considered highly favorable terms.

Andrew Johnson appointed William L. Sharkey, who opposed secession in 1861, as provisional governor of Mississippi, and Sharkey called a constitutional convention that met in Jackson in August 1865. During the convention, delegates actually argued over the abolition of slavery with some delegates still claiming that Mississippi was a sovereign state and could therefore not be forced to accept emancipation. More realistic voices prevailed and the convention voted to abolish slavery by a count of 87 to 11. The convention also produced a new constitution and elections were scheduled for state and local officials. In October, former Confederate General Benjamin G. Humphreys was elected governor, although he had to wait for his official pardon from Andrew Johnson before taking office. The elections also produced a state legislature filled with men who had served the Confederacy and who were dedicated to reestablishing some semblance of the old social order.

Once in office, the newly elected body passed a series of controversial laws that were collectively known as the Black Code. They were designed to regulate the activities of the newly freed slaves and keep the freedmen subordinate. At the time viewed as moderate legislation by many Mississippi whites, the laws did give the former slaves certain rights. They could testify in court when involved in litigation. They could own land under certain circumstances, and their marriages were legalized. However, the legislation also placed serious restrictions on the African-American community. The freedmen could not rent or lease some rural land, they could not own firearms, and they had to have a license to do many jobs. The legislature also passed vagrancy laws under which former slaves could be arrested and, if they could not pay the required fine, "hired out" to their former masters or other whites. During the period one major Mississippi newspaper counseled "We must keep the ex-slave in a position of inferiority. We must pass such laws as will make him feel his inferiority." During Humphreys's tenure as governor (he served until 1867), federal troops were ordered to look out for the physical safety of the former slaves, but they were also told not to interfere to any great degree with Mississippi's civilian authorities. As a result, federal officials in Mississippi did little to counter the laws restricting freedmen and, despite subsequent claims to the contrary, military and civil authorities in the state generally coexisted peacefully.

As one of the first states to begin reconstruction, Mississippi became a model, emulated by other Southern states, of how to reestablish some degree of the old political and social order. Very quickly other Southern states elected former Confederates to their legislatures and passed restrictive Black Codes. This generated loud protests from the North. Thousands of federal soldiers had died during the Civil War and it seemed to many as if the Southerners were attempting to turn back the clock and negate their defeat. The Southern states also elected many former Confederates to national office, men who many in the North believed had committed treason by supporting the rebellion. Congress countered this situation in December 1865 by refusing to seat the Southern congressmen, leaving the status of the new Southern governments unresolved. The Northern backlash also included calls for the South to extend full civil and political rights to the freedmen.

In 1866, congressional elections changed the course of Reconstruction. So-called Radical Republicans won solid control of congress, effectively neutralizing President Andrew Johnson as a political force. The Radicals immediately took over the administration of Reconstruction, and they refused to recognize the state governments that had been set up under the leadership of former Confederates. In March 1867, Congress passed a series of Reconstruction Acts that reorganized the South. These acts created five military districts, each of which was placed under martial law. The Fourth Military District included Mississippi and Arkansas, with General E. O. C. Ord in command. As part of the Reconstruction Acts, only those adult males in the state who could swear an "ironclad oath" that they had never given aid to the rebellion against the

United States could participate in creating a new state government. This initially excluded many Democrats and former Confederates from the process, and also allowed many freedmen to take an active role in setting up Mississippi's government.

As a result, the Republican Party governed Mississippi for several years. Three general classifications of citizens made up the Republican Party in the state. First, there were those who came from outside the state to live in Mississippi and support Reconstruction policies, particularly those tenets dealing with the newly freed slaves. Their critics referred to them as "carpetbaggers," individuals who had supposedly come into the state to take advantage of the situation and hopefully enrich themselves. Second, there were native white Mississippians who cooperated with federal authorities in implementing Reconstruction policies. Critics referred to this group as "scalawags" who similarly wanted to use the post-war chaos to line their pockets. Finally, the largest block of Republican votes during the period came from the freedmen community, and a number of African Americans held public office during the period.

A new constitutional convention convened in January 1868. This convention included twenty-six carpetbaggers, thirty-three scalawags, and sixteen African Americans in addition to twenty-nine white conservatives dedicated to preserving antebellum ways. Despite the fact that there were relatively few blacks at the convention, some conservative newspapers later disparaged the meeting as the "Black and Tan Convention" and downplayed its accomplishments. The 1868 Mississippi Constitution that the convention produced was patterned after state constitutions in the North. Among other things, it declared that all persons residing in Mississippi who were citizens of the United States were citizens of the state and had equal civil and political rights. The constitution also provided for a system of free public education and for no discrimination in the use of public facilities. One of the convention delegates later wrote, "This new constitution dodged nothing. Under its provisions the Negro was a man, and all men were to be equal." Provisions in the new constitution also provoked bitter opposition from conservatives, and from many whites who soon regained their right to vote. Regardless, the constitution was ratified, new elections were held, and Mississippi officially reentered the Union in 1870 under Republican control.

The Republicans controlled Mississippi for about five years, during which time they repaired or rebuilt railroads, bridges, levees, and public buildings. The School Law of 1870 established Mississippi's first public school system and the legislature passed a Civil Rights Act prohibiting discrimination in public places and on public conveyances. While African-American voters had influence, African Americans never dominated Mississippi's government during the period as some would later claim. No African American was ever elected governor, nor were African Americans ever a majority in the legislature. At the local level where the county sheriff was the most important elected office, only twelve of seventy-four counties ever had a black sheriff—this in a state where African Americans represented roughly half of the population and 70 to 80 percent of the population in some counties.

During the early 1870s, a significant backlash against Reconstruction policies in Mississippi developed among conservative whites whose goal was to reclaim the state for the Democratic Party and to put in place, in one form or another, the social structure of the antebellum period. Conservatives formed political "White Men's Clubs" to appeal to the white masses and "Taxpayer Leagues" to protest the Republicans' fiscal policies. These groups served two purposes. They unified many white voters based on race and they successfully circulated anti-Republican propaganda throughout the state. During the period, terror groups such as the Ku Klux Klan, the Knights of the White Camellia, and the Sons of Midnight harassed and sometimes killed black and white Republicans alike. During local elections in 1874 and the statewide legislative elections of 1875, violence prevailed as the Democrats implemented the "Mississippi Plan," which generally involved race-based appeals to white voters, stuffed ballot boxes, falsified election returns and violence and intimidation designed to keep African Americans and white Republicans away from the polls. During the 1875 political season, serious race riots broke out at Water Valley, Louisville, Macon, Columbus, Vicksburg, and other places. In Clinton, more than twenty African Americans died during several days of rioting and many others were forced to flee the town.

The statewide elections of 1875 represented a triumph for the Mississippi Plan. Widespread voter fraud and intimidation resulted in legislative victories for the Democrats in sixty-two of the state's seventy-four counties. Once seated, the new legislature impeached the Republican governor Adelbert Ames and "convinced" other Republican politicians to give up their offices. Although the disputed presidential election of 1876 and subsequent Compromise of 1877 that gave Rutherford Hayes the presidency marked the official end of Reconstruction in the South, the 1875 elections marked the end of Reconstruction in Mississippi and the beginning of a hundred years of Democratic dominance of the state.

Because it was so successful, the Mississippi Plan became the blueprint used by other Southern states to rid themselves of Republican rule. Meanwhile, the federal government did nothing to combat the abuses. By the mid-1870s, much of the Northern public had grown tired of the Reconstruction debate and so many Northern politicians lost interest as well. Civil rights for African Americans was not an issue that excited the Northern electorate, and a financial panic in 1873 made economic concerns a priority in many circles. In general, Northern officials were more interested in industrial development than in committing significant resources to prop up state governments in the South against massive white resistance. They believed it more prudent to allow the Democrats back into congress on their own terms, and then work with them within that body. After four years of war, and several years of Reconstruction, the North was tired of fighting, and it gave the South back to the Democratic Party at the expense of the African-American population. Soon most African Americans in Mississippi, and in the rest of the South, would be excluded from the political system, and legally segregated into a "separate but equal" world of their own.

Later, a number of myths sprang up concerning Reconstruction, most of which were used for decades as propaganda to keep the Democratic Party in power, and to insure that Mississippi whites (and Southern whites in general) would never forget who "rescued" them from the alleged evils of Republican rule. Even today many of these myths are wrongly accepted by some as fact. For instance, one of the great myths of Reconstruction held that the helpless South suffered great abuses under federal military rule, and that the South was under martial law through the entire Reconstruction period. In reality, military rule in the South only lasted about three years following the end of the war, and relatively few troops were stationed in the Southern states. In Mississippi the total number of troops in the state never exceeded 6,900 and by 1869, only four years after the Confederate surrender, there were only 716 federal soldiers in the state, an average of less than ten per county.

Another myth alleged that the Reconstruction period was one of great political corruption in the South—that the carpetbaggers had come South to take advantage of the chaos and enrich themselves and that the Scalawags had helped them. In Mississippi, there were some Republican officials who were corrupt, and many who were not. Overall, there was no evidence that the Republican governments in the state were any more or less corrupt than Democratic governments either before or after Reconstruction. In fact, during the four decades after the war there were three major financial scandals involving state treasurers stealing funds. These took place in 1866, 1890, and 1902 when Democrats were in control.

Once national Reconstruction ended, the Southern states were suddenly free to reconstruct themselves as they saw fit, which is exactly what happened in Mississippi. The Democratic Party, with a commitment to white supremacy as one of its central tenets, regained control of the state government. Former slaves were disenfranchised, white and black Republicans were banished from office, and the legislature passed laws segregating society. In addition, white Mississippians quickly began to reconstruct the record of the events that took place from 1861 to 1865. In doing so, they molded a new record to fit an ideal that never actually existed, in an attempt to dull the pain of a defeat that was very real.

Despite the end of the war, and the turbulence of the Reconstruction period, the mutual commitment between the men who had fought for the Confederacy and their communities remained intact. The veterans were no longer soldiers—most returned to their former lives as small farmers—but they were called upon again after Reconstruction to serve in a new capacity as living symbols of the virtues of the war effort. In 1861, the men had gone to war to protect a community ideal and in the years following the surrender their communities would battle to protect the soldiers' legacy, and the idea that their initial enthusiasm for the war was justified. As was the case in other parts of the South, it took little time for Mississippi communities to impress upon their veterans a collective identity as vanquished heroes. Regardless of their post-war activities, for the rest of their lives the men who had gone to war would be recognized first and foremost as Confederate veterans in a new, ongoing struggle fought with words and rituals instead of bullets.

As the South weathered the Reconstruction period, the seeds of Southern mythology regarding the collective service of the former Southern soldiers began to take root in the states of the Old Confederacy. Defeated militarily, the South in the decades following Reconstruction struggled to vindicate the ideals and decisions that had led it into the Civil War and cost so many men their lives. From the ashes of war, and the turbulence of the Reconstruction period, a cultural identity took shape grounded in ideas and attitudes referred to collectively as the Lost Cause. Celebrations of the Lost Cause took many forms: annual civil and religious services honoring the Confederate dead, veterans' reunions, the deification of Confederate military leaders, the erection of Confederate monuments, and the emergence of groups such as the United Confederate Veterans (UCV), United Sons of Confederate Veterans (SCV), and United Daughters of the Confederacy (UDC). Politicians on the stump used the language of the Lost Cause—language denoting moral superiority based on abstract notions of honor and chivalry—to garner votes, and ministers espoused Lost Cause virtues from the pulpit. Textbooks "educated" generations of Southern school children on the nature of the war as a noble struggle of principle, lost only in the face of superior Northern resources. For a century after the war the Lost Cause gave cultural authority to Confederate symbols, most prominently the so-called "stars and bars" rebel flag. As they entered the twentieth century, the states of the former Confederacy did their best to maintain this cultural identity by accenting the New South with many of the cosmetic trappings of an idealized Old South. From a practical standpoint, while salving the psychological wounds of defeat, such a course also helped maintain both white supremacy and the political dominance of the Democratic Party in the region.

Democratic politicians, over the span of the next few decades, would glorify and glamorize the prewar South, spinning tales of great mansions, endless cotton fields, and loyal, happy slaves. These revisionists never missed an opportunity to remind their white constituents that it was the Republican Party that sponsored the federal war effort that had left so many Southerners dead or maimed for life, and that during Reconstruction it was the party of Lincoln that sought to destroy the Southern "way of life" by placing the newly freed slaves on the same social level as the white population. Given the opportunity, they argued, the Republicans would do so again and therefore the white population in the South should always be on guard. It was precisely the same type of racially-charged rhetoric espoused by Democrats of the 1850s concerning abolitionists, but here it was placed in the context of the post-war, post-Reconstruction South.

The Lost Cause also spawned a number of veterans' groups, the most prominent being the United Confederate Veterans (UCV), founded in New Orleans in 1889. With chapters in all the states of the Old Confederacy and in hundreds of communities, the group served as a social outlet for veterans at the local level, particularly in rural areas, and institutionalized a host of Southern myths concerning the war. The UCV also published a monthly magazine, *Confederate Veteran*, between 1893 and 1932. At its peak just after the turn of the twentieth century, the organization boasted more than 47,000 active members and another 35,000 inactive members in 1,523 camps. The national organization gave a numerical designation to local chapters, but allowed their membership to designate the chapters with names of their choosing. In many cases members named their group after a Confederate general or former commanding officer that they admired. In 1896, at the behest of a number of UCV leaders, the Sons of Confederate Veterans (SCV) was formed so that the descendents of the rapidly-aging former soldiers could perpetuate the legacy and ideals associated with the Confederacy and the Lost Cause.

Local UCV chapters formed throughout Mississippi and veterans were quick to enroll. Depending on their location, these groups ranged in size from about 50 to 150 men, and usually included former soldiers from various commands. In Grenada, veterans named their chapter after William Barksdale, Mississippi's hero at Gettysburg, while Corinth's former Confederates called their group the Albert Sidney Johnston Chapter after the fallen commander at Shiloh. At Cedar Bluff, the veterans named their organization in honor of the fiery cavalry leader Nathan Bedford Forrest. In 1894, there were thirty-four chapters of the United Confederate Veterans in Mississippi and by the turn of the twentieth century that number had risen to almost eighty. While the national organization governed the UCV, the practical functions of the group took place on the local level. Just as Mississippi's volunteer companies had entered the war as community enterprises, the individual UCV chapters were sources of community pride. By 1900, the community sons that had fought in the war were community fathers and grandfathers, but the reverence that locals held for their service to the Confederacy never faded. Through their support of the veterans, and of the local veterans' groups, citizens in communities across the state paid homage to the Lost Cause in the post-war era in the same manner that they had supported the cause of 1861.

Another group that played a large role in perpetuating the Confederate ideal and the myths of the Lost Cause was the United Daughters of the Confederacy (UDC), founded in Nashville in 1894. Originally conceived as an auxiliary to the UCV, the UDC took its name from Varina Anne Davis, daughter of Jefferson Davis, who was referred to by some as the "Daughter of the Confederacy." The UDC was organized in much the same manner as the UCV and SCV, with state divisions and local chapters that were highly social in nature. The group also had its own auxiliary, the Children of the Confederacy, created to indoctrinate future generations of white Southerners into the cult of the Lost Cause. Mississippi's first chapter of the United Daughters of the Confederacy was chartered in Meridian and named for Varina Anne Davis. On April 27, 1897, the Mississippi division of the UDC was created, including the Meridian group and chapters in Columbus, Okolona, Greenville, and Vicksburg, and soon other chapters formed throughout the state. As with the UCV, the practical functions of the UDC took place at the local level as the organization helped organize reunions, raise memorials, and recognize the achievements of the Confederacy and Confederate veterans. In most communities, the United Daughters of the Confederacy was the most important social organization for women just as the United Confederate Veterans, and later the Sons of Confederate Veterans, were the most important organizations for men.

While community support for the former Confederate soldiers took many forms, its most public manifestation involved annual gatherings of the surviving veterans, their families, and their friends. Reunions of surviving Confederate veterans became a sacred ritual in the post-war South. The national or state organizations of the United Confederate Veterans sponsored many, but most were community events sponsored by local UCV chapters or other civic groups. Not long after the war's conclusion, many of Mississippi's surviving veterans began holding informal regimental reunions, and later more organized events after they established their local UCV chapters. The reunions were well attended by both the ex-soldiers and the community at large, and were usually marked by speeches from prominent veterans and local politicians. More importantly, they also served as a primary venue for the communal celebration of the Lost Cause, and for the men to pay homage to the war itself as the central event of their lives.

In 1908, Columbus hosted a typical local reunion for the veterans of Lowndes County complete with a feast of Brunswick stew and barbecue and a band that played the standards of the day. Hundreds of veterans and spectators gathered to enjoy the daylong festivities, as one participant recorded in the flowery language of the period for publication in *Confederate Veteran*:

> There was a fine orchestra present, and with song and music the day passed delightfully.... A memorial service was held to honor those veterans who died during the past year, and a committee was appointed to draft resolutions to their memory—some of the most gallant men that represented Lowndes County in the great internecine struggle.... At twelve o'clock dinner was served, and a sumptuous repast it was, too. The veterans and their friends were first served with Brunswick stew, which was faultlessly prepared, followed by a meat course, and in the barbecued meat the same degree of perfection was obtained. Fragrant coffee accompanied the meat, the whole making a repast fit for a king. After the dinner was over the speech making commenced, and short addresses by several veterans.... A graceful compliment to the Confederate veterans on the occasion of their annual barbecue was bestowed by the Columbus Railway, Light, and Power Company in providing for them free transportation to Washington Park.[1]

In addition to local gatherings, the Mississippi division of the UCV also held more elaborate statewide reunions well into the twentieth century. In 1910 a crowd that included more than 600 aging veterans gathered at Vicksburg, where "the city, for the second time in its history, made a complete surrender, this time in hospitable welcome to the grizzled soldiers, many of whom had fought bravely in the memorable siege." Edmund Noel, Mississippi's governor and himself a Spanish-American War veteran, gave a lengthy address celebrating the former Confederates, as did several other dignitaries. After a grand meal at the Carroll Hotel downtown, the veterans climbed into automobiles for a trip around the old siege lines. Three years later the state reunion was held at Greenwood where, according to one observer, "the spirit of patriotism was manifest in everything done." The Greenwood meeting included about 500 veterans along with their friends and family. In the afternoon, those in attendance

---

[1] "Reunion at Columbus, Miss.," *Confederate Veteran* 16/10 (October 1908): 491.

were well fed and that evening most attended a reception on the courthouse square sponsored by local chapters of the UDC. Because the veterans were old men who in some instances found it difficult to get around, dozens of volunteers manned automobiles to carry the honorees from one place to another. According to one correspondent, "Greenwood never looked better.... Automobiles await on every corner; the tramp, tramp, tramp is never seen, and the old soldiers are gleaming with appreciation." In 1926, John L. Collins, at the time one of Mississippi's few remaining veterans, attended the state UCV reunion held at Corinth. After speeches and a parade, he and other former Confederates were taken by automobile 20 miles north to the Shiloh battlefield. Still firm in the belief that the Civil War was linked to the South's revolutionary heritage, Collins later reported that as he toured the grounds he "saw the spot where so many of [Mississippi's] distinguished citizens fell as martyrs to the cause of the South—even martyrs as our brave sires who fell in '76 for American independence."[2]

By the time the generation of Southern males that had fought the war began passing from the scene, their exploits as Confederate soldiers had already entered the realm of legend. In the South every veteran, regardless of rank, became a larger than life hero and every battle—large or small, won or lost—drew comparisons with the great battles of history. As the old soldiers disappeared, the communities in which they lived, and particularly the UDC, made efforts to preserve their memory forever. At hundreds of sites throughout the states of the Old Confederacy, recognition of the veterans took the form of some type of statue or monument bearing appropriate names and inscriptions. The unveilings of these Confederate monuments were central rituals in the celebration of the Lost Cause. They were usually conducted as part of a grand ceremony with patriotic

---

[2] "Veterans at Vicksburg," *Confederate Veteran* 18/1 (January 1910): 25; "Mississippi Veterans at Greenwood," *Confederate Veteran* 21/11 (November 1913): 516; "Reunion of Mississippi Comrades," *Confederate Veteran* 34/11 (November 1926): 424–25.

speeches and emotional appeals reminiscent of the flag presentation ceremonies that had sent so many young men off to war in 1861.

Mississippi's first Confederate monuments appeared in Amite County at Liberty and in Marshall County at Holly Springs in 1871.Eventually more than sixty Mississippi counties recognized their Confederate veterans with monuments on courthouse squares and in special sections of cemeteries dedicated to the Confederate dead. More often than not, local chapters of the UDC and SCV were in charge of raising funds for these projects, which could be a difficult task in a state where few citizens had significant disposable income. Some monuments were relatively simple while others were elaborately carved depending on the monies available. On June 3, 1909, large crowds lined the streets of Greenville in Washington County for a typical unveiling ceremony preceded by "a long parade of Veterans, sons of Veterans, school children, carriages containing the UDC and floats on which were young ladies representing the different Confederate states." Built using stone quarried from Kennesaw Mountain, Georgia, the Greenville monument was larger than most. It had a 10-foot base and a height of more than 37 feet with a hand-carved figure of a Confederate soldier at the top. The Columbus (Mississippi) Marble Works, which was ultimately responsible for many of the state's Confederate monuments, built the Greenville tribute at a total cost of around $4,000 (approximately $85,000 in today's money).[3]

The largest and most significant monument dedication in Mississippi took place at the capital in Jackson on June 3, 1891, when the state unveiled its massive tribute to all of Mississippi's Confederate soldiers and sailors. More than 20, 000 people from all over the state attended the celebration. "They have been coming slowly but steadily for a week," one observer wrote of the crowd, "They came upon horseback, in carriages, buggies and on foot. Excursion trains arrived on all the railroads from all directions. Each train was a long one, and was packed and jammed." Those in attendance witnessed the prerequisite parade that included veterans,

---

[3] "Greenville (Miss.) Monument," *Confederate Veteran* 18/2 (February 1910): 68.

officers from the UDC and SCV, members of the state's political elite, and floats depicting various scenes evoking an idealized Confederacy. After the parade, the crowd assembled near the state capitol building where they listened to testimonials and political speeches. United States senator and former Confederate general Edward Carey Walthall gave the keynote address after which Jefferson Hayes Davis, grandson of the former Confederate president, lifted the veil from the great obelisk. Funded through private donations and an appropriation from the state legislature, the monument stood more than 60 feet tall. It had a large marble vault at its base and was crowned by a granite likeness of a common soldier. On top of the vault stood a life-size statue of Jefferson Davis, Mississippi's most notable Confederate son. "A generation has well nigh come and gone since this open tribute was due," Walthall told the crowd during a speech that summed up the essence of the Lost Cause creed, "and its payment is now proof that we act upon no transit impulse, but a strong and stable sentiment which has endured and *will* endure."[4]

By far the most active of the Confederate heritage groups in the twentieth century was the UDC. In addition to leading the charge to raise funds for monuments, local chapters were instrumental in founding another central ritual of the Lost Cause when they promoted annual celebrations paying homage to the Confederate dead. One of the first "Decoration Day" celebrations in Mississippi (and in the United States) took place in April 1866, one year after the final surrender, at Friendship Cemetery in Columbus. It was a simple ceremony. Four local UDC members brought fresh flowers to the burial ground to decorate the graves of Confederate soldiers, many of whom were casualties brought to Columbus by rail following the Battle of Shiloh. After decorating the graves of the former Confederates, the women also placed flowers on the graves of the few Union soldiers buried in the cemetery. The fact that the women decorated both Confederate and Union graves was reported widely in

---

[4] "Confederate Soldiers' Day," *Jackson* (MS) *Daily Clarion Ledger*, June 3, 1891, 1–2.

newspapers and taken as a symbolic sign of sectional healing. Even in New York, Horace Greeley's *New York Herald Tribune* ran a brief account of the event. Other towns in both the North and the South held similar ceremonies at around the same time and collectively these were said to inspire the national Decoration Day that evolved into the Memorial Day holiday that we recognize today.

While Confederate heritage organizations sponsored reunions and helped erect monuments, they also undertook projects that would have deeper, more long-range effects on the South. Paramount among these was the promotion of histories written from a distinctly "Southern" perspective. Writing—or in most cases rewriting—the history of the Civil War was an important component of the Lost Cause with the "Southern" version of the years 1861–1865 serving as a foundation on which Lost Cause ideology rested. Southern histories of the war were based on a number of premises, all of which were designed to salve the wounds of defeat and, in fact, turn the concept of Confederate defeat into a virtue, a moral victory of sorts. From an emotional or psychological standpoint, this is understandable. If white Southerners of the late nineteenth and twentieth centuries could not rationalize positive reasons that their fathers and grandfathers had gone to war in 1861, as well as a positive version of the war's outcome, they would be forced to face two grim realities. First, their ancestors had taken up arms against the land of their birth, an act that certainly meets most definitions of treason. In addition, because the Confederacy failed to accomplish its military objectives, and from a political standpoint the Southern nation no longer existed, the soldiers who had fought for the South and lost their lives had indeed died in vain. White Southerners were naturally quick to latch on to any "history" of the war that portrayed their ancestors and the entire Confederate experience in a nobler light.

Most Confederate histories followed the same general formula. First, they discounted the institution of slavery and its racial implications as having been a cause of the war. The conflict, they said, was a struggle over the higher concept of states' rights. For those writing Confederate history the fact that slaveholding was the

primary "states' right" discussed during the years leading up to the
war was merely a coincidence, as was the fact that only slaveholding
states were members of the Confederacy. They also argued that
Southern slaves were well taken care of, happy, docile, and content to
be slaves before "outside influences" led them astray. Second,
Southern histories made it plain that the Confederacy was fighting
on the side of right, and that the Southerners were forced to
surrender only because of superior Northern resources. Third, all
Confederate soldiers were heroic characters regardless of rank or the
battles in which they took part. Desertion and courts martial in the
Confederate military was rarely if ever mentioned and strategic
errors by Southern commanders were usually overlooked, even those
that caused massive loss of life. In contrast, Northern officers and the
men under their command were many times shown in a negative
light. Finally, Southern histories universally claimed that
Reconstruction was a harsh period during which ruthless Yankees
took advantage of the South's defeat to pad their own pockets and
manipulate the black population with the help of a few unscrupulous
white Southern natives. Again, writers promoting this line of
thinking tended to ignore the fact that had Reconstruction actually
been harsh, Southern leaders like Jefferson Davis and Robert E. Lee
might have been executed for treason and segregation would have
never become the law throughout the South.

The UCV, UDC, and SCV were especially eager to "educate"
Southern school children to have proper reverence for their
Confederate heritage. "We are doing much," one of the founders of
the Mississippi division of the UDC wrote in 1901, "to cancel false
impressions made upon younger generations by Northern versions of
our history, and trust that soon these untruthful and unjust records
will be replaced." Mississippi took a leading role in scrutinizing state
textbooks to make sure that only those books containing the
"correct" version of events found their way into the state's
classrooms. In September 1920, the national leadership of the UCV

lauded Mississippi's efforts "in adopting histories from which the young will be taught the truths of Confederate history."[5]

The most glaring example of Confederate revisionism dealt with the historical record of the Ku Klux Klan. Dedicated to white supremacy, the Klan used violence, murder, and other forms of intimidation to terrorize black and white Republicans during the Reconstruction period. By the turn of the century, however, many white writers in the South promoted the lawless Klansmen as heroes rather than criminals. In 1913, Mrs. S. E. F. Rose, president of the Mississippi division of the UDC, authored a booklet on the history of the "famous and mysterious" Ku Klux Klan that the UDC sold as a fundraiser. As with many other Southern accounts of the Civil War and Reconstruction eras, the work was an exercise in fabrication and rehabilitation. Mrs. Rose concluded in no uncertain terms that the Ku Klux Klan was a noble group dedicated to "patriotism, justice, protection, preservation of real law and good government, and the establishment of white supremacy forever." According to *Confederate Veteran*, where the book was advertised, the history was "in suitable form for school study, and [Mrs. Rose] will endeavor to secure its adoption as a supplementary reader in schools, thus bringing the true history of this great organization direct to the young people of the Southland." For decades all textbooks accepted by the state for distribution in the public schools portrayed the Klan in a positive light. Pearl Vivian Guyton, in *Our Mississippi*, published in 1952, wrote that "the purpose of the Klan was to protect the weak, innocent, and defenseless people, especially the widows and orphans of Confederate soldiers." She went on to praise "the Ku Klux Klan and other patriotic organizations" for helping restore political power into "the hands of responsible citizens." Not until the 1970s would a textbook appear in Mississippi that was not clouded by Confederate myth, and then only after a legal battle. The Mississippi Textbook

---

[5] Mrs. Albert G. Weems, "Work of the Daughters of the Confederacy," in *Publications of the Mississippi Historical Society*, 4 vols. (Oxford: Mississippi Historical Society, 1901) 73–74; "Mississippi Veterans at Greenwood," *Confederate Veteran* 21/11 (November 1913): 518.

Commission tried to keep a 1974 book, *Mississippi: Conflict and Change*, edited by James W. Loewen and Charles Sallis, off the list of acceptable state histories because it included what some commission members believe was too much information about past racial conflict in the state. The courts decided the matter and the book was eventually accepted.[6]

In the post-war South, the Lost Cause also represented a significant political force. Democratic leaders were quick to realize that veterans who were perceived as heroes in their communities also made good candidates for office. After Reconstruction, Lost Cause imagery and rhetoric helped Confederate veterans win state and local offices throughout the former Confederacy. In post-Reconstruction Mississippi, former Confederate officers held most of the state's highest offices for years and veterans filled many local offices such as sheriff, chancery clerk, or mayor. No politician could expect to be successful if he was not affiliated with the UCV and no campaign was complete without newspaper articles and flyers that included accounts of the candidates' service to the South. After the Confederate generation began to disappear around the turn of the twentieth century, politicians continued to practice their trade in the shadow of the Civil War. Candidates could not win an election without the backing of the UDC and SCV and office seekers routinely passed out Confederate flags at political rallies.

Despite their status as aging symbols of an idealized Confederate heritage, most of Mississippi's veterans lived out quiet lives, struggling to make a living on their farms in the beleaguered, post-war South. Throughout their lifetimes, Mississippi remained one of the nation's poorest states with small farmers, both white and black, occupying the lower rungs of the economic ladder. While their status as veterans established the men's reputations in their communities, it could not feed their families. The former soldiers took part in periodic celebrations of their service, but for most their day-to-day

---

[6] "Ku Klux Clan and 'The Birth of a Nation,'" *Confederate Veteran* 24/4 (April 1916): 157–59; Pearl Vivian Guyton, *Our Mississippi* (Austin TX: Steck Company, 1952) 218–20, 229.

existence remained tied to the land and to the elements. Upon returning from the war, they also settled back into their communities' traditional social hierarchies, which paralleled those of the antebellum period. Generally, among the veterans, wartime rank translated into post-war status. Veterans who were community leaders during the post-war era were usually former officers. They held most public offices, were leaders in their local UCV chapters, and they took part in what little commercial enterprise was available. Conversely, most of the enlisted men, the common foot soldiers, returned to their lives as part of their state's struggling majority of small farmers.

While the state of Mississippi lauded the service of its veterans in the post-Reconstruction era, it did little in terms of offering economic relief to those "faithful adherents of the Lost Cause" who were in need. In 1888, the state established a pension fund to aid veterans who were "incapacitated for manual labor by a wound received in [Confederate] service," and for their widows and servants who met certain qualifications. The pensions were meager to say the least, providing those who qualified with $17.85 (approximately $366 in current money) annually. The state legislature periodically amended the pension law and by 1920, after most of Mississippi's veterans had passed away, yearly pensions had risen to a maximum of $200 (approximately $1900 in current money) depending on the circumstance. While the 1920 pension law provided a stipend for all soldiers "who were honorably discharged, or paroled, or did not desert the Confederate service," only those veterans or their widows owning less than $3000 in personal and real property qualified. For servants the limit on personal and real property was $2,500.[7]

The funeral service for a Confederate veteran was one of the most hallowed Lost Cause rituals of the post-war South, providing in

---

[7] Mississippi, *Laws of the State of Mississippi, Passed at a Regular Session of the Mississippi Legislature, Held in the City of Jackson, Commencing Jan'y 3, 1888, and Ending March 8, 1888* (Jackson MS: R.H. Henry State Printers, 1888) 30–31; Mississippi, *Laws of the State of Mississippi, Passed at a Regular Session of the Mississippi Legislature, Held in the City of Jackson, Commencing January 6, 1920, and Ending April 3, 1920* (Jackson MS: Tucker Printing House, 1920) 372–75.

the minds of many further vindication of the lofty ideals that led the antebellum South into the war. Regardless of their status, the death of a former soldier in Mississippi was recognized with a hero's funeral in his community. Fellow veterans, many times in their tattered Confederate uniforms, usually served as pallbearers or as honorary pallbearers and offered eulogies that praised the service of their deceased comrade. Such tributes extended to obituaries in local newspapers, or in the *Confederate Veteran*, the national organ of the UCV.

As in the rest of society, the more prominent the veteran, the greater the tributes after his death, with former officers, and particularly former generals, receiving the greatest accolades. In 1898, former Major General Edward C. Walthall died in Washington DC, after a long illness. Walthall was by far the most famous of Mississippi's Confederate generals to survive the war. He led troops during some of the conflict's bloodiest engagements including Chickamauga, the Atlanta Campaign, and Franklin, Tennessee. After the war, Walthall returned to Mississippi where he practiced law and became heavily involved in politics, finally ascending to a seat in the United States Senate. After Walthall's death, and a funeral service in Washington, his body was brought back to Mississippi by train for burial in his hometown of Holly Springs. The depot was crowded as the funeral train pulled into town, as was the church where another service was held. Finally, Walthall's body was taken to the local cemetery, trailed by a throng that included hundreds of aging veterans who had once been under the general's command. It was the largest funeral that Holly Springs had ever witnessed, and the occasion was dutifully reported by the state's largest newspaper in Jackson:

> Before the arrival of the train several hundred old Confederate soldiers who had followed General Walthall during the Civil War and about the entire population of Holly Springs had assembled at the depot to pay a sad duty to their departed friend. From the time the body was placed in the church till its removal a steady stream of people passed through to look for the last time upon the face of him who was so highly beloved—the man against whom no

unkind word had ever been spoken—the popular idol of the people of Mississippi.[8]

If Walthall was the most famous Confederate officer from Mississippi to return from the war, Jefferson Davis was certainly the most famous person from the state who was associated with the conflict. His unique status as the Confederacy's only president gave him a special place in American history as well as in the history of his state. After his capture in 1865, Davis was indicted for treason but never brought to trial. While federal authorities held him for two years, they eventually dropped all charges and set the former Confederate president free. Davis participated in a number of unsuccessful business ventures that left him perpetually strapped for funds. In 1877, he accepted the invitation of a wealthy widow and admirer, Mrs. Sarah Dorsey, to take up residence in a small cottage on the property of her estate, *Beauvoir*, near Biloxi, Mississippi, on the Gulf Coast. Mrs. Dorsey offered the cottage rent-free but Davis insisted on paying her a small rent. There he began writing his massive two-volume Civil War history *The Rise and Fall of the Confederate Government* with the help of Mrs. Dorsey, who took his dictations, and his assistant W. T Walthall, whose skills as a researcher and writer ultimately came into question. Because she was somewhat jealous of Mrs. Dorsey, Davis's wife Varina initially would not live on the Gulf Coast, choosing instead to move in with her daughter's family in Memphis. She eventually changed her mind and came to *Beauvoir*, where she also helped her husband with his writing. Mrs. Dorsey died in 1879 and left the property to Davis, after which he and Varina moved from the cottage into the larger house on the estate. Jefferson Davis lived out his final years on the Gulf Coast, defending the Lost Cause and his role in the Confederate experience until the very end. He fell ill and died while on a visit to New Orleans on December 6, 1889. After a huge funeral, he was laid to rest temporarily in Metairie Cemetery in New Orleans, but four

---

[8] "Funeral for E. C. Walthall," *Jackson* (MS) *Daily Clarion Ledger*, April 25, 1898, 1.

years later his remains were reburied at Hollywood Cemetery in Richmond, Virginia, near other prominent Confederates.

In 1902, Varina Davis sold *Beauvoir* to the Mississippi division of the United Sons of Confederate Veterans, attaching two stipulations to the sale. Mrs. Davis insisted that the group preserve the estate as a shrine to her husband's memory and also maintain the site as a home for aging Confederate veterans. The state of Mississippi eventually constructed twelve barracks there for housing some of the state's veterans, their wives, and their widows with a maximum capacity of 288 residents. On December 2, 1903, J. R. Climer of Madison County became the first veteran admitted and from that point until 1957 the home cared for around 2,000 residents. Smith County veteran James A. Thrasher, who died in 1951 at the age of 100, was the last Confederate veteran to live at *Beauvoir*, and two Confederate widows, Mollie Lavinia Bailey of Rosedale and Mollie Cottle of Rolling Fork were the home's last residents. Almost 800 Confederate veterans and their wives were buried in a cemetery maintained on the property.

In the modern era, the *Beauvoir* property is probably Mississippi's greatest shrine to the complexities and contradictions of the Lost Cause. While the state's battlefields, especially Vicksburg and Corinth, draw thousands of visitors each year who are interested in the Civil War, Jefferson Davis' former home is a monument to a different type of struggle. The actual house in which Davis lived out his final years is open to the public as a tribute to his place as an important figure in American history, but the grounds also include another large building. Through the efforts of the Mississippi Sons of Confederate Veterans, and with a great deal of state funding, the 13,500-square-foot Jefferson Davis Presidential Library opened in 1998, and the fact that it even exists represents a Confederate past that has never been able to reconcile with the American present. The building contains a great deal of Davis memorabilia and could have easily been called the Jefferson Davis Museum, but those behind its construction and operation instead chose another name. Their stated purpose was to create a library "comparable to other existing presidential libraries." They chose to call the structure a "Presidential Library" in an effort to legitimize Davis's role as president of the

Confederacy by comparing his legacy to the legacies of former presidents of the United States. In truth, while the so-called presidential library on the Gulf Coast is certainly an impressive building that houses legitimate historical papers and artifacts, its name is merely a façade, a uniquely Southern attempt to have it both ways. Existing presidential libraries in America were built to honor past presidents of the United States, an existing nation that continues to thrive. Davis, on the other hand, was president of a short-lived political entity that was barely a nation even at its height, a political entity whose primary aim was to break the United States apart. Herein lies the great irony, and the great flaw in Lost Cause ideology. No matter how many monuments are built, no matter how many buildings are named, no matter how many "Southern" histories are written, no matter how many parades are held or graves decorated in the South, it is impossible to change the outcome of the Civil War. While paying homage to the individual Confederate soldier, whose willingness to face hostile fire or charge impregnable positions during the war certainly meets the definition of heroism, is a legitimate form of celebrating heritage, revering the political Confederacy is a suspect practice at best. The Confederacy and the twin pillars of secession and slavery on which its government was founded were discredited by defeat. If imitation is indeed the sincerest form of flattery, then calling the Davis shrine a "Presidential Library" pays great homage to the United States of Lincoln, Grant, and Sherman, the political entity whose armies crushed the Confederacy, saved the Union, and ended Davis's political career.[9]

On April 17, 2001, Mississippians went to the polls to vote in an unusual—and highly controversial—election that concerned the adoption of an official flag for the state. Voters had two choices. One was the existing state standard that prominently displayed the "stars and bars" Confederate battle flag in its upper left corner. The other

---

[9] In 2005, Beauvoir, the former home of Jefferson Davis, and the Jefferson Davis Presidential Library were heavily damaged by Hurricane Katrina. Both structures survived and currently (2006) are being repaired and restored.

was a similar banner that included a circular grouping of stars in place of the Confederate emblem. In a vote that was primarily, but not exclusively, along racial lines, Mississippians cast ballots by a margin of two to one to keep the existing flag in place. Some claimed that the election's outcome was a victory for heritage while others called it a triumph for hate. After the election, Mississippi found itself the only state in the Union to prominently include the controversial Confederate battle flag as part of its official state flag design. As a result, the Confederate battle flag continued to fly over Mississippi's public buildings more than 130 years after the Confederacy ceased to exist.

For months prior to the referendum on the flag, tempers flared around the state as citizens discussed among themselves and at a series of public meetings the propriety of Confederate imagery. While many of the state's residents who were interested in the subject discussed it intelligently, angry fringe elements also emerged to promote their own agendas and their own slanted, often irrational, definitions of heritage, hate, and history. Race was an overriding part of their arguments as they opened old wounds and tried to appeal to the lowest common denominators of the human existence. "It's the worst thing I've ever dealt with," one state legislator lamented after the issue was decided. "I've been cussed. One fellow called and said he was going to have me knocked off. We saw a dark side of personalities on both extremes."[10] The issue was one of the most divisive that Mississippi faced since the Civil Rights era and few in the state's mainstream, black or white, were sad to see the election finally come and go. Events surrounding the election garnered a great deal of negative national publicity for the state, but in reality the outcome was not surprising. In fact, it was predictable. When Mississippi's electorate voted to keep the Confederate battle flag flying over their state they simply confirmed the words of acclaimed Mississippi novelist William Faulkner, himself the descendant of a

---

[10] Quoted in John M. Coski, *The Confederate Battle Flag: America's Most Embattled Emblem* (Cambridge MA: Belknap Press of Harvard University Press, 2005) 265.

Confederate officer. "The past is never dead," Faulkner once wrote. "It's not even past."

Appendix

The Cause

In January 1861, the Mississippi Secession Convention passed an ordinance of secession that took the state out of the Union. In addition to the ordinance itself, the convention published a document outlining the delegates' specific reasons for voting in favor of radical action. Alexander M. Clayton drew up the document, which left little doubt as to what motivated Mississippi to sever its ties with the United States. While advocates of secession often used the term "state's rights" in association with their cause, the convention's official explanation outlined in no uncertain terms the fact that the protection of the institution of slavery was at the heart of the matter.

A Declaration of the Immediate Causes Which Induce and Justify the Secession of the State of Mississippi from the Federal Union, 1861

In the momentous step which our State has taken of dissolving its connection with the government of which we so long formed a part, it is but just that we should declare the prominent reasons which have induced our course.

Our position is thoroughly identified with the institution of slavery—the greatest material interest of the world. Its labor supplies the product which constitutes by far the largest and most important portions of commerce of the earth. These products are peculiar to the climate verging on the tropical regions, and by an imperious law of nature, none but the black race can bear exposure to the tropical sun. These products have become necessities of the world, and a blow at slavery is a blow at commerce and civilization. That blow has been long aimed at the institution, and was at the point of reaching its consummation. There was no choice left us but submission to the mandates of abolition, or a dissolution of the Union, whose principles had been subverted to work out our ruin.

That we do not overstate the dangers to our institution, a reference to a few facts will sufficiently prove.

The hostility to this institution commenced before the adoption of the Constitution, and was manifested in the well-known Ordinance of 1787, in regard to the Northwestern Territory.

The feeling increased, until, in 1819-20, it deprived the South of more than half the vast territory acquired from France.

The same hostility dismembered Texas and seized upon all the territory acquired from Mexico.

It has grown until it denies the right of property in slaves, and refuses protection to that right on the high seas, in the Territories, and wherever the government of the United States had jurisdiction.

It refuses the admission of new slave States into the Union, and seeks to extinguish it by confining it within its present limits, denying the power of expansion.

It tramples the original equality of the South under foot.

It has nullified the Fugitive Slave Law in almost every free State in the Union, and has utterly broken the compact which our fathers pledged their faith to maintain.

It advocates negro equality, socially and politically, and promotes insurrection and incendiarism in our midst.

It has enlisted its press, its pulpit and its schools against us, until the whole popular mind of the North is excited and inflamed with prejudice.

It has made combinations and formed associations to carry out its schemes of emancipation in the States and wherever else slavery exists.

It seeks not to elevate or to support the slave, but to destroy his present condition without providing a better.

It has invaded a State, and invested with the honors of martyrdom the wretch whose purpose was to apply flames to our dwellings, and the weapons of destruction to our lives.

It has broken every compact into which it has entered for our security.

It has given indubitable evidence of its design to ruin our agriculture, to prostrate our industrial pursuits and to destroy our social system.

It knows no relenting or hesitation in its purposes; it stops not in its march of aggression, and leaves us no room to hope for cessation or for pause.

It has recently obtained control of the Government, by the prosecution of its unhallowed schemes, and destroyed the last expectation of living together in friendship and brotherhood.

Utter subjugation awaits us in the Union, if we should consent longer to remain in it. It is not a matter of choice, but of necessity. We must either submit to degradation, and to the loss of property worth four billions of money, or we must secede from the Union framed by our fathers, to secure this as well as every other species of property. For far less cause than this, our fathers separated from the Crown of England.

Our decision is made. We follow their footsteps. We embrace the alternative of separation; and for the reasons here stated, we resolve to maintain our rights with the full consciousness of the justice of our course, and the undoubting belief of our ability to maintain it.[1]

---

[1] Mississippi Commission on the War Between the States, *Journal of the State Convention and Ordinances and Resolutions Adopted in 1861*, 86.

Augustus Hervey Mecklin at Shiloh, 1862

In spring 1861, enthusiasm for the Confederate cause ran high and thousands of Mississippians volunteered to fight for their state. Among them was twenty-six-year-old Augustus Hervey Mecklin of Choctaw County. Mecklin enrolled as a private in a local company that eventually entered Confederate service as part of the 15th Mississippi Infantry. Like many other Mississippi soldiers in the western theater of the war, Mecklin saw his first major combat on April 6 and 7, 1862, at the Battle of Shiloh on the Tennessee River. He kept a journal that included a detailed record of his actions and observations during the exceedingly bloody two-day struggle. Though he and his fellow Southerners were ultimately driven from the field and forced to retreat, Mecklin ends his journal entry for the battle's second day with claims of a Confederate victory. Regardless of his questionable interpretation of the struggle's final outcome, Mecklin's account of the Battle of Shiloh represented a young Mississippians first realization of the true horrors of war.

Battlefields on the Tenn. River Sun. [April] 6 1862

No day of my life has been so full of stirring terrible events as this. Never may I see such another. Even now my mind is agitated & as I think of what I have seen this day visions dark & bloody float before my eyes & sounds of death & suffering fill my eyes. After marching a short distance, we halted to rest. We were standing & sitting in this position when the sound of musketing was heard just in front of us. Judging from the frequent peals that it was the enemy, we tried our guns to ascertain if all was clear then loaded. We had gone but a short distance when we were ordered into line of battle.

I thought of the hundreds, perhaps thousands that this day must pass into eternity. I thought of the many widows & of those that must this day be made. I thought of weeping mothers & sisters...of lovers & minds. I thought of my own liability to fall a victim, —perhaps in one more hour—then came up the momentous questions. Am I prepared[?] As often in my past history as I have made this inquiry of my heart, never before I think did I so honestly seek to know the truth. As often as I have endeavored to look into the unknown future, never before did I gaze so earnestly mentally into that dark unknown world & seek to the position I must occupy there. At this moment I trust I made a sincere, honest surrender of myself to God, the maker, the preserver of my life. I told him my desire to live, if by so doing, I might honor his name & benefit my fellow creatures. I trust I was honest in this. I asked for life if that might be a useful one. Let me remember this in future years.

Shortly after we loaded our pieces we ascertained that the heavy firing in front was not a collision with the enemy, but the men of Gen. Breckenridge firing their guns to dry them. From the formation of our men into line of battle until we entered the battle in good earnest, we went through a series of movements, whose object I am unable to explain & where made I cannot now tell. Our brigade under command of Genl. Statham was composed of our Reg. with those of Col. Shellier's 22d Miss., Col. Bottle's 45th Tenn., Col. Cummings', & Col Mitchel's. Sometimes we would advance in columns of attack. Then we would march by the right flank Sometimes our move was to the right & sometimes to the left, but always forward.

From early in the morning the battle had been raging. In front of us we heard a continual roar of musketry & far above this, the deep mouthed cannon uttered uproarous thunder. Word was brought us occasionally that our men were successful in every move. That the enemy were driven & that their camps were in our possession. Our men answered these favorable reports by loud cheers, our movements became more brisk & our officers more excited. It was evident from all these indications that we were near the scene of action & must soon be into it. Our muskets were thrown aside & a guard placed over them. Just at this juncture while making a rapid march at double quick one of our Liets was shot through the hand accidentally by his own pistol & just at the same moment almost, our adjutant, the Lieut's Bro., was stabbed accidentally in the thigh. With a bayonet.

Resting for some time we went on towards the firing. We passed several wounded men & occasionally squads of wounded men & occasionally squads of wounded yankees. Soon we were on the battlefield. Here & there we saw the bodies of dead men — friends & foes lying together. Some torn to mince meat by cannon balls. Some still writhing in the agonies of death. We halted for a short time near where a poor fellow was lying leaning against a tree severely wounded. The cannon appeared to be carrying on this contest wholly among themselves. Though at some distance from us. Some of the balls reached us & while we were halted one struck a tree nearly a foot through & splitting it a sunder tore a poor fellow who was behind it into a thousand pieces. We moved on. The trees were spotted with bullet holes. Many branches & tree tops not budding into the tender leaf of spring. bowed [sic] their heads, torn partly from the forest stem by the balls of both sides.

It was very warm. The sky was clear and but for the horrible monster death who now pile high carnival, this might have been such a Sabbath morn as would have called pleasant recollections of Sabbath bells & religious enjoyment. Again we halted near the evening camp in a long level open field apparently used by them for a drill ground. There had been a hot contest; on all sides lay the dead & dying. Before us were the rifle pits dug by the Yankees, behind them lay the camp. The sight was beautiful, viewed aside from the scenes of blood that now surrounded it. The country was level. The trees were budding into the first leaf of spring.

While resting here, Genl. Beauregard, as I suppose, came charging by. Our men greeted his appearance with deafening cheer. We were not allowed to rest long, but filing to the right we hastened on. We passed another camp & halted in the woods. We advanced from this position in line of battle. Far to the right we heard heavy firing. All was still just before us & had been the greater part of the morning. We ascended a hill & beyond it lay another encampment of the enemy & a line of men. We knew not whether they were friends or foes. Orders came to advance. We were worried that they were our friends. No sooner were we near them than orders came to advance rapidly to the assistance of our men on the left where there was a heavy firing & where we afterwards learned, there was a heavy force of the enemy. This was about the center of their lines. We advanced rapidly to the point designated & taking our position on the left of the encampments were no sooner ascended the bow of the hill than we were saluted with a violent volley from the enemy.

For the first time in my life, I heard the whistle of bullets. We took shelter behind the tents & some wagons & a pile of corn & returned the fire of the enemy with spirit. The bullets whistle around my ear. I was near the front & firing. lay [sic] down to load soon men were falling on all sides. Two in Co. E just in front of me fell dead shot through the brain. On my left in our own Co., W. Wilson, W. Thompson & Ben. Stewart. Bro. Geo. & James Boskins were wounded. I fired until my gun got so foul that I could not get my ball down. Taking a short stick that lay near, I drove the ball down. Again the tube became filled up & not being able to get it off, I called to one of Co. E. to throw me the gun of a wounded man by him. I fired this until the tube became filled. Throwing it down I went to the rear & picking up my gun held on until the battle was over.

We had fired but a few more rounds when we were ordered to cease firing & fall back. We did so & formed under cover of the hill. Some ordered to charge bayonet. We rushed forward. The enemy had fallen back & taken a position opposite their battery. We had some distance to go. We ran forwards as rapidly as we could. But being nearly exhausted we were unable to make but little speed. The mini balls were falling thickly around us. Capt. Aldridge fell & Capt. Gage, Maj. Brantley was wounded in the hand. We fired upon the enemy at a distance of 100 yds. & fell back to a deep valley. Many of our boys fell in this fatal charge. Never was such firing. Taking shelter in the deep recess we were sheltered from the balls & bombs of the enemy. Our men were nearly exhausted for want of water. The dead of the enemy lay thickly... Our boys rushed to the water with their cups and drank deeply. If the water had been mixed with blood it would have been all the same. We were out of ammunition. We sent for some. We lay here some time The enemy appeared to be aware of our stopping there. They fired upon us and their bombs. No one was hurt seriously. A shell struck a rock & it struck me on the back. The blow was slight & I did not long feel it. We lay here a long time until completely rested.

Then we fell back to the right of the encampment that we just occupied when our Brigade was into action. Here we halted & formed & counted off, & lay down to rest. While here, we were shelled severely by one of the enemy's gun boats. But they were mistaken in our position & the shells all passed over us. Here we lay for some time, soon orders came to push forward & assist Leut. Jackson. We did so pushing thro the woods in line of battle until we came to a small field on the right of which a small squad of our men were sheltered. In front was heavy firing. I expected again to be into it. But before we reached the place, the enemy driven from this position & we charged up on the fragments of their forces. A few scattered prisoners were taken. Here we came in sight of the enemy's camp. We charged down a declivity & led on by Col. S—we rushed through the camp. Here a Reg. had stacked their arms. We went but a little distance beyond there when we were halted.

No demonstration was made by either side for some time. Our cannon we sent forward to feel the disposition of the enemy. After firing several rounds, the enemy opened up on us with their boats. These boats had been so placed that they commanded exactly our camp. The shell fell thickly in all parts of the camp. We being beyond it did not suffer, but some Regs. were cut up badly. We were ordered to fall back, we did so, still the shells fell fast around us. Many were killed here. Genl. Bragg sent orders to fall back from beyond the range of the gunboats. We did so & halted. It was now dark.

Long had I looked for the kind hand of darkness to lay its peaceing [sic] hand upon this savage conflict. The noise of battle had passed away except an occasional bomb sent from the enemy's boat which circling through the air fell home deeply in the ground. Our men fell upon the damp ground & were soon sound asleep. I attempted it myself but the balls would whistle & the musketry would roar around my ears. Our men many of them had lost their provisions. We were ordered to fall back to another encampment &

feed upon the enemy's provisions. We did so. Throwing my blankets down or the one we had taken from the enemy, I was soon asleep.

About midnight we were awakened, with orders to fall in. The rain began to fall in torrents. The darkness was so intense that I could scarcely see my file leader. Passing on the more gloomy sights and sounds I could scarcely imagine. I have said it was dark, but frequent vivid peals of flashings of lightning rent the heavens & revealed objects clearly all around. Then when the veil of night was rent & the curtain of darkness was lifted it was then sickening sights fell before my eyes. Near me at one time lay a dead man, his clothes ghastly, bloody face turned up to the pattering rain drops that fell fast upon that brow cold in death. Perhaps a brow often kissed by fond & loving sister, mother or wife, who now await for the dear objects of their love, no longer to feel their kind manifestations of love. Not far off on their rear revealed a body half covered up in a pool of water. At another flash I saw one of our men stumble over a corpse that lay in the road. Once as the light of heaven flashed across this scene of blood I saw a large piece of ground literally covered with dead heaped & piled upon each other. I shut my eyes upon the sickening sight [b]ut a loud moan came to my ears cry, "water, water... O for a little water."...

We passed on & halting I lay down upon the damp ground & slept until the sun once more rose on earth. The events of this day were certainly in our favor. If we hold our position a victory. If they are reinforced then the result is still doubtful. We have certainly driven the enemy back from all points & are this night in possession of the enemy's camp.

Two miles from the enemy's camp. Mon. 7th. April 1862

By daylight we were in line of battle being commanded to "order arms" & "rest". We got a good supply of Yankee crackers & meat. Eating our breakfast & examining our guns, we were ready for the conflict again, which we felt was upon us. While our Reg. still rested I walked across the branch near by. Dead men were all around. One sitting against a bank & leaning his head upon his hands & knees.

The position was as natural as if he had fallen asleep, yet he was dead. Near us where we lay in line of battle was a dead body. Some of our men very coolly examined his wounds & took his cartridges. Another boy not far off with his hat over his face. In vain I attempted to close my eyes to these shocking spectacles: wherever I turned I saw men pail [sic] in death. Saw pale faces upturned & besmeared with mud & water—hair matted with gore & hair. O it was too shocking too horrible. God grant that I may never be the partaker in such scenes again. My resolution is set. When released from this I shall ever be an advocate of peace.

Once more we are ordered to "forward march." We advanced our lines beyond the enemy's camp. Here we halted & receiving new orders we "right flanked" & "filing right" went farther up the river, where even now we heard the roar of cannon. Here I began to have my doubts as to the issues of this contest. I knew that the enemy were reinforced & stoutly. I knew that we had received no reinforcement. Halting near the place where we first met the enemy, we formed a line of battle behind a fence. Stanford's battery was on our right.

We lay here for some time & I saw some of the boys of my acquaintance in the battery. Bro. Robt. had been with them but had left that morning being somewhat unwell. Soon they began & I knew that our time would soon begin. [S]ure enough[,] we were ordered to advance. Going across a field we halted for the cannon to play a while. Lying down upon the ground the cannon of the enemy began to play upon us. Their shot came near us—uncomfortably near—the battery near us could not find the right kind of ammunition of any kind. I think this was a misfortune at this juncture. Here we were ordered to charge. We did so. Running two hundred yds. We began to fire upon those who were in our front. The fire was not returned for some time & our officers began to think that we were firing upon our friends & ordered our men to "cease firing." but we saw their blue coats & knew too well that they were foes. Soon they opened a most furious fire upon us. Never was any force exposed to such a shower of balls. They must have been ten to one. Our men fell behind trees & logs & returned the fire with spirit. The balls came swarming like bees. I was behind a tree & I think a dozen or more balls struck that tree nearly on a level with my body. I fired several rounds when my gun was again choked I made several attempts before I succeeded. Soon it became evident that we could not long stand such heavy fire. I saw our men falling back one by one. [T]hen I saw whole squads retreating. Soon the whole Reg. was in a full retreat. The retreat was a perfect rout. The men scattered in every direction. Our reg. never again formed itself that day. Many of them made no halt.

This was a most disastrous charge. Some of our men fell dead here. Two Reg. were fighting against a most tremendous force. We fell back across the hill & the officers succeeded in getting the stragglers together. Here we were reinforced & advancing again we forced the enemy back. They had taken one of our batteries. We drove them back & took it again. We reached first position & here was the most tremendous firing I ever heard. We drove the enemy back & the firing appeared to bear to the left. I was ordered to set fire to some houses near by. Soon they were wrapped in flames. I was completely exhausted & falling back with Cap't. Collins rested a while. The firing continued towards the left. It was evident that our men were falling back. I saw the enemy filing rapidly by & then I knew that we must fall back. I walked slowly to the rear & halted. Capt. Ferrill's Co. where I had been sent put on skirmish & came up after the charge. This Co. formed a nucleus after which to form the stragglers of our Reg. The firing by this time had pretty well ceased & the straggling men came thick & fast & were halted as they went by. It was evident that we had been repulsed & that we must now leave the field to the foe.

We turned & marched slowly away, gathering men as we went. I was completely exhausted & felt that if the march continued forward, I could not last long. We halted about 2 miles from the scene of action. Our company was counted off, only ten present out of 48 that came to action… Some companies were not represented. We halted on a little gravelly knoll & made us a fire and ate something. Soon we were ordered to march & fell back a short distance & halted. I built a little fire & lay down & was soon asleep. But again I was disturbed &

we were marched back & chose a new camp ground. We understood this as being our resting place for the night.

I had no blanket. It had been raining & the ground was damp & muddy I lay down having only my gun under me to keep me out mud & my cartridges dry. I did not lie long before I was sound asleep and lay there until I was aroused by the rain which began to fall. I covered my face & slept on for sometime. At last after getting thoroughly soaked, I arose & attempted to enter the tent of Leut. Breckenridge. He did not wish anyone to enter his tent as he would have some business to attend to during the night. We might be in the way. But the tent was already crowded and I concluded that I had as good a right as any of them and accordingly took my position. I scarcely had space to stand but after stamping around for sometime, I found room to sit down & finally got a place to lay my head. It was in a puddle of water but I slept finely. We were not allowed to have any fire. Some of the boys attempted to make fires, but they were put out. I struggled through the night in this way. [S]oon the light so long & ardently wished for came we forced ourselves into line were anxious to go. Thus ended the 2d day. Every thing this day was against us. We were fighting fresh troops & our scattered & disorganized troops were not able to contend against them. I do not think our loss was great though not as great as that of enemy. We left the enemy in the possession of the field. Our men destroyed several of their camp grounds. All things compared we have gain a dear fought victory.[2]

---

[2] August H. Mecklin Papers, diary entries for April 6 and 7, 1862.

William Tecumseh Sherman's Socio-Political Assessment of Mississippi Whites, 1863

In August 1863, a few weeks after the United States's successful Vicksburg campaign, Henry W. Halleck wrote to William T. Sherman in Mississippi. At the time the federal government was already looking to the future and to potential plans for allowing the Southern states back into the Union once the Civil War ended. In his letter, Halleck asked Sherman to "consult with Grant, McPherson, and others of good, cool judgment and write me your views fully, as I may wish to use them with the President." Sherman's response, penned on September 17, 1863, outlined his opinion on how the Deep South might be reconstructed. In so doing, he advised Halleck that "in order to deal with the inhabitants of that part of the South which borders on the great river, we must recognize the classes into which they have divided themselves." Sherman then gave a concise socio-political evaluation of the four classes to which he believed Mississippi whites and whites in the other cotton states belonged in 1863:

First. The large planters, owning lands, slaves, and all kinds of personal property. These are, on the whole, the ruling class. They are educated, wealthy, and easily approached. In some districts they are bitter as gall, and have given up slaves, plantations, and all, serving in the armies of the Confederacy; whereas, in others, they are conservative. None dare admit a friendship for us, though they say freely that they were at the outset opposed to war and disunion. I know we can manage this class, but only by action. Argument is exhausted, and words have lost their usual moaning. Nothing but the logic of events touches their understanding; but, of late, this has worked a wonderful change. If our country were like Europe, crowded with people, I would say it would be easier to replace this class than to reconstruct it, subordinate to the policy of the nation; hut, as this is not the case, it is better to allow the planters, with individual exceptions, gradually to recover their plantations, to hire any species of labor, and to adapt themselves to the new order of things. Still, their friendship and assistance to reconstruct order out of the present ruin cannot be depended on. They watch the operations of our armies, and hope still for a Southern Confederacy that will restore to them the slaves and privileges which they feel are otherwise lost forever. In my judgment, we have two more battles to win before we should even bother our minds with the idea of restoring civil order—viz., one near Meridian, in November, and one near Shreveport, in February and March next, when Red River is navigable by our gunboats. When these are done, then, and not until then, will the planters of Louisiana, Arkansas, and Mississippi, submit. Slavery is already gone, and, to cultivate the land, negro or other labor must be hired. This, of itself, is a vast revolution, and time must be afforded to allow men to adjust their minds and habits to this new order of things. A civil government of the representative type would suit this class far less than a pure military rule, readily adapting itself to actual occurrences, and able to enforce its laws and orders promptly and emphatically.

Second. The smaller farmers, mechanics, merchants, and laborers. This class will probably number three-quarters of the whole; have, in fact, no real interest in the establishment of a Southern Confederacy, and have been led or driven into war on the false theory that they were to be benefited somehow—they knew not how. They are essentially tired of the war, and would slink back home if they could. These are the real tiers etat of the South, and are hardly worthy a thought; for they swerve to and fro according to events which they do not comprehend or attempt to shape. When the time for reconstruction comes, they will want the old political system of caucuses, Legislatures, etc., to amuse them and make them believe they are real sovereigns; but in all things they will follow blindly the lead of the planters. The Southern politicians, who understand this class, use them as the French do their masses—seemingly consult their prejudices, while they make their orders and enforce them. We should do the same.

Third. The Union men of the South. I must confess I have little respect for this class. They allowed a clamorous set of demagogues to muzzle and drive them as a pack of curs. Afraid of shadows, they submit tamely to squads of dragoons, and permit them, without a murmur, to burn their cotton, take their horses, corn, and every thing; and, when we reach them, they are full of complaints if our men take a few fence-rails for fire, or corn to feed our horses. They give us no assistance or information, and are loudest in their complaints at the smallest excesses of our soldiers. Their sons, horses, arms, and every thing useful, are in the army against us, and they stay at home, claiming all the exemptions of peaceful citizens. I account them as nothing in this great game of war.

Fourth. The young bloods of the South: sons of planters, lawyers about towns, good billiard-players and sportsmen, men who never did work and never will. "War suits them, and the rascals are brave, fine riders, bold to rashness, and dangerous subjects in every sense. They care not a sou for niggers, land, or any thing. They hate Yankees and don't bother their brains about the past, present, or future. As long as they have good horses, plenty of forage, and an open country, they are happy. This is a larger class than most men suppose, and they are the most dangerous set of men that this war has turned loose upon the world. They are splendid riders, first-rate shots, and utterly reckless. Stewart, John Morgan, Forrest, and Jackson, are the types and leaders of this class. These men must all be killed or employed by us before we can hope for peace. They have no property or future, and therefore cannot be influenced by any thing except personal considerations.[3]

---

[3] W. T. Sherman to H.W. Halleck, September 17, 1863. Quoted in William T. Sherman, *Memoirs of General William T. Sherman, by Himself*, 335–38.

Charles Clark Concedes Defeat, 1865

In 1863 Mississippians elected Charles Clark as governor of their war-ravaged state. By the time he took office Vicksburg was lost, Jackson was heavily damaged, Union forces controlled the Gulf Coast, and the state's railroads were crumbling. As a result, simply keeping the state government functioning occupied most of Clark's time during an administration cut short by the defeat of the Confederacy. After the final surrender of Confederate military forces Clark, who was soon afterwards placed under arrest by federal authorities, published a brief address to the people of Mississippi urging them to accept the consequences of war and maintain order in their communities:

Meridian, Miss., May 6, 1865
To the People of Mississippi:
General Taylor informs me that all the Confederate armies east of the Mississippi River are surrendered, with all government cotton, quartermaster, commissary and other stores. Federal commanders will only send such troops as may be necessary to guard public property. All officers and persons in possession of public stores will be held to a rigid accountability, and all embezzlers certainly arrested. Arrangements will be made to issue rations to the destitute. I have called the legislature to convene at Jackson on Thursday, the 18th inst. They will doubtless order a convention.

The offices of the state government will immediately return with the archives to Jackson. County officers will be vigilant in the preservation of order and the protection of property. Sheriffs have power to call out the posse comitatus, and the militia will keep arms and obey orders for that purpose, as in times of peace. The civil laws must be enforced, as they now are, until repealed. If the public property be protected and the peace be preserved, the necessity for Federal troops in your counties will be avoided. You are therefore urged to combine to arrest marauders and plunderers.

The collection of taxes should be suspended, as the laws will doubtless be changed. Masters are responsible, as heretofore, for the:

protection and conduct of their slaves, and they should be kept at home as heretofore. Let all citizens fearlessly adhere to the fortunes of the State, aid the returned soldiers to obtain civil employment, maintain law and order, condemn all twelfth-hour vaporers, and meet stern facts with fortitude and common sense.

Charles Clark, Governor of Mississippi.[4]

---

[4] Rowland, *History of Mississippi*, 831–32.

BIBLIOGRAPHY

Official Documents

Ames, Herman V., ed. *State Documents on Federal Relations: The States of the United States*. Philadelphia: University of Pennsylvania Department of History, 1906.

Compiled Service Records of Soldiers from Mississippi Serving during the Civil War [microfilm], Mississippi Department of Archives and History Library, Jackson, Mississippi.

Massachusetts. *State Papers on Nullification: Including the Acts of the Convention of the people of South Carolina, Assembled at Columbia, November 19, 1832 and March 11, 1833; The Proclamation of the President of the United States, and the Proceedings of the Several State Legislatures Which Have Acted Upon the Subject*. Boston: Dutton and Wentworth, 1834.

Mississippi. *Journal of the State Convention, and Ordinances and Resolutions Adopted in January, 1861,With an Appendix*. Jackson MS: Mississippi State Convention, 1861.

——. *Laws of the State of Mississippi*. 1821–1920. Jackson MS: Various printers.

Mississippi House of Representatives. *Journals*, 1817–1865. Jackson MS: Various printers.

Mississippi Senate. *Journals*, 1817–1865. Jackson and Meridian MS: Various printers.

US Bureau of the Census. *Census of the United States*, 1820–1920.

US War Department, compiler. *The Official Records of the Union and Confederate Navies in the War of Rebellion*. 30 volumes. Washington, DC: Government Printing Office, 1894–1922.

————. *The War of the Rebellion: Official Records of the Union and Confederate Armies*. 130 volumes. Washington, DC: Government Printing Office, 1880–1901.

Personal Narratives, Diaries, Books, Letters or Articles

Aughey, John H. *Tupelo*. Lincoln NE: State Journal Company, 1888.
Augustus Hervey Mecklin Papers. Mississippi Department of Archives and History Library, Jackson, Mississippi.
Augustus to T. J. Edmondson, 9 April 1862. Gladys Boyette personal papers. Copy in the possession of the author.
Baldwin, Joseph G. *Flush Times of Alabama and Mississippi. A Series of Sketches*. New York: D. Appleton and Co., 1853.
Bergeron, Arthur W., Jr., editor. *The Civil War Reminiscences of Major Silas T. Grisamore, C.S.A.* Baton Rouge LA: Louisiana State University Press, 1993.
Bestor, Arthur E., Jr. "Letters from a Southern Opponent of Sectionalism, September, 1860, to June, 1861." *Journal of Southern History* 12/1 (February 1946): 106–21.
Bettersworth, John K., editor. *Mississippi in the Confederacy: As They Saw It.* Baton Rouge LA: Louisiana State University Press, 1961.
Binford, James R. "Recollections of the Fifteenth Mississippi Infantry, C.S.A." Patrick Henry Papers. Mississippi Department of Archives and History. Jackson, Mississippi.
Brannon, John W. *The John F. Johnson Journal of 1902*. Eupora MS: self-published, 1984.
Cappleman, Josie Frazee. "Local Incidents of the War Between the States." In Franklin L. Riley, editor. In *Publications of the Mississippi Historical Society*, 79–87. Volume 4. Jackson MS: Mississippi Historical Society, 1901.
Chambers, William Pitt. *Journal of William Pitt Chambers*. Jackson MS: Mississippi Historical Society, 1925.
Christie, T. D. to "My Dear Sister," 21 September 1862. Minnesota Historical Society, St. Paul, Minnesota.
Confederate Reminiscences and Letters, 1861–1865. 21 volumes. Atlanta GA: Georgia Division, United Daughters of the Confederacy, 2000.

Cramer, Clayton E. *By the Dim and Flaring Lamps: The Civil War Diary of Samuel McIlvaine, February through June, 1862.* Monroe NY: Library Research Associates, 1990.

Crist, Lynda Lasswell, et. al., editors. *The Papers of Jefferson Davis.* Baton Rouge LA: Louisiana State University Press, 1983.

Davidson, W. J. "The Diary of Private W. J. Davidson." In *The Annals of the Army of Tennessee and Early Western History*, 55–62. Volume 1. Jackson TN: The Guild Bindery Press, 1878.

Davis, Reuben. *Recollections of Mississippi and Mississippians*, rev. ed. Hattiesburg MS: University and College Press of Mississippi, 1972.

Dicken. James T. "Long Creek Rifles." *Kosciusco (MS) Star Ledger*, 1 January, 1898.

Dimond, E. Gray and Herman Hattaway, editors, *Letters from Forest Place: A Plantation Family's Correspondence.* Jackson: University Press of Mississippi, 1993.

Deupree, J. G. "The Capture of Holly Springs, Mississippi, Dec. 20, 1862." In Franklin L. Riley, editor. *Publications of the Mississippi Historical Society*, 49–61. Volume 4. Oxford MS: Mississippi Historical Society, 1901.

An English Combatant. *Battlefields of the South, From Bull Run to Fredericksburg; With Sketches of Confederate Commanders, and Gossip of the Camps.* New York: John Bradburn, 1864.

Feemster, Zenas E. *The Traveling Refugee; or the Cause and Cure of the Rebellion in the United States;Embracing a Sketch of the State of Society in the South, Before, and at the Commencement of the Rebellion.* Springfield IL: Baker and Phillips, 1865.

Foote, Henry S. *Casket of Reminiscences.* Washington, DC: Chronicle Publishing Co., 1874.

———. *War of Rebellion; or, Scylla and Charybdis. Consisting of Observations Upon the Causes, Course, and Consequences of the Late Civil War in the United States.* New York: Harper & Brothers Publishers, 1866.

Foxworth, Jobe M. Diary. Mississippi Department of Archives and History. Jackson, Mississippi.

Francis Marion Aldridge Papers. Mississippi Department of Archives and History Library, Jackson, Mississippi.

Frierson, Charles, to parents, 28 January 1862. Gay Carter personal papers. Copy in possession of the author.

Frierson, James to mother, 28 January 1862. Letter owned by Gay Carter personal papers. Copy in possession of the author.

Fulkerson, H. S. *A Civilian's Recollections of the War Between the States*. Baton Rouge LA: Otto Claitor, 1939.

George W. Jones diary. Greenville Public Library. Greenville, Mississippi.

Gunn, D. B. "Reminiscences of the War." John J. Thornton Papers. Mississippi Department of Archives and History. Jackson, Mississippi.

Grammer, George A. Diary. Mississippi Department of Archives and History. Jackson, Mississippi.

Grant, Ulysses S. *Personal Memoirs of U.S. Grant*. Mineola NY: Dover Publications, Inc, 1995.

"Greenville (Miss.) Monument." *Confederate Veteran* 18/2 (February 1910): 68.

Hamilton, W. F. *Military Annals of Carroll County*. Carrollton MS: self-published, 1906.

Harwell, Richard, editor. *The Journal of Kate Cumming, Confederate Nurse 1862–1865*. Savannah GA: The Beehive Press, 1975.

"History of the Water Valley Rifles, Company F, Fifteenth Mississippi Infantry." Supplement to the WPA Historical Research Project, Yalobusha County, 16 February 1937. Special Collections, J. D. Williams Library, University of Mississippi, Oxford.

Inge, Mrs. F. A. "Corinth, Miss. in Early War Days." *Confederate Veteran* 17/9 (September 1909): 442–43.

John A. Cato letters. Mississippi Department of Archives and History. Jackson, Mississippi.

Johnson, Robert Underwood and Clarence Clough Buel, editors. *Battles and Leaders of the Civil War*. 4 volumes. New York: The Century Company, 1887.

Jones, Katherine M. *Heroines of Dixie: Confederate Women Tell Their Story of the War*. Indianapolis IN: The Bobbs-Merrill Company, Inc., 1955.

"The Ku Klux Klan and 'The Birth of a Nation.'" *Confederate Veteran* 24/4 (April 1916): 157–59.

Liddell, St. John R. "Liddell's Record of the Civil War." *The Southern Bivouac* 1/9 (February 1896): 529–35.

Logsdon, David R. compiler and editor. *Eyewitnesses to the Battle of Franklin*. Nashville TN: Kettle Mills Press, 1991.

Lyon, James A. "Journal of Reverend James A. Lyon, Columbus, Mississippi, 1861–1870." Typed manuscript. Mississippi Department of Archives and History. Jackson, Mississippi.

McGavock Family Papers. Tennessee State Library and Archives. Nashville, Tennessee.

Miller, Letitia Dabney. "The Recollections of Letitia Dabney Miller" (unpublished manuscript). Mrs. Cade Drew Gillespie Collection. Department of Archives and Special Collections, J. D. Williams Library, University of Mississippi, Oxford.

"Mississippi Veterans at Greenwood." *Confederate Veteran* 21/11 (November 1913): 516–18.

Montgomery, Frank A. *Reminiscences of a Mississippian in War and Peace.* Cincinnati: The Robert Clarke Company Press, 1901.

Niles, Jason. Scrapbook. Southern Historical Collection. University of North Carolina Library.

"Recollections of Vicksburg During the Siege." *The Southern Bivouac* 1/1 (September 1882): 2–11.

"Reunion at Columbos, Miss." *Confederate Veteran* 16/10 (October 1908): 491.

"Reunion of Mississippi Comrades." *Confederate Veteran* 34/11 (November 1926): 424.

Sherman, William T. *Memoirs of General William T. Sherman, by Himself.* Bloomington: Indiana University Press, 1957.

"Veterans at Vicksburg." *Confederate Veteran* 18/1 (January 1910): 25.

Wallace, Jim. "History and Reminiscences of Attala County" [photocopy], 1916. Mississippi Department of Archives and History Library, Jackson, Mississippi.

Watson, Joel Calvin. Diary. Grenada Public Library, Grenada, Mississippi.

Weems, Mrs. Albert G. "Work of the Daughters of the Confederacy." In *Publications of the Mississippi Historical Society*, 73–78. Volume 4.Oxford: Mississippi Historical Society, 1901.

Wood, John W. *Union and Secession in Mississippi.* Memphis: Saunders, Farrish, and Whitmore Printers, 1863.

Woods, Thomas H. "A Sketch of the Mississippi Secession Convention of 1861, Its Membership and Work." In *Publications of the Mississippi Historical Society*, 91–103. Volume 6. Oxford: Mississippi Historical Society, 1902.

Zinser, Samuel. Letters. Cullom Davis Library, Bradley University. Peoria, Illinois.

Newspapers

Attala (MS) *Democrat*
Brandon (MS) *Republican and Advocate*
Carrollton (MS) *Conservative*
Carrollton (MS) *Democrat*
Columbus (MS) *Democrat*
Davenport (IA) *Daily Gazette*
Holly Springs (MS) *Gazette*
Kosciusco (MS) *Star Ledger*
Liberty (MS) *Planter*
Mississippian (Jackson)
Memphis (TN) *Daily Appeal*
Natchez *(MS)* Daily Courier
Natchez (MS) *Free Trader*
New York Times
Vicksburg (MS) *Whig*
Water Valley (MS) *Progress*
Yazoo City (MS) *Democrat*
Yazoo City (MS) *Whig*

Books

Attala County Historical Society. *Kosciusko-Attala County History*. Kosciusko MS: self-published, 1976.
Ballard, Michael B. *Civil War Mississippi: A Guide*. Jackson: University Press of Mississippi, 2000.
———. *Pemberton: A Biography*. Jackson: University Press of Mississippi, 1991.
———. *Vicksburg: The Campaign that Opened the Mississippi*. Chapel Hill: University of North Carolina Press, 2004.
Barney, William L. *The Road to Secession*. New York: Praeger Publishers, 1972.
———. *The Secessionist Impulse: Alabama and Mississippi in 1860*. Princeton: Princeton University Press, 1974.

Bearss, Edwin C. *The Campaign for Vicksburg.* 3 volumes. Dayton OH: Morningside House, Inc., 1986.

——. *Decision in Mississippi: Mississippi's Important Role in the War Between the States.* Jackson: Mississippi Commission on the War Between the States, 1962.

——. *Forrest at Brice's Cross Roads and in North Mississippi.* Dayton OH: Morningside Press, 1979.

——, and Warren Grabau. *The Battle of Jackson, May 14, 1863; The Siege of Jackson, July 10–17, 1863; Three Other Post-Vicksburg Actions.* Baltimore: Gateway Press, 1981.

Bearss, Margie Riddle. *Sherman's Forgotten Campaign: The Meridian Expedition.* Baltimore: Gateway Press, Inc., 1987.

Beringer, Richard E., Herman Hattaway, Archer Jones, and William N. Still, Jr. *Why the South Lost the Civil War.* Athens: University of Georgia Press, 1986.

Bettersworth, John K. *Confederate Mississippi: The People and Policies of a Cotton State in Wartime.* Baton Rouge: Louisiana State University Press, 1943.

Biographical and Historical Memoirs of Mississippi. Chicago: The Goodspeed Publishing Company, 1891.

Bond, Bradley G. *Political Culture in the Nineteenth-Century South: Mississippi, 1830–1900.* Baton Rouge: Louisiana State University Press, 1995.

Brown, A. J. *History of Newton County, from 1834 to 1894.* Jackson: Clarion-Ledger Company, 1894.

Brown, D. Alexander. *Grierson's Raid.* Urbana: University of Illinois Press, 1954.

Cain, Cyril Edward. *Four Centuries on the Pascagoula: History and Genealogy of the Pascagoula River Country.* 2 volumes. Spartanburg SC: The Reprint Company Publishers, 1983.

Carter III, Samuel. *The Final Fortress: The Campaign for Vicksburg, 1862–1863.* New York: St. Martin's Press, 1980.

Cashin, Joan E. *A Family Venture: Men and Women on the Southern Frontier.* New York: Oxford University Press, 1991.

Castel, Albert. *General Sterling Price and the Civil War in the West.* Baton Rouge: Louisiana State University Press, 1968.

Claiborne, John Francis Hamtramck. *Life and Correspondence of John A. Quitman.* Volume 1. New York: Harper and Bros., 1860.

Clark, Thomas D., and John D.W. Guice. *The Old Southwest, 1795–1830: Frontiers in Conflict*. Norman: University of Oklahoma Press, 1996.

Clayton, James D. *Antebellum Natchez*. Baton Rouge: Louisiana State University Press, 1968.

Cochran, Fan Alexander, editor and compiler. *History of Old Tishomingo County, Mississippi Territory*. Oklahoma City: Barnhart Letter Shop, 1969.

Coleman, James P. *Choctaw County Chronicles*. Ackerman MS: self-published, 1974.

Cooper, William J. *Liberty and Slavery: Southern Politics to 1860*. New York: Alfred A. Knopf, 1983.

Cooper, Jr., William J., and Thomas E. Terrill. *The American South: A History*. New York: McGraw-Hill, Inc., 1991.

Coski, John M. *The Confederate Battle Flag: America's Most Embattled Emblem*. Cambridge: The Belknap Press, 2005.

Cozzens, Peter. *The Darkest Days of the War: The Battles of Iuka & Corinth*. Chapel Hill: The University of North Carolina Press, 1997.

Daniel, Larry J. *Shiloh: The Battle That Changed the Civil War*. New York: Simon and Schuster, 1997.

Davis, William C. *Jefferson Davis: The Man and His Honor*. Baton Rouge: Louisiana State University Press, 1991.

Degler, Carl. *The Other South: Southern Dissenters in the Nineteenth Century*. New York: Harper and Row, Publishers, 1974.

Dubay, Robert W. *John Jones Pettus*. Jackson: University Press of Mississippi, 1975.

Eaton, Clement. *A History of the Old South*. 3rd edition New York: Macmillan Publishing Company, 1975.

———. *Jefferson Davis*. New York: The Free Press, 1977.

Ellis, Richard E. *The Union at Risk: Jacksonian Democracy, States' Rights and the Nullification Crisis*. New York: Oxford University Press, 1987.

Evans, Robert G. *The 16th Mississippi: Civil War Letters and Reminiscences*. Jackson: University Press of Mississippi, 2002.

Fairley, Laura Nan and James T. Dawson, *Paths to the Past: An Overview History of Lauderdale County, Mississippi*. Meridian MS: Lauderdale County Department of Archives and History, 1988.

Faulkner, William. *Requiem for a Nun*. New York: Trade Paperback, 1975.

Foster, Gaines M. *Ghosts of the Confederacy: Defeat, the Lost Cause, and the Emergence of the New South*. New York: Oxford University Press, 1987.

Freehling, William W. *The Road to Disunion, Secessionists at Bay, 1776–1854*. New York: Oxford University Press, 1990.

Greenberg, Kenneth H. *Masters and Statesmen: The Political Culture of American Slavery*. Baltimore: The Johns Hopkins University Press, 1985.

Hankinson, Alan. *Vicksburg 1863: Grant Clears the Mississippi*. London: Ospry, 1993.

Hartje, Robert G. *Van Dorn: The Life and Times of a Confederate General*. Nashville TN: Vanderbilt University Press, 1967.

Hattaway, Herman. *General Stephen D. Lee*. Jackson: University Press of Mississippi, 1976.

Hathorn, J. C. *A History of Grenada County*. Grenada MS: self-published, 1972.

Hearon, Cleo. "Nullification in Mississippi." In *Publications of the Mississippi Historical Society*, 37–71. Volume 12. University: Mississippi Historical Society, 1912.

Hoehling, A. A. *Vicksburg: 47 Days of Siege*. New York: Fairfax Press, 1991.

Howell, H. Grady. *Going to Meet the Yankees: A History of the "Bloody Sixth" Mississippi Infantry, CSA*. Madison MS: Chickasaw Bayou Press, 1981.

Hurst, Jack. *Nathan Bedford Forrest: A Biography*. New York: Knopf, 1993.

Keating, Bern. *A History of Washington County, Mississippi*. Greenville MS: The Greenville Junior Auxiliary, 1976.

Korn, Jerry. *War on the Mississippi: Grant's Vicksburg Campaign*. Alexandria VA: Time-Life Books, 1985.

Lamers, William M. *The Edge of Glory: A Biography of General William S. Rosecrans, USA*. New York: Harcourt Brace and World, 1961.

Leckie, Robert. *None Died in Vain*. New York: Harper Collins Publishers, 1990.

Livermore, Thomas L. *Numbers and Losses in the Civil War in America: 1861–1865*. Bloomington: Indiana University Press, 1957.

Loewen, James W., and Charles Sallis, editors. *Mississippi: Conflict and Change*. New York: Random House, Inc., 1974.

Long, E. B., with Barbara Long. *The Civil War Day by Day: An Almanac* New York: Da Capo Press, Inc., 1971.

Lowry, Robert, and William H. McCardle. *A History of Mississippi, from the Discovery of the Great River by Hernando DeSoto, Including the Earliest Settlement Made by the French Under Iberville, to the Death of Jefferson Davis*. Jackson MS: R. H. Henry and Company, 1891.

Marszalek, John F. *Sherman: A Soldier's Passion for Order*. New York: Free Press, 1993.

May Robert E. *John A. Quitman: Old South Crusader*. Baton Rouge: Louisiana State University Press, 1985.

Mayes, Edward. *Lucius Q.C. Lamar: His Life, Times and Speeches, 1825–1893*. Nashville TN: Publishing House of Methodist Episcopal Church, South, 1896.

Martin, David G. *The Shiloh Campaign, March–April, 1862*. Conshohocken PA: Combined Books, Inc., 1996.

McCurry, Stephanie. *Masters of Small Worlds: Yeomen Households, Gender Relations, and Political Culture of the Antebellum South Carolina Low Country*. New York: Oxford University Press, 1995.

McDonough, James Lee and Thomas L. Connelly. *Five Tragic Hours: The Battle of Franklin*. Knoxville: University of Tennessee Press, 1983.

McFeely, William S. *Grant: A Biography*. New York: W. W. Norton & Company, 1981.

McLemore, Richard A., editor. *A History of Mississippi*. 2 volumes. Hattiesburg: University and College Press of Mississippi, 1973.

McMurry, Richard. *John Bell Hood and the War for Southern Independence*. Lincoln: University of Nebraska Press, 1982.

McPherson. James M. *Battle Cry of Freedom: The Civil War Era*. New York: Ballantine Books, 1988.

———. *Marching Toward Freedom: The Negro in the Civil War 1861–1865*. New York: Alfred A. Knopf, 1967.

Miers, Earl S. *The Web of Victory: Grant at Vicksburg*. New York: Knopf, 1955.

Montgomery County Historical Society. *History of Montgomery County*. Dallas: Curtis Media Corp., 1993.

Morris, Christopher. *Becoming Southern: The Evolution of a Way of Life, Warren County and Vicksburg, Mississippi, 1770–1860*. New York: Oxford University Press, 1995.

Nevins Allen. *The War for the Union*. New York: Charles Scribner's Sons, 1959.

Pereyra, Lillian A. *James Lusk Alcorn: Persistent Whig*. Baton Rouge: Louisiana State University Press, 1966.

Polk, Noel, editor. *Mississippi's Piney Woods: A Human Perspective*. Jackson: University Press of Mississippi, 1986.

Quarles, Benjamin. *The Negro in the Civil War*. New York: Russell and Russell, 1953.

Rainwater, Percy Lee. *Mississippi: Storm Center of Secession 1856–1861*. Baton Rouge LA: Otto Claitor, 1938.

Ranck, James B. *Albert Gallatin Brown, Radical Southern Nationalist*. New York: Appleton-Century Co., Inc., 1937.

Robertson, Jr., James I. *Soldiers Blue and Gray*. Columbia: University of South Carolina Press, 1988.

Rowland, Dunbar. *Encyclopedia of Mississippi History*. 4 volumes. Madison WI: Selwyn A. Brant, 1907.

———. *History of Mississippi, The Heart of the South*. 4 volumes. Jackson MS: S. J. Clarke Publishing Co., 1925.

———. *Military History of Mississippi 1803–1898*. Spartenburg SC: The Reprint Company, 1988.

Ryan, J. S., and T. M. Murphree. *History of Calhoun County, Miss*. Pittsboro MS: The Calhoun Monitor, 1904.

Sansing, David G. *The University of Mississippi: A Sesquicentennial History*. Jackson: University Press of Mississippi, 1999.

Scharf, J. Thomas. *History of the Confederate States Navy From Its Organization to the Surrender of Its Last Vessel*. New York: Gramercy Books, 1996.

Shea, William L., and Terrence J. Winschel. *Vicksburg Is the Key: The Struggle for the Mississippi River*. Lincoln: University of Nebraska Press, 2003.

Sifakis, Stewart. *Who Was Who in the Civil War*. New York: Facts on File, Inc., 1988.

Silver, James W. *Mississippi in the Confederacy: As Seen in Retrospective*. Baton Rouge: Louisiana State University Press, 1961.

Smith, Frank E. *The Yazoo River*. Jackson: University Press of Mississippi, 1988.

Smith, Page. *Trial by Fire: A People's History of the Civil War*. New York: McGraw-Hill, 1985.

Snay, Mitchell. *The Gospel of Disunion: Religion and Separatism in the Antebellum South*. New York: Cambridge University Press, 1993.

Sword, Wiley. *Shiloh: Bloody April*. New York: William Morrow and Co., Inc., 1974.

———. *Southern Invincibility: A History of the Confederate Heart*. New York: St. Martin's Griffin, 1999.

Symonds, Craig L. *Joseph Johnston: A Civil War Biography*. New York: W. W. Norton, 1992.

Thomas, Emory M. *The Confederate Nation: 1861–1865*. New York: Harper & Row, 1979.

Trudeau, Noah Andre. *Out of the Storm: The End of the Civil War, April–June, 1865*. New York: Little, Brown, and Company, 1994.

Wayne, Michael. *The Reshaping of Plantation Society: The Natchez District, 1860–1880*. Baton Rouge: Louisiana State University Press, 1983.

Webster County Historical Society. *The History of Webster County*. Dallas: Curtis Media Corporation, 1985.

Wheeler, Richard. *The Siege of Vicksburg*. New York: Thomas Y. Crowell Co., 1978.

———. *Voices of the Civil War*. New York: Thomas Y. Crowell Company, 1976.

Wiley, Bell Irvin. *The Life of Johnny Reb*. Baton Rouge: Louisiana State University Press, 1978.

Wilson, Charles Reagan. *Baptized in Blood: The Religion of the Lost Cause, 1865–1920*. Athens: The University Press of Georgia, 1980.

Wilson, Harold S. *Confederate Industry: Manufacturers and Quartermasters in the Civil War*. Jackson: University Press of Mississippi, 2002.

Wyatt-Brown, Bertram. *Honor and Violence in the Old South*. New York: Oxford University Press, 1986.

Wyeth, John A. *That Devil Forrest: Life of General Nathan Bedford Forrest*. Baton Rouge: Louisiana State University Press, 1989.

Wynne, Ben. *A Hard Trip: A History of the 15th Mississippi Infantry, CSA*. Macon GA: Mercer University Press, 2003.

Yalobusha County Historical Society. *Yalobusha County History*. Dallas: National Share Graphics, 1982.

Periodicals

Biel, John G. "The Evacuation of Corinth." *Journal of Mississippi History* 24/24 (Spring 1962): 40–56.

Blain, William T. "William Felix Brantley, 1830–1870." *Journal of Mississippi History* 37/4 (November 1975): 359–80.

———. "Banner Unionism in Choctaw County." *Mississippi Quarterly* 29/2 (Spring 1976): 207–20.

Brown, D. Alexander. "Battle at Chickasaw Bluffs." *Civil War Times Illustrated* 9/4 (July 1970): 4–9, 44–48.

Chesebrough, David B. "Dissenting Clergy in Confederate Mississippi." *Journal of Mississippi History* 55/2 (May 1993): 115–32.

Crowther, Edward R. "Mississippi Baptists, Slavery, and Secession, 1806–1861." *Journal of Mississippi History* 56/2 (May 1994): 129–48.

Ezell, John. "Jefferson Davis Seeks Political Vindication." *Journal of Mississippi History* 26/4 (November 1964): 307–21.

Gunn, Jack W. "Mississippi in 1860 as Reflected in the Activities of the Governor's Office." *Journal of Mississippi History* 22/3 (July 1960): 167–78.

Hesseltine, William B., and Larry Gara. "Mississippi's Confederate Leaders after the War." *Journal of Mississippi History* 13/2 (April 1951): 88–100.

Jordan, Daniel P. "Mississippi's Antebellum Congressmen: A Collective Biography." *Journal of Mississippi History* 38/2 (May 1976): 157–82.

Kelley, Donald Brooks. "Harper's Ferry: Prelude to Crisis in Mississippi." *Journal of Mississippi History* 27/4 (November 1965), 351–72.

———. "Intellectual Isolation: Gateway to Secession in Mississippi." *Journal of Mississippi History* 36/1 (February 1974): 17–38.

Montgomery, Goode. "Alleged Secession of Jones County." *Publications of the Mississippi Historical Society*. Volume 8. Jackson MS: Mississippi Historical Society, 1904.

Orr, J. A. "A Trip from Houston to Jackson, Miss., in 1845." *Publications of the Mississippi Historical Society*. Volume 9. Jackson MS: Mississippi Historical Society, 1906.

Phillips, Adrienne Cole. "The Mississippi Press's Response to John Brown's Raid." *Journal of Mississippi History* 48/2 (May 1986): 119–34.

Rawson, Donald M. "Democratic Resurgence in Mississippi, 1852–1853." *Journal of Mississippi History* 26/1 (February 1964): 1–27.

Stone, James H. "General Absalom Madden West and the Civil War in Mississippi." *Journal of Mississippi History* 42/2 (May 1980): 135–44.

Sumner, Mary Floyd. "Politics in Tishomingo County, 1836–1860." *Journal of Mississippi History* 28/2 (May 1966): 133–51.

Sweatt, Gregory. "Mystery in Mississippi: Reverend Sweatt Has Disappeared." *Civil War Times Illustrated* 21/6 (October 1982): 42–44.

Wooster, Ralph A. "The Membership of the Mississippi Secession Convention of 1861." *Journal of Mississippi History* 16/4 (October 1954): 242–57.

Miscellaneous

Collection Files. Mississippi State Historical Museum, Jackson, Mississippi.

Confederate Grave Registrations [microfilm]. Mississippi Department of Archives and History Library. Jackson, Mississippi.

Subject Files. Mississippi Department of Archives and History. Jackson, Mississippi.

Unveiling Ceremonies of the Holmes County Confederate Monument, at Lexington, Mississippi, December 2, 1908 (program). Mississippi Department of Archives and History Library. Jackson, Mississippi.

INDEX

A.M. West, 90
A.O. Tyler, USS, 47
Abbeville, MS, 81
Aberdeen, MS, 20, 43, 80, 154
Adams County, MS, 48, 89
Adams, William Wirt, 151, 152, 168
Alabama, 5, 125, 143, 151, 153
Alamucha Infantry, 44
Albert Sidney Johnston Chapter (UCV), 188
Alcorn, James L., 1, 25, 28, 29, 32, 34, 35
Ames, Adelbert, 184
Amite County, MS, 193
Annandale Plantation, 37
Appomattox Courthouse, VA, 138
Arkansas, 145
Arkansas, CSS, 73, 74
Army of Northern Virginia, 48
Army of Tennessee, 48, 164, 168, 169
Army of the Ohio, 60
Atlanta Campaign, 155, 158, 199
Atlanta, GA, 164
Attala County, MS, 25, 30, 37
Aughey, John H., 27
Autry, James L., 72
Bailey, Mollie Lavinia, 201
Ball's Bluff, Battle of, 54
Bankston Textile Mills, 167
Bankston, MS, 167
Barksdale, Ethelbert, 21, 173
Barksdale, William, 48, 49, 50, 135, 173, 188
Barksdale's Mississippi Brigade, 50
Baron de Kalb, USS, 98

Barry, William L., 28
Barteau, Clark R., 101
Baton Rouge, LA, 71, 72, 102
Beauregard, P.G.T., 60, 64, 68, 69, 70, 110, 148, 210
Beauvoir, 200, 201
Bedford County, TN, 149
Bell, John, 22, 23
Bellefontaine, MS, 166
Benton, USS, 103
Big Black River Bridge, Battle of, 115-116, 118
Big Black River, 128, 135, 138, 151
Biloxi, MS, 200
Black and Tan Convention, 182
Black Codes, 181
Bolivar County, MS, 35, 37
Bolton, MS, 116
Bonnie Blue Flag, 32, 117
Booneville, MS, 160, 166
Bowen John S., 81, 106, 107, 113, 115, 131, 132, 133
Bowling Green, KY, 58, 59, 60
Bowman House, 111, 112
Bozeman, Peter H., 44
Bragg, Braxton, 60, 63, 69, 74, 76, 82, 110, 149
Brandon, MS, 136, 150
Branham, Henry B., 67
Breckinridge, John C., 22, 23, 63, 72
Brice's Cross Roads, Battle of, 160, 161, 163
Brookhaven, MS, 102, 166

Brown, Albert Gallatin, 13, 14, 15, 21, 23, 24, 28
Brown, Isaac N., 73
Brown, John, 19, 25, 47
Bruinsburg, MS, 105
Buchanan, John H., 37
Buell, Don Carlos, 60, 61, 64, 74
Buena Vista, Battle of, 31, 88
Bull Run (1st), Battle of, 49, 51, 55, 56, 89
Burt, E.R., 49
Byers, Samuel H.M., 113
Cadwallader, Sylvanus, 129, 130
Calhoun, John C., 6, 7, 8
California, 15
Canby, Richard S., 175
Carondelet USS, 73, 103
Carroll County, MS, 55, 56, 57
Cedar Bluffs, MS, 188
Chambers, William Pitt, 147
Champion Hill, Battle of, 113-115, 117, 118, 146, 151
Champion, Matilda, 146
Charleston, SC, 21
Chase, William Henry, 88
Chattanooga, TN, 149, 157, 158
Chewalla, MS, 77
Chicago Tribune, 120
Chickamauga, Battle of, 199
Chickasaw Bayou, 91, 129, 148
Chickasaw Indians, 4, 84
Chillicothe, USS, 98
Choctaw County, MS, 27, 166, 167
Choctaw Indians, 4
Choctaw, USS, 127
Choppin, Samuel, 65
Cincinnati, OH, 34
Cincinnati, USS, 122
Citronelle, AL, 175
Clark, Charles, 32, 34, 145, 147, 155, 165, 166, 170, 173, 174, 175, 176, 220
Clayton, Alexander M., 30, 205
Cleveland, Grover, 29
Climer, J.R., 201
Clinton, MS, 13, 113, 183
Coahoma County, MS, 1, 35, 149
Cobb, Howell, 172
Coffeeville, MS, 83, 156
Cold Harbor, Battle of, 155
Coldwater River, 98
Collins, John L., 191

Columbus Marble Works, 192
Columbus, KY, 58, 60
Columbus, MS, 143, 158, 170, 183, 189, 193
Compromise of 1850, 15
Confederate Congress, 2
Confederate Veteran, 187, 190, 196, 199
Conscription, 68, 71, 166
Constitutional Union Party, 22
Copiah County, MS, 13
Corinth, Battle of, 77-81, 152
Corinth, MS, 2, 36, 58, 59, 60, 61, 62, 63, 65, 66, 67, 68, 69, 70, 71, 74, 76, 77, 78, 79, 80, 81, 157, 191
Corona Female College, 66
Cottle, Mollie, 201
Crump, William, Jr., 170
Crystal Springs, MS, 115
Cumberland Gap, 58
Cumming, Kate, 58, 66
Daily Courier (Natchez), 20
Dana, Charles A., 127
Dartmouth College, 125
Davis Bend, 142, 143
Davis, Jefferson Hayes, 193
Davis, Jefferson, 10, 14, 23, 24, 31, 34, 52, 61, 68, 69, 80, 92, 93, 96, 116, 118, 128, 136, 141, 143, 152, 164, 172, 176, 193, 200, 201, 202
Davis, Joseph, 116, 143
Davis, Reuben, 23, 24, 145
Davis, Varina Anne, 188, 189
Davis, Varina Howell, 200
Decatur, MS, 151
Democratic Party (Mississippi), 8, 13, 22, 25, 27, 29, 183, 184, 185
Democratic Party (National), 21, 22
Demopolis, AL, 153
Desertion, 137, 138, 139
District of Columbia, 15
Dixie, 117
Dorsey, Sarah, 200
Douglas, Stephen, 22
Duck Hill, MS, 90, 91
Durant, MS, 168
Eaton, John, 126, 142, 143
Edwards Station, MS, 113, 116, 151
Election of 1859 (state), 18
Emancipation Proclamation, 141, 142, 144, 172

Emory College, 28
England, 28
Enterprise, MS, 36, 110, 143
Evans, Nathan, 54
Falkner, William C., 48, 50
Farragut, David G., 71, 72
Faulkner, William, 51, 178, 203
Featherston, Winfield Scott, 48, 49
Flags in the Dust, 51
Florida, 51
Foote, Andrew, 59
Forest Queen, USS, 103
Forney, John H., 131
Forrest, Jeffrey, 154
Forrest, Nathan Bedford, 148, 149, 152,
 153, 154, 155, 156, 157, 158, 160,
 161, 162, 163, 164, 188
Fort Donelson, 59
Fort Henry, 58
Fort Lafayette, 56
Fort Pemberton, 98
Fort Pillow, 161
Fort Pulaski, 177
Fort Sumter, SC, 40, 148
Fort Warren, 56
France, 28
Franklin County, MS, 19
Franklin, Battle of, 155, 168, 199
Free State of Jones, 138
Freedman's Bureau, 179
French, Samuel Gibbs, 88, 150
Galveston, TX, 176
Garlandville, MS, 102
Garrett, Henry A., 34, 40
General Order Number 11, 86
Georgia, 5, 80, 106, 125, 155, 163
Gettysburg, Battle of, 135, 188
Gift, George W., 73
Glenn, David C., 21
Grand Gulf, MS, 105, 106
Grand Junction, TN, 82
Grant, Fred, 115, 116
Grant, Jessie, 86
Grant, Mrs., 85
Grant, Ulysses S., 59, 60, 63,64, 75, 82,
 84, 85, 86, 87, 96, 97, 98, 103, 105,
 106, 108, 110, 111, 112, 113, 114,
 118, 119, 121, 122, 123, 126, 128,
 130, 132, 133, 134, 137, 144, 149, 202
Gray, Nicholas, 125

Greeley, Horace, 194
Green, Joshua, 111
Green, Thomas, 111
Greensboro, MS, 167
Greenville, MS, 99, 189, 192
Greenwood, 98, 190, 191
Gregg, John, 108
Grenada, MS, 36, 90, 168, 188
Grierson, Benjamin, 99, 101, 102, 102,
 106, 166, 167
Guntown, MS, 160
Guyton, Pearl Vivian, 196
Hail Columbia, 134
Halleck, Henry W., 65, 68, 75
Hardee, William J., 63
Harper's Ferry, VA, 19, 20, 37
Hayes, Rutherford, 184
Haynes, M.D., 140
Hazlehurst, MS, 102
Hebert, Louis, 77, 79
Helen Johnstone Guards, 37
Henry Clay, USS, 103
Hinds County, MS, 48, 108
Holly Springs Female Institute, 45
Holly Springs, MS, 45, 49, 81, 82, 83, 84,
 85, 86, 91, 155, 156, 170, 192, 199
Holmes County, MS, 37
Hood, John Bell, 88, 157, 164, 165, 168,
 172
House, James, 170
Houston, MS, 49, 166
Humphreys, Benjamin G., 135, 180
Hurlbut, Stephen A., 112, 144
Illinois Troops: 6th Illinois Cavalry, 101;
 7th Illinois Cavalry, 101
Illinois, 22, 35, 47
Indiana, 57
Inge, Rebecca, 65
Inge, William H., 60
Iowa Troops: 2nd Iowa Cavalry, 101
Irwinville, GA, 176
Isom, Thomas D., 67
Iuka, Battle of, 75-76, 152
Iuka, MS, 36, 75, 76
Jackson, A.M., 174
Jackson, Andrew, 6, 7
Jackson, Battle of, 110-111
Jackson, MS, 15, 90, 102, 110, 111, 112,
 113, 115, 125, 127, 128, 136, 138,
 143, 144, 149, 176

James Brown, 90
Jeff Davis Legion, 34, 89
Jefferson College, 13
Jefferson County, MS, 35, 174
Jefferson Davis Presidential Library, 201, 202
Johnson, Andrew, 143, 176, 179, 180, 181
Johnston, Albert Sidney, 59, 61, 64, 65, 70, 71
Johnston, Joseph, 89, 96, 109, 110, 112, 115, 118, 119, 127, 128, 131, 135, 136, 148, 157, 158, 164, 169, 175
Johnstone, Helen, 37
Jones County, MS, 138, 139
Kansas, 15, 25
Kemper County, MS, 18, 174
Kennesaw Mountain, GA, 192
Kentucky, 2, 35, 58, 74, 75, 89, 152
Kimball, Nathan, 129
Kingston, MS, 144
Kirby, Peter, 90
Knight, Newton, 138, 139
Knights of the White Camellia, 183
Knox County, TN, 50
Kopperl, Charles, 55, 56, 57
Kosciusko, MS, 25
Ku Klux Klan, 183, 196
Lafayette County, MS, 28
Lafayette, USS, 103
LaGrange, TN, 101, 162
Lake Providence, LA, 97
Lake, MS, 151
Lamar, Lucius Q. C., 24, 28
Lamar, Mirabeau, 28
Lamar, MS, 166
Lauderdale County, MS, 44
Lauderdale Springs, MS, 67
Leaf, MS, 33
Leake County, MS, 37, 165
Lee, Robert E., 61, 135, 168, 169, 175, 195
Lee, Stephen D., 91, 120, 148, 160, 161, 162, 163, 164, 158
Leesburg, VA, 54
Lexington, USS, 127
Liberty, MS, 144
Lieb, Hermann, 127
Lincoln, Abraham, 2, 22, 23, 25, 26, 40, 55, 72, 97, 99, 141, 142 , 143, 181, 175, 179, 202

Lockett, Samuel, 113
Lockhart's Station, MS, 44
Lodi, MS, 168
Loewen, James W., 197
Longstreet, James, 88
Lookout Mountain, TN, 157
Loring, William W. 49, 98, 113, 150
Lost Cause, 186, 188, 189, 191, 193, 194, 197, 198, 201
Loughborough, Mary, 123
Louisiana Troops (Federal): 8th Louisiana (US) Cavalry, 156
Louisiana, 97, 152
Louisville, MS, 183
Louisville, USS, 103
Lovell, Mansfield, 77, 79, 81
Lowndes County, MS, 28, 190
Mack and Brothers, 86
Macon, MS, 67, 143, 158, 165, 183
Madison County, MS, 37, 48, 201
Manifest Destiny, 9
Manship, Charles H., 110
Marion County, MS, 19
Marshall County, MS, 35, 49, 83, 84, 192
Martin, William Thompson, 88, 89
Massachusetts, USS, 47
Maury, Dabney H., 77, 79
McClernand, John A. 107, 113, 115, 120
McCulloch, Henry E., 126, 127
McElroy, Sophronia, 44
McGehee, Miles, 37
McPherson, James B., 107, 108, 109, 113, 117, 132
Meade, George, 135
Mecklin, Augustus Hervey, 208
Memphis and Charleston Railroad, 59
Memphis, TN,
Memphis, TN, 37, 83, 112, 144, 149, 158, 162, 165, 166
Meridian, MS, 67, 102, 143, 148, 149, 150, 151, 152, 153, 154, 155, 157
Metairie Cemetery (New Orleans), 200
Mexican War, 9, 10, 11, 12, 31, 37, 40, 41, 50, 70, 88
Mill Springs, Battle of, 59, 157
Miller, Horace, 90
Milliken's Bend, 91, 98, 126, 127, 156
Minnesota, 76
Mississippi Cavalry Units (Federal): 1st Mississippi (US) Cavalry, 156

Mississippi Central Railroad, 90, 110, 168
Mississippi Infantry Units (Confederate):
   2nd, 45, 48, 50; 5th, 51; 7th, 51; 9th, 45;
   10th, 51; 11th, 48; 12th, 37; 13th, 45;
   14th, 51; 15th, 37, 45, 51, 59, 156, 157;
   17th, 48, 50; 18th, 48, 50; 20th, 37; 21st,
   50; 22nd, 209; 24th, 37; 46th, 147
Mississippi Infantry Units (Mexican War):
   1st, 9, 80; 2nd, 34
Mississippi Manufacturing Company, 167
Mississippi Plan, 183, 184
Mississippi Secession Convention, 2, 24,
   28, 29, 32, 205
Mississippi Society, 47
Mississippi Textbook Commission, 197
Mississippian (Jackson), 1, 21, 23, 173
Missouri Troops: 6th Missouri Infantry
Mobile and Ohio Railroad, 59, 67, 149,
   154, 158, 166
Mobile, AL, 88
Monroe County, MS, 80
Montgomery, AL, 32
Montgomery, L.M., 132
Montrose, MS, 102
Moore, John C., 79, 80
Moore, William H., 48
Morton Pine Knots, 37
Morton, MS, 37, 136
Mott, Christopher, 32, 34
Mound City, USS, 103
Mudd, John J., 87
Murphy, Robert C., 84, 87
My Cave Life in Vicksburg, 123
Nashville, Battle of, 155, 168, 199
Nashville, TN, 60, 164
Natchez, MS, 3, 8, 13, 20, 71, 72, 141,
   144, 156, 177
Negro Soldier Law, 173
New Albany, MS, 154, 162
New Jersey, 88
New Orleans, Jackson, and Great
   Northern Railroad, 102
New Orleans, LA, 47, 65, 71, 72, 187, 200
New York Herald Tribune, 194
New York, 37, 55, 56, 57, 125, 194
Newton County, MS, 174
Noel, Edmund, 190
Norfolk, VA, 96
North Carolina, 57, 157, 169
Nueces River, 10

Nullification Crisis, 6, 13
O'Connor Rifles, 37
O'Conor, Charles, 37, 38
Ogden, Mrs., 66
Ohio, 105
Okolona, MS, 58, 149, 154, 157, 158, 166,
   189
Opposition Party, 19, 22, 30
Ord, E.O.C., 75, 132, 181
Osband, E.D., 177
Our Mississippi, 196
Oxford, MS, 28, 67, 82, 83, 86, 164
Palo Alto, MS, 101
Pea Ridge, AR, 59
Pearl River, 4, 151
Pemberton, John C., 82, 96, 99, 106, 108,
   112, 113, 114, 117, 118, 119, 121,
   124, 128, 130, 131, 132, 133
Pennsylvania, 2, 11, 56, 96, 101, 135
Perryville, Battle of, 82
Peters, George B., 88
Petersburg, Battle of, 155
Pettus Rifles, 37
Pettus, John A., 54
Pettus, John Jones, 17, 18, 19, 20, 21, 23,
   24, 26, 36, 51, 52, 53, 54, 85, 110,
   143, 144, 145
Pettus, William W., 54
Pierce, Franklin, 31
Piney Woods, 4, 26
Pittsburg Landing, 68
Pittsburg, USS, 103
Polk, Ellen, 65
Polk, James K., 9
Polk, Leonidas, 60, 88, 148, 150, 151,
   152, 153. 157
Pontotoc, MS, 50, 154, 162
Pope, John, 69
Port Gibson, Battle of, 107
Port Gibson, MS, 175
Porter, David, 102, 106, 119, 122, 134
Prairie Station, MS, 154
Price, Sterling, 74, 75, 76, 81
Price, USS, 103
Putnam County, GA, 28
Quincy, Adeline, 125
Quitman, John A., 8, 15, 37
Ramsey, Abiezer Clarke, 33
Rankin County, MS, 19, 30
Ransom, T.E.G., 144

Rawlins, John A., 129, 130
Raymond, Battle of, 108-109
Raymond, MS, 108, 109
Reconstruction Acts, 181
Reconstruction Myths, 184, 185
Reconstruction, 181-185, 186, 197, 198
Republican Party, 16, 17, 18, 21, 182, 183,
    184, 187
Requiem for a Nun, 178
Rhinebeck, NY, 8
Richland, MS, 37
Richmond, VA, 78, 81, 137, 139, 156,
    166, 175
Rio Grande River, 10
Ripley, MS, 45, 50, 81, 160, 162, 166
Rise and Fall of the Confederate Government,
    200
Robinette, Henry C., 79
Rogers, William Peleg, 80
Rolling Fork, MS, 201
Rose Cottage, 60, 65
Rose, Mrs. S.E.F., 196
Rosecrans, William, 74, 75, 77, 79
Rosedale, MS, 201
Runnels, Daniel, 60
Russia, 28
Rutherford County, TN, 49
Sallis, Charles, 197
Satartia, MS, 129
Savannah, GA, 106
School Law of 1870, 183
Seddon, James A, 128
Seven Days, Battle of, 49
Seward, William H., 56
Sharkey, William L., 19, 23, 25, 180
Sherman, William T., 83, 92, 99, 110,
    111, 113, 116, 128, 136, 137, 143,
    144, 149, 151, 152, 154, 157, 158,
    161, 162, 168, 175, 202, 217
Shiloh, Battle of, 63-65, 70, 71, 72, 74,
    106, 193, 208
Ship Island, 47, 156
Ship Island, Ripley and Kentucky
    Railroad, 50
Shirley House, 126
Shirley, Alice, 125
Shirley, Frederick, 125
Shirley, James, 125, 126
Silver Wave, USS, 103
Singleton, Otho R., 23, 24

Smith County, MS, 201
Smith, Andrew Jackson, 162, 163, 164
Smith, Edmund Kirby, 176
Smith, Martin Luther, 131, 132
Smith, William Sooy, 149, 154, 155
South Carolina, 2, 6, 7, 13
Southern Mississippi Railroad, 101
Spanish-American War, 180
Spring Hill, TN, 88
St. Louis, MO, 131
St. Thomas Hall, 156
Starkville, MS, 101, 154
Steele, Frederick, 99
Stevenson, Carter L., 113, 131
Stone, Charles P., 54
Stone, John M., 135
Stuart, J.E.B., 87, 89
Sturgis, Samuel, 158, 160
Summit, MS, 102
Sunny South (Aberdeen), 20
Swain, Martha T., 44
Tallahatchie River, 98
Tariffs, 6, 7, 8, 9
Taylor, Richard, 164, 169, 175
Taylor, Zachary, 80, 164
Tennessee Troops: 45th Tennessee
    Infantry, 209
Tennessee, 9, 58, 74, 75, 76, 88, 138, 155,
    161, 164, 172
Texas Troops: 2nd Texas Infantry, 80
Texas, 9, 10, 28, 80
The Unvanquished, 51
Thomas, George H., 59
Thompson, Martha, 96
Thornton, John J., 30
Thrasher, James A., 201
Tippah County, MS, 37, 38, 45, 149
Tishomingo County, MS, 175
Tishomingo Hotel, 59, 66, 79
Tullahoma, TN, 109
Tunica County, MS, 55
Tupelo (Harrisburg), Battle of, 163, 164
Tupelo, MS, 75, 158, 163, 164, 169
Tuscumbia, AL, 168
Tuscumbia, USS, 103
Union Church, MS, 102
Union City, TN, 51
United Confederate Veterans (UCV),
    186, 187, 188, 189, 190, 192, 195,
    198, 199

United Daughters of the Confederacy (UDC), 186, 188, 189, 191, 192, 193, 195, 196

United Sons of Confederate Veterans (SCV), 186, 188, 189, 190, 192, 193, 195, 200

United States Military Academy, 31, 88, 106, 110, 114, 126, 148

University Greys, 40

University of Mississippi, 28, 29, 40, 67

Van Dorn, Earl, 34, 35, 59, 72, 77, 78, 79, 80, 81, 82, 84, 87, 88, 91

Vaughn, John, 115

Vera Cruz, Mexico, 80

Vicksburg Campaign, 105-135

Vicksburg Military Park, 126

Vicksburg, MS, 3, 10, 47, 71, 72, 73, 74, 82, 83, 91, 95, 97, 99, 103, 105, 106, 113, 114, 115, 116, 117, 118, 119, 120, 121, 122, 123, 124, 125, 126, 127, 128, 130, 131, 132, 133, 134, 135, 137, 138, 141, 142, 143, 144, 146, 148, 151, 152, 154, 156, 166, 168, 170, 183, 189, 190

Virginia, 2, 5, 25, 49, 51, 53, 57, 87, 88, 105, 138, 155, 156, 172

Walnut Hills, 91, 92

Walter, Harvey W., 19, 85

Walthall, Edward Carey, 156, 157, 193, 199, 200

Walthall, W.T., 200

Washburn, Cadwallader, 161

Washington County, MS, 29, 192

Washington, DC, 15, 20, 31, 75, 86, 199

Water Valley, MS, 45, 82, 183

Wesson, James M., 167

West Point, MS, 101, 154

West, Absalom M., 90, 145

West, MS, 168

Wexford Lodge, 125, 126

Wheeler, Joseph, 89

Whig Party, 13, 19, 30

Whiting, William H.C., 89

Wilmington, NC, 89

Wilmot Proviso, 11, 13

Wilmot, David, 11

Winona, MS, 168

Winslow, E.F. 151

Wisconsin Troops: 8th Wisconsin Infantry, 84

Wood, John W., 25, 26, 30

Woodall Mountain, 75

Woodville, MS, 144

World War II, 105

Yalobusha County, MS, 45, 156

Yazoo City, MS, 156

Yazoo County, MS, 45, 48

Yazoo River, 73, 98, 122, 156

Yellow Tavern, Battle of, 88

Yerger, J. Shall, 29

Zollicoffer, Felix K., 59